D1556416

FROM MAKING TO MUSIC

FROM MAKING TO MUSIC

The History of THORN EMI

S. A. Pandit

Hodder & Stoughton

Copyright © S. A. Pandit 1996

First published in 1996
by Hodder and Stoughton
a division of Hodder Headline PLC

The right of S. A. Pandit to be identified as the Author of
the Work has been asserted by him in accordance with the
Copyright, Designs and Patents Act 1988.

10 9 8 7 6 5 4 3 2 1

All rights reserved. No part of this publication may be
reproduced, stored in a retrieval system, or transmitted,
in any form or by any means without the prior written
permission of the publisher, nor be otherwise circulated
in any form of binding or cover other than that in which
it is published and without a similar condition being
imposed on the subsequent purchaser.

A CIP Catalogue record for this title is
available from the British Library

ISBN 0 340 68045 8

Typeset by Hewer Text Composition Services, Edinburgh

Printed and bound in Great Britain by
Mackays of Chatham PLC, Chatham, Kent

Hodder and Stoughton
A division of Hodder Headline PLC
338 Euston Road
London NW1 3BH

CONTENTS

LIST OF ILLUSTRATIONS

Thorn
Sir Jules Thorn
Sir Richard Cave
Thorn factories in Great Cambridge Road, Enfield
An early television set, 1930
Ferguson television set, 1949
Radio Rentals, 1995
Thorn House, St Martin's Lane, London
Tricity cooker from the early sixties
Kenwood Chef, circa 1968
Lighting fixtures
Rent-a-Center, USA
Thorn Group logo

EMI
Alfred Clark
Sir Alexander Aikman
Sir Joseph Lockwood
Sir John Read
'His Master's Voice' by Francis Barraud
Enrico Caruso
Maria Callas
Sir Edward Elgar
Abbey Road Studios
Frank Sinatra
Nat 'King' Cole
Aerial photograph of the Hayes site
Capitol Records
The Beatles
The Beach Boys
Pink Floyd

ABC Cinemas
CAT Scanner
HMV UK logo

THORN EMI
Peter Laister
Sir Graham Wilkins
Sir Colin Southgate
James G. Fifield
Michael Metcalf
Simon Duffy

ACKNOWLEDGEMENTS

A number of people associated with THORN EMI, currently and in the past, have made the writing of this book possible and I gratefully acknowledge their help. Most of all, I would like to thank those who generously made time to talk to me about the events covered. Their names are listed in Appendix i. Their contribution to the book has been invaluable, although I should emphasise that the opinions in it are, except where otherwise stated, my own.

I have had liberal access to THORN EMI's archives and have drawn heavily on material from them. I am grateful to the management of the company for making this possible. My thanks to them also for allowing use of the illustrations in the book and use of extracts from the company's publications.

Last but not least, special thanks to Claire Enders, who took on the role of editor and constructive critic and was an invaluable source of information on, and insight into, the entertainment industries.

The following copyright holders have granted permission for reproduction of material in this book: Macmillan Press Ltd. for the extract from *The General Theory of Employment, Interest and Money* (1935) by J. M. Keynes in the Introduction; *Times* Newspapers Ltd. for the extract from *The Times* leader of 17 July 1967 in Chapter 2 and for the extract from an article by Sue Summers in *The Sunday Times* of 8 December 1985 in Chapter

12; *The Observer* for the extract from an article by John Davis (1975) in Chapter 4; Some of the material in Chapters 5 and 6 on the development of EMI was drawn from research done by Dr Peter Martland of Cambridge University and his assistance is hereby acknowledged; Management Today Publications Ltd. for the extract from an article by Cheryll Barron in *Management Today* of February 1979 in Chapter 7; the *Financial Times* Ltd. for extracts from the *Financial Times* dated 10 November 1979, 13 July 1984, 7 February 1985 and 11 December 1985 in Chapters 8, 10, 11 and 12 respectively; and Pinter, a Cassel imprint, for the extract from *The Inmos Saga* (1985) by M. McLean and T. Rowland in chapter 11.

INTRODUCTION

The Great Cambridge Road is a busy thoroughfare which struggles out of the choking sprawl of north-east London towards the open countryside of Hertfordshire. For much of its length, it is lined with pre-war, semi-detached houses, grimy with traffic smoke, interspersed with drab, institutional buildings and muddy playing fields. The northern end is a complete contrast – all shiny paint and new brickwork, shopping malls, supermarkets and theme restaurants. Something about this area, however, gives one the uncanny feeling that these glossy new constructions stand on the graveyard of a recently departed era. The layout and angle of the roads suggest an entirely different purpose to that to which the place is now devoted.

The Borough of Enfield, through which the Great Cambridge Road runs, has had a long association with making things. Its most famous product is the Lee-Enfield rifle, the standard infantry weapon of the British Army through two world wars. But in the recent past, the most important manufacturer in the borough was Thorn Electrical Industries, generally known as Thorn, whose factories lined the northern end of the road. In its heyday, Thorn's seventy-odd factories in the borough and elsewhere in Britain made light-bulbs, televisions, stereo equipment, video recorders, cookers, refrigerators, food mixers, domestic heating equipment – in fact, almost all of the appliances used in the modern home – together with a range of industrial goods. Sir Jules Thorn, its founder, was able to claim that 'every household in the country has one of our products'.

Sir Jules was an inspirational figure to those concerned about the fading performance of Britain's manufacturing businesses after the Second World War. Starting with little but his enthusiasm and commercial acumen, he had challenged the industrial estab-lishment of the day with a level of energy and aggression alien to the prevailing culture. By spotting new markets in the expansive climate of post-war Britain, and by a shrewd mixture of alliances and acquisitions, he had built the tenth-largest company in the country. In 1968, a stockbroker's report described its development as 'one of the romances of British industry'.

Yet there is little trace of Sir Jules's legacy on the Great Cambridge Road today. In a symbolism that captures the changes wrought on the industrial landscape of Britain in the 1980s, the sites of his factories are now occupied by Safeway and Sainsbury, TGI Friday and Toys 'R' Us.

Sir Jules retired twenty years ago and the history of his company since then divides neatly into two halves. In the first, his successors sought to diversify the company away from its dependence on manufacturing durable goods for the British consumer. The key event in this period was the acquisition, in 1979, of EMI. EMI was a company whose origins went back to the invention of recorded music in the late nineteenth century. By the late 1970s, it was itself a very diverse company, with interests ranging from military equipment to bingo clubs. It was also a highly innovative company. Both these characteristics are exemplified by the fact that it brought both The Beatles and the CAT scanner to the market. Following this acquisition, Thorn changed its name to THORN EMI.

The period of diversification came to an end in 1985, following an ill-fated venture into the semiconductor industry. For the owners of the company – the ordinary shareholders – the decade since Sir Jules Thorn's retirement had been disastrous. Relative to the stock market as a whole, the value of their shares had fallen by two-thirds. In the decade since 1985, the previous policies were reversed and diversification gave way to a relentless pruning, on a scale unprecedented in Britain. This process reached its logical conclusion in 1996, with the demerger of THORN EMI into two separate companies, Thorn and EMI, formally reversing the merger of 1979.

For the shareholders, this latter period was a rewarding one, with the value of their shares sextupling in absolute terms, from the low point of ten years ago. Relative to the stock market as a whole, the value of the shares has doubled. However, the policies followed by the company during this period have not been without criticism. In particular, there are those who bemoan the fact that, having been one of the country's largest manufacturers, by the time it demerged, THORN EMI now makes nothing but recorded music products – that its withdrawal from manufacturing is another example of the defeatism that grips British industrialists.

This book traces the histories of both Thorn and EMI from their origins, but it is primarily an account of the last twenty years of THORN EMI, which corresponds to the time since Sir Jules Thorn retired from active business life. These were years of radical change both for the company and for its peers in British industry, driven by the emergence of competition on a global scale, rapid technological change and increasing social and economic volatility. In this new environment, the ideas that had guided management decisions in the past were found to have lost their applicability.

Commenting on the influence of ideas on political affairs, the economist John Maynard Keynes wrote:

> The ideas of economists and political philosophers, both when they are right and when they are wrong, are more powerful than is commonly understood. Indeed, the world is ruled by little else. Practical men, who believe themselves to be quite exempt from any intellectual influences, are usually the slaves of some defunct economist.

(*The General Theory of Employment, Interest and Money*, 1935)

Keynes's comments, suitably paraphrased, can also be applied to the world of business. The prevailing doctrine among the high priests of business thinking in the 1960s encouraged size, diversity and a balanced portfolio. Balance and diversity were important objectives for EMI's management in the 1960s and 1970s, in particular the perceived need to balance its main business of selling recorded music with other, unrelated, activities. Similar considerations encouraged Thorn's management to try to balance the company's dependence on the sale of consumer durable goods in the UK by diversifying into unrelated areas.

Balance, however, came at a price. It meant passing up on opportunities to become dominant in one business, either to avoid upsetting the balance, or because the company's resources had been deployed elsewhere. More subtly, it meant distancing strategy-making for the company as a whole from what was really important in the competitive arenas of each of its businesses. The portfolio as a whole became more important than the health of each of its components.

The merger of Thorn and EMI was partly driven by a quest for balance, but it also gave rise to a new, and extremely ambitious, objective: that of orchestrating a group of diverse businesses, whose products had some natural links, to gain commercial advantage. This idea also laid more stress on the portfolio – on the links between the components – than on the separate strength of each component. It was, however, flawed in two respects. It underestimated the problems of achieving the links it sought, and it overlooked the fact that links between the components brought little advantage if each of the businesses was not competitive in its own sphere.

Since 1985, focus, in some ways the antithesis of balance, has been the dominant theme in THORN EMI's strategy. It is responsive both to the increasing need in many industries to achieve a strong competitive position in a global sense, and to the preference of increasingly sophisticated investors to allocate, or balance, their portfolios as they themselves see fit. The transition from balance to focus characterises much of British industry over the past decade. Few companies, however, were as diverse as THORN EMI a decade ago, or have pursued the idea of focus as relentlessly.

Some of the events in this book have been written about before – in particular, the success and failure of EMI's CAT scanner and the rise and fall of Inmos, the first and so far only British attempt to build a mass-market semiconductor business. What this book attempts to do is to thread these separate events into the larger fabric of which they were a part. Writing on business often runs the risk of taking crucial events outside the broader context in which they occurred. However, business decisions are the result not only of the relevant circumstances in which they are taken, but also of the backgrounds and characters of the participants who make them. An important role of business history is to provide this context.

To set the THORN EMI story in context, one needs to start with its founder. Surprisingly, for someone who was regarded as one of the most brilliant post-war industrialists, very little has been written about Sir Jules Thorn and no biography exists. It seems appropriate, therefore, to start where he started.

1

Thorn Electrical Industries –
The First Thirty Years

Jules Thorn was born on 6 February 1899 in Vienna, the youngest of three brothers in a Jewish family. He was just old enough to be of the generation that provided the cannon fodder for the First World War. His eldest brother fought in the Austro-Hungarian Army on the Russian front, where he was taken prisoner, and Jules himself was conscripted on leaving school. It would be surprising if the war, in which Austria had a disastrous involvement, and the economic and social chaos that followed, had not coloured his later attitudes.

Soon after he was demobilised, he entered the Vienna Handelshochschule – the commerce school in Vienna. His first job was with an Austrian manufacturer of gas mantles (the globe-shaped devices that provided the illumination in gas lamps) called Olso – gas was still used for street lighting at the time. It was as Olso's sales representative that he first came to Britain in 1923. The association was not, however, a lengthy one. By 1926, Olso had gone into liquidation, leaving him in a foreign country without a job.

Precisely when Jules Thorn decided to make Britain his home is unclear. It has been suggested that he felt obliged to stay on to pay off debts incurred in connection with the Olso trade. On the other hand, by 1926, the prospect of returning to Austria may not have had much appeal. The country was in political turmoil with, on one side, the spectre of Marxism inspired by the Russian revolution and, on the other, the rise of home-grown fascism and Nazism across the border in Germany. Both his brothers subsequently emigrated from Austria, the eldest coming to Britain, where he set up in the timber business, and the younger, who had trained as a doctor, going to the USA. Jules himself had married an English girl, Dorothy Tanner, in 1928. In any event, he had, by this time, established enough of a reputation to go into business in Britain on his own. The particular opportunity he spotted was in the lighting industry, but this time in electric rather than gas lighting.

The incandescent electric lamp had been invented in 1879 and fifty years later the lamp industry had settled into comfortable middle age. There had been little change in the product since before the First World War, and the next major innovation in electric lamps was not to occur until the development of the fluorescent tube in 1936. The established British companies had long realised that competition was futile. Light bulbs were quintessentially the type of product that economists describe as price-inelastic. Within limits, the customer will buy what he needs – no more and no less – irrespective of price. To this problem, which has dogged the lighting industry throughout its history, a convenient solution had been found: prices and market shares were fixed by a happy band of lamp manufacturers who called themselves the Electric Lamp Manufacturers Association, or ELMA for short. From palatial offices in a prestigious part of London, this gentleman's club cheerfully handed out sales quotas to members, and these were enforced by a system of fines. Today, in an era of Offices of Fair Trading and laws to promote competition, such behaviour seems close to criminality. At the time, it was completely legal and above board and not uncommon in a number of manufacturing industries. In fact, it was not until 1954 that the Monopolies and Restrictive Practices Commission investigated the lighting industry and uncovered a number of anti-competitive practices.

Inevitably, ELMA's arrangements were not watertight and there were a small number of suppliers outside the club. These largely depended on imported lamps, since ELMA controlled the domestic supply of the components necessary to manufacture lamps – glass bulbs, tungsten wire, and so forth – and restricted supply to non-members. Jules Thorn, no doubt taking advantage of his connections in central Europe, started importing lamps from the Hungarian Tungsram company. His vehicle for this trade was the Electric Lamp Service Company Limited, dealers in electrical and radio goods, which he incorporated in March 1928.

By the early 1930s, with the onset of the Great Depression, the protection of national manufacturers against imports was a popular cause. The British Government, no doubt under pressure from ELMA, introduced stiff import duties on lamps. By now, Jules Thorn was obtaining some of his lamp supplies from a small British manufacturer that was not a member of the ELMA club. However, this supplier was shortly to be gobbled up by one of the club members, which then promptly cut off his supplies. Faced with this double blow, he had to consider either manufacturing for himself, or going out of business. He came across a small company, also not a member of the ELMA club, which was in financial trouble. Its factory, the Atlas Lamp Works in Angel Road, near the southern end of the Great Cambridge Road, was acquired in 1932, and thus began a long association with the Borough of Enfield.

By late 1933, the Electric Lamp Service Company had started making its own lamps, which it sold under the Atlas brand. Although ELMA's arrangements meant that lamp prices allowed for good profits, the company had a number of problems to contend with. Not being a member of the ELMA club, it had difficulty obtaining component supplies and was forced into the expensive business of making its own components much earlier than it would otherwise have done. ELMA also had the habit of cutting off supplies to any retailer who purchased lamps from non-club members. As a result, the company's business was with the smaller, less successful dealers and, for many years, it had no representation among the top flight of retailers. However, by offering slightly better discounts and credit terms than the ELMA members, it was able to make progress.

While lamps were by far the largest business at this stage, Jules Thorn had also been developing a trade in importing and selling radio valves and radios. Public broadcasting had begun in Britain in 1922 with the formation of the British Broadcasting Company Ltd, a private company controlled by the makers of radio receivers, who received half the revenue from the ten-shilling licence fee. However, it was not until this company was wound up in 1927 and replaced by a public corporation, the BBC, that radio's popularity began to take off. In 1928, when Jules Thorn was setting up in business on his own, the radio boom was under way. The manufacture of radio valves and light bulbs required similar skills and the radio valve business was a sensible diversification for a lamp manufacturer. A chance encounter with a fellow Austrian, Alfred Deutsch, in 1928, gave Jules Thorn access to the radio engineering knowledge he lacked. Alfred 'Freddy' Deutsch had trained as an electrical engineer at the University of Vienna and had come to Britain for a holiday when he was persuaded by Jules Thorn to join him as his technical adviser. The partnership was to last for four decades.

The interest in radio also led, somewhat accidentally, into what was to become Jules Thorn's most profitable business. Early radios were unreliable and expensive to repair, the valves being the most troublesome items. As a result, many radios were rented and a number of specialist rental shops had sprung up in the early 1930s. One such shop, in Twickenham near London, got into financial difficulty while owing a large debt to Jules Thorn and, as a result, was taken over by him. At the time, he had no wish to develop it and it remained an oddity among his business interests for many years. It was not until two decades later that he was persuaded to open his second rental shop.

At about the time that Jules Thorn was acquiring his first rental shop, a few miles away in Hayes, near the present Heathrow Airport, a company called Electric and Musical Industries was setting up a television research group under a brilliant scientist called Isaac (later Sir Isaac) Shoenberg, to develop a practical system for television broadcasting. This was the system eventually adopted by the BBC. It is worth digressing for a moment to compare the two companies, which were to merge nearly half a century later, at this stage in their development. On one side, Electric and Musical Industries, later to change its name to EMI, a world leader in the recorded music industry and at the forefront of crucial technologies, setting standards for the future. On the other, a small company making a mundane commodity product in a second-hand factory, barred from the gentleman's club of the industry, with no technology of its own and with one rental shop.

Certainly, the idea that his company would one day acquire Electric and Musical Industries would have seemed laughable to Jules Thorn at the time. He would, in any event, have been far too busy to spare time for idle speculation. There was much to do on the business front. In August 1932, he acquired control of the Chorlton Metal Company, which dealt in electric lamps and radios in Manchester. In October 1933, he acquired the designs and goodwill of the Lotus Radio Company, which allowed him to start manufacturing his own radio receivers. The original Atlas Lamp Works were soon working to capacity and new buildings and machinery were required to meet the growing demand for lamps. Direct sales to municipalities and other large users were going particularly well, elegantly foiling ELMA's grip on the retail distribution channels.

By 1936, Jules Thorn felt confident enough to float his company on the London Stock Exchange. The business was on a roll – the prospectus showed a threefold increase in profits to £37,014 in the two years to 31 March 1936. The Electric Lamp Service Company changed its name to Thorn Electrical Industries and increased its issued share capital from £2,000 to £150,000, partly by capitalising retained profits. Jules Thorn raised £101,475 by selling part of his holding, but he still owned one-third of the ordinary shares. The company raised £72,300 to finance its working capital requirements. At the issue price, the ordinary shares were valued at six times the pre-tax profits of the last full year and were thirty times oversubscribed. They immediately rose to a 20 per cent premium over the issue price.

Flotation was not allowed to interrupt the development of the business. The Ferguson Radio Corporation was acquired late in 1936. This company had been founded by J.B. Ferguson, a Canadian who had come to Britain in 1933 and had started importing parts and assembling radio receivers in a factory in Chiswick. Although the business grew rapidly in the radio boom, by 1935 it was in difficulty as a result of over-trading, giving Jules Thorn the opportunity to buy it cheaply. The business was moved to Enfield, alongside Thorn's existing radio manufacturing. Ferguson himself returned to Canada in 1940 but his name lived on in Britain as the leading Thorn brand in the consumer electronics market of the future.

In Britain, 1936 was also a landmark year for a technical development that was to have momentous consequences for consumer electronics. John Logie Baird had demonstrated television in

January 1926, using a mechanical device for scanning the film and transmission by wire. It did not, however, fulfil the requirements of a practical broadcasting system and it was not until ten years later that Isaac Shoenberg's team at EMI was to finish the development of the system that enabled the BBC to start the world's first television service. The system developed was so robust that it formed the basis of British television broadcasting until the 1960s. The outside broadcast of the coronation of King George VI, from Hyde Park Corner, in November 1937, demonstrated that television was a practical proposition.

Thorn, with its interests in radio, seized the new opportunity and started assembling television sets in Enfield. A set the size of a refrigerator, but with a tiny screen, was on the market by 1938, under the Ferguson brand name. However, the outbreak of war put an end to the BBC television service and television manufacture went into hibernation for the duration of the hostilities.

The demands of the wartime economy inevitably affected Thorn's business. The Ferguson factory was given over to making military radios for tanks, aircraft and small boats, but a few domestic radio sets were still made. Some of the lamp factory's output was also switched towards military supplies – items for aviation such as signal lamps, identification lamps and airfield lighting. Various types of lamps that had previously been imported from what was now occupied Europe had to be made in the UK. However, with no business of its own outside Britain, the company's organisation remained intact. Operating under a strict regime of controls, Thorn made steady rather than spectacular progress. By its 1946/47 financial year, pre-tax profits had grown to just under £93,000, from £42,500 in 1936/37, its first year as a public company.

Post-war Britain, with consumers bursting with cash but starved of goods and with a war-weary infrastructure in urgent need of refurbishment, was to be a time of rich pickings for manufacturers. It was also the time when Thorn established its pre-eminent position in its two main markets, lighting and consumer electronics. Jules Thorn's first move was into a new opportunity in lighting.

The discharge lamp, in which light is produced by passing an electric current through an inert gas, had been invented by

Georges Claud in France before the First World War. However, it had a number of drawbacks which limited its use to special applications such as neon signs. Its descendant, the modern fluorescent tube, appeared in America shortly before the Second World War. Because it converted electricity to light much more efficiently than the incandescent lamp, it was quickly adopted for commercial and industrial lighting. While the principles of the fluorescent tube were well known, the secret of commercial success lay in efficient production. It was known that the Sylvania Electric Products Company, a large US electrical company with excellent manufacturing technology, was looking for a European partner. With characteristic chutzpah, Jules Thorn presented himself at Sylvania's offices in Massachusetts and suggested to its executives that they should share their technology with him.

The deal he struck with them was probably his greatest personal business coup. Sylvania subscribed for new share capital in Thorn to give them a shareholding of around 20 per cent, and Sylvania and Thorn agreed to share their technology in the area of fluorescent lamps. Since the amount of technology owned by Sylvania and Thorn, respectively, was far from equal, it was a very good deal for Thorn. What, apart from Jules Thorn's undoubted charm, persuaded Sylvania to enter into it is uncertain. However, Jules Thorn almost certainly held out as an inducement the possibility of selling Thorn to Sylvania at some time in the future. Whether he ever had any intention of doing so is another matter. However, the deal must have pleased him greatly: in one move he had outflanked the gentlemen of the ELMA club, who had so vexed his early business life, and ensured that he, and not they, would dominate the British lighting industry. The Great Cambridge Road was to be the site of the new fluorescent tube factory and, by the early 1950s, Thorn dominated the British fluorescent tube market – a market that was to provide much of the cash for its growth during the decade.

Relations with Sylvania remained cordial for a number of years and, by the late 1960s, it was the largest shareholder in Thorn. There were attempts to collaborate in other areas, in particular in television picture tubes and in telecommunications equipment, but neither of these was successful. Although Sylvania had a representative on the Thorn board, Jules Thorn was too much his own man to let Sylvania have any say in running his company. Later proposals by Sylvania to acquire Thorn were rebuffed, and Sylvania's patience must have been sorely tried when Thorn went off in directions very different from those it would have chosen. It finally decided to part company with Thorn in the late 1960s.

Meanwhile, developments in television broadcasting were also creating lucrative opportunities for Thorn. The timing of these developments in Britain, however, well ahead of the rest of Europe, was to have a singular effect on British manufacturers. We will return to this in a later chapter, but it is worth noting here that because the BBC was committed to the pre-war 405-line standard, Britain was not able to agree a common standard with other European countries, which had not made the same investment in television before the war. The number of lines determines the quality of the picture, and post-war technology had made possible higher definitions of up to 625 lines. As a result there were three different standards in Europe, the French having also gone their own way, for different reasons. The British market was therefore, in practice, open only to British manufacturers, at least until the standards changed in the late 1960s. By the same token, exports from Britain were small and British manufacturers gained no advantage from the country's crucial role in the development of television. As a result, the British market developed in a rather hothouse, boom-and-bust atmosphere – with no imports to take up the excess in the boom and no export markets to take up the slack in the bust.

The BBC resumed its television service in June 1946 and, by 1947, Thorn had a television set on the market, assembled from valves and tubes obtained from Philips. This set retained the gargantuan proportions of its pre-war ancestor and it was not until 1949 that the company launched a satisfactory product at a competitive price. By then, the market had begun to take off. In 1947, total British production had amounted to 28,000 sets. By 1952, it had risen to 812,000. The Ferguson radio factory in Enfield was given over entirely to television manufacture, the radios and radiograms being moved first to a factory in Wales and then to Spennymoor in the north-east of England when the Welsh factory was destroyed by fire. Commercial television broadcasts began in 1954, but sets sold until then could not receive the new frequencies and they either required converters or had to be replaced. To accommodate this development, the Enfield factory had to be enlarged yet again as the market rose to 1.8 million sets in 1955. By 1957, Enfield had produced its millionth set and there were twenty-nine British television manufacturers. In 1959, total production was running at 2.9 million sets per year. That, however, was the peak, the high-water mark of British television production, never to be seen again. The bust that followed was precipitous. By 1961, production had fallen to 1.25 million sets and there followed the inevitable shake-out among the manufacturers.

The immediate cause of the collapse was the introduction by the Macmillan government of credit controls of an unprecedented ferocity, the first in a sequence of booms and busts that would bedevil British manufacturers from then on. Television was particularly hard hit as the market was approaching saturation by the late 1950s and sales would have slowed down of their own accord. For reasons explained earlier, manufacturers did not have the option of switching to exporting and, as a result, the devastation among them was immense. By the mid-1960s, only eight of the twenty-nine manufacturers of 1957 were still in business.

For those strong enough to survive the devastation, there were juicy pickings in the aftermath. One casualty of the shake-out was EMI. It will be recalled that EMI almost single-handedly developed the television broadcasting system adopted by Britain, and its primary motive in doing this had been to sell television sets. However, although EMI was a brilliant technological innovator, the company's sets, though well engineered, cost too much to make. By the end of the boom, EMI had merged its business, which traded under the His Masters Voice and Marconiphone brands, with Thorn's to form a joint venture – the British Radio Corporation – in which Thorn had majority ownership and control. It was not a happy experience for EMI. Jules Thorn effectively ignored their presence in the joint venture and would not allow them any meaningful information on it. The partnership did not last long and EMI sold its holding to Thorn for a pittance. Thus, the company that had done more than any other to give Britain its lead in television made little money out of making television sets.

Thorn's robustness in the boom and bust of the 1950s was

due in part to its manufacturing efficiency and in part to its Ferguson brand. The fact that Thorn was also in the television rental business, which was to be critical for its manufacturing interests in later years, was unimportant at this stage. Although, as we have seen, Thorn acquired its first rental shop for radios in the 1930s, in 1947 it still had just the one shop, trading under the Domestic Electric Rentals brand. The Radio Rentals company, which Thorn was to acquire in 1968, was a much earlier believer in the rental concept and had a much bigger business at the time.

The man who should be given credit for introducing Thorn to the television rental business in the first place was an Irishman called Tom Ludlow, manager of the rental shop in Twickenham in the late 1940s. His immediate boss was Henry Moss, who was responsible for various peripheral operations within the company, including, for example, the factory that made lamp caps for light bulbs. Ludlow persuaded Moss to open a second rental outlet in Tottenham. Shortly thereafter, Jules Thorn decided to close both rental outlets. Ronald 'Ronnie' Davis, the finance director of Thorn, was sent to close the business, accompanied by Jack Strowger, the chief accountant, presumably to make sure that he did so – a mode of operation often used by Jules Thorn. Ludlow, however, was a charming and persuasive man and convinced Davis that, rather than close it down, Thorn should expand it. Ronnie Davis, to his credit, saw how it could become a profitable business and, in turn, managed to convince Jules Thorn to give it a try. By 1954, ten outlets had been opened and the business never looked back. In spite of its success, Jules Thorn himself had an ambivalent attitude to rental and worried that its existence would upset his other customers. Domestic Electric Rentals is not listed as a subsidiary in the company's annual report until 1962, and the first mention of it in the chairman's statement is in 1963: 'Through our subsidiary company, Domestic Electric Rentals Limited, we are favourably placed to cater for the increasing requirement of those who prefer to rent their receivers.'

Although the later success of his rental companies identified Jules Thorn with the business, he saw himself as a manufacturer. Certainly, neither rental nor any of the other businesses his company diversified into in later years were as close to his heart as lamp-making and television manufacturing. It was probably after the 1950s boom that Jules Thorn began to appreciate the value of the rental business, not only as offering more stable income than retail sales, but also as a way of smoothing loading on the factory. Retail sales tended to be heavily seasonal – skewed towards the autumn. Sales to the rental business could smooth the troughs. A further factor was the favourable tax treatment accorded to television rental companies in Britain. Rental sets were treated as fixed assets for income tax (and later, corporation tax) purposes and were eligible for the same allowances as plant and machinery. The early growth of television in the UK, compared to the rest of Europe, when sets were unreliable and expensive and the changes in broadcasting standards which made early sets redundant when commercial television started, helped to establish the habit. In the early days of black and white television in Britain, most sets were purchased. It was only as the market grew that renting became more prevalent and by 1967, just before the arrival of colour television, nearly half of all sets were rented. Interestingly, the experience was reversed in the colour era: initially, the vast majority of sets were rented but purchased sets increased as the market matured.

While lamps and televisions contributed most of Thorn's profits throughout the 1950s, it had started some of the diversification that was to become a feature of the company in the next two decades. One of the first examples was the acquisition, in 1951, of the Tricity Cooker business, which manufactured small electric cookers in what was no more than a garage in Enfield. The business had been owned by the London Electricity Company, for which Ronnie Davis had been an auditor before joining Thorn. It was moved to a new factory in Spennymore, a move that nearly finished it off as the designs suitable for the hand-built cookers in Enfield proved unsuitable for mass production in Spennymore. The initial losses were so large that the auditors were convinced that fraud was involved. Jules Thorn wanted to close the business down but was persuaded to persevere. A new design proved much more successful and making cookers was to be a profitable business for the company for many years.

The collaboration with Sylvania had shown Thorn the importance of lighting fittings as an adjunct to lamps and led to the acquisition of the Smart and Brown fittings business and of George Forrest & Son Ltd, makers of candelabra and decorative fittings for

170 years. While the former was to grow and prosper, the latter, alas, was not to celebrate its second centenary.

Jules Thorn's head office had been in a modest building near King's Cross station – a shabby, run-down area of London. However, in 1958, in a move that marks a rite of passage, he had constructed for his company a new headquarters in the West End of London. Designed by Sir Basil Spence in the brutalist style that was to become so popular in the 1960s, it was hailed, at the time, as a landmark of modern architecture. With its rough concrete cladding, its no-nonsense, block-like shape and its eighty-foot abstract sculpture in bronze high on its walls, it seemed to challenge its neighbours from a more ornate and leisurely age. By 1958, sitting in his new offices on the twelfth floor, looking out across Trafalgar Square at Big Ben and the Houses of Parliament, Jules Thorn could feel proud of what he and his company had achieved since the end of the war. Starting with under 2,000 employees in 1947, Thorn now had nearly 15,000 employees. Pre-tax profits had risen over fifteen times to nearly £1.5 million. It was the leading British television manufacturer and one of the largest lighting manufacturers. As Harold Macmillan, the Prime Minister, assured the British that 'they had never had it so good', the chairman of Thorn should have been able to look forward to the next decade with confidence.

2

Deal Making

By his sixtieth birthday, in 1959, Jules Thorn had become a member of the industrial establishment. The knighthood had yet to arrive – it would come in 1964 – but his success in lighting and television manufacturing had made him a figure to be reckoned with. What was he like, at this time, as a person? Physically, he was tiny, but he conveyed a sense of energy and authority which masked his lack of stature. He was always immaculately dressed and groomed, in a formal style. He was, however, without affectation or stuffiness and there was something of the clever but incorrigible schoolboy about his manner.

Despite his considerable wealth and notwithstanding his dress sense, he was a man of simple, almost frugal, tastes. Even his new head office, although it towered over a smart area of London, had a drab, utilitarian feel to its interior – the grey walls unadorned with paintings, the flooring plain carpet tiles, the furniture out of a mass-market office catalogue. Business entertainment was frowned upon. An investment analyst recalls an interview that ran on well past lunchtime. On confirming that his guest would like some lunch, Jules Thorn sent out for ice-cream bars for the two of them. He took an unabashed pleasure in simple things. Nigel Graham Maw, whose law firm had been advisers to Thorn from its early days, recalls calling in at his office late one evening to pay his compliments. Jules Thorn was seated at his desk, a diminutive figure in a large, bare office, listening to *The Archers* on a small radio. His guest took a chair and waited in silence till the programme came to an end, his presence unacknowledged. Fifteen minutes at the end of the working day were always devoted to *The Archers*. Late in life, he started collecting some of the toys of rich men: racehorses – of which he was a notably successful owner – and Impressionist paintings, but his consuming interest, almost till the end, was the company he had founded.

For much of his life he lived on his own. He married soon after settling down in Britain – in 1928 – and had a son and a daughter, Cedric and Anne. However, the family were sent off to the US on the outbreak of war and the marriage appears never to have recovered from this separation. The couple formally separated in 1950 and Jules Thorn kept his personal life very much to himself thereafter. He did not remarry until 1972, and the arrangements for the wedding give an indication of his retiring nature. Nigel Graham Maw and his father were the only guests invited to the ceremony at Marylebone Town Hall, and even they were only told about it the week before. Afterwards, the two guests and the newly married couple went out to lunch at the Mirabelle in Curzon Street. Jules Thorn's closest colleagues were unaware of his wedding until after the event.

In his business style he was very much the hands-on manager who liked to see and touch his products and his factories. Not for him the dispassionate analysis of figures in a remote head office, followed by lofty summons to his subordinates. He was happiest visiting one of his lamp factories, talking to the women on the production line and occasionally lecturing them on the importance of avoiding waste. In this, of course, he had retained the method of management he had successfully employed when he started off with one factory in north London and, as long as the company's breadth of interests remained fairly narrow, it worked well. However, once it had diversified beyond lighting and television manufacture, this approach was less appropriate, but by then he was probably too set in his ways to change.

His talent for deal-making was to remain impeccable throughout his working life and was much exercised in the acquisitive climate of the 1960s. He also had an audacity and a willingness to flout convention which would, at times, raise eyebrows and hackles, but often gave him the edge over more conventionally minded opponents. At the same time, he could be surprisingly naïve – for example, while buying a central heating business from the Shell Oil Company, he was genuinely taken aback to find that he had not bought the right to use the Shell logo.

In the early sixties, the senior executives of the company were, in the main, people who had joined at the start of their careers and would serve until the end. Of the five board members in 1961, four had been on the board since 1948 and the fifth, Don Mitchell, an American nominated by Sylvania, had joined the board in 1949. The longest-serving board member, apart from Jules Thorn himself, was Freddy Deutsch, who had joined Jules Thorn in 1928. He retired in 1974 – a career span almost matching that of Jules Thorn himself. Ronnie Davis, the finance director in 1961, had joined the company in 1943, been appointed company secretary in 1946 and was a director when he died in 1968. By 1970, only Jules Thorn and Freddy Deutsch remained from the board of 1961, but most of the new appointees were long-serving Thorn men, from the generation that had joined the company just after the Second World War. They included Dennis Neill, who played a key role in building the company's manufacturing capability in consumer electronics and domestic appliances, and Jack Strowger, who ended his career with the company as managing director. The tradition of long service was to be a feature of Thorn's senior executives during Jules Thorn's career.

His relationship with this steadfast group was, however, complex. They clearly had considerable influence over a number of key decisions and, as the company became more diverse, their role was crucial. However, working for him was not easy. Part grand patriarch and part irascible old rogue, he was quick to criticise and slow to give credit when it was due. Outsiders got the impression that he regarded his senior executives as not very competent youths, who would be quite incapable were it not for him. Moreover, he appears to have had a deep sense of insecurity, which made him irrationally suspicious of those close to him and vindictive when he felt vulnerable: one executive who threatened to resign over a matter of principle was told that he would never find work again if he did.

Since he also had a reputation as a bad paymaster, it may seem surprising that he led such a dedicated and long-serving team. However, Thorn was, at the time, a highly successful company, and being part of that success would itself have been both rewarding and motivating. Also, Jules Thorn had a way of disarming the victims of his unreasonableness which made them forget the hurt caused.

Leslie Hill, who became managing director of Thorn Lighting
in the mid-seventies, recalls that board meetings were unusual
affairs. The agenda would soon be cast aside as Jules Thorn laid
into whatever subject was uppermost in his mind – as often as
not the lighting business – accompanied by a tirade against the
individual responsible. However, immediately after the meeting
he would come up to Leslie Hill and say: 'You didn't mind me
having a go at you, Les, did you?'

Although his colleagues often found him unreasonable and
crusty, the relationship was not without a tinge of affection on
both sides. A story about the naming of his first racehorse captures
some of the flavour. Puzzling over what to call the animal, he asked
his long-serving secretary, Jean Orr, for advice. She replied: 'Why
don't you call it what you call your directors – Spoilt Lad?' So the
horse, a very successful race-winner, was christened Spoilt Lad.

Although outwardly Thorn had, by the early 1960s, all the
trappings of a large company, inside it still had many of the
habits of a small one. Harold Mourgue, one of the newcomers to
the company in the 1960s – he joined in 1961 when the business
he was working for, Ultra, was taken over – remembers it as
being a very aggressive company but also a very unsophisticated
one. In keeping with small company habits, the bank balance
was scrutinised daily, but other information for managing the
business was poor. The information that came into the head
office was patchy: Jules Thorn would study the figures showing
daily sales orders for light bulbs, but the barons heading other
parts of his empire would tell him only what they wanted to.
Other functions operated with a similar informality: executives
were not incentivised through a formal bonus system but would
unexpectedly receive a letter from the chairman offering them
shares in the company – often out of his personal shareholding
– because they had pleased him in some way.

The working style of the company was informal: job titles
counted for little and job descriptions did not exist. Jules Thorn
consulted the same small group of people on almost all issues.
As one of his colleagues put it: 'All meetings were attended
by the same people: you simply changed your title depending
on what the meeting was about.' Although the expansion of the
company's share capital base had reduced his personal holding

to a small minority, Jules Thorn's approach was still that of a proprietor rather than that of a general manager. In an attempt to strengthen his control, the company had adopted a policy of issuing two classes of ordinary shares, identical in all respects save for the fact that one class had voting rights and the other, the A shares, did not. As a result, Jules Thorn was able to control a much higher proportion of the votes than his share of the company's capital might suggest. By 1968, for example, he controlled 25 per cent of the votes but his share ownership, direct and through trusts, was 13 per cent. This device, common at the time in companies with still-active founding shareholders, became increasingly unpopular with outside shareholders, but was dropped by Thorn only after Jules Thorn's retirement.

By the early 1960s, it would have been possible to discern a distinctive approach to business, a strategy – although Jules Thorn himself would not have used that word – that had accounted for the company's success. It was founded on being a follower rather than a trail-blazer into new product markets; borrowing or buying technology – thereby minimising both the cost and the risk of backing the wrong one; efficient, low-cost manufacturing using, wherever possible, assets cheaply acquired; and opportunistic deal-making to consolidate a market position. It was an essentially conservative strategy, albeit applied to some fast-changing markets, and in the climate of the 1950s, an extremely successful one. Thorn's major advantage was its ability to think more imaginatively and to move faster than its more hide-bound and lethargic domestic competitors.

By 1960, the long post-war British consumer boom had come to an end. As we have seen, the television market was one of the first and most dramatically affected. Thorn, the most successful and aggressive company in the field, was in the thick of the restructuring that followed. In addition to acquiring EMI's television brands, it bought, in 1961, the television business of Ultra Electronics, which came with a new factory in Gosport on the south coast. Thorn's television brands now covered three different segments of the market: Ferguson was the set for the family; the EMI brands – HMV and Marconiphone – were aimed at the technophile who wanted the latest features; and Ultra, which was heavily promoted by advertising featuring a chic Afghan hound, was aimed at smart young couples with a taste for stylish living-room furniture.

The slump also gave Thorn an opportunity to rectify what had, hitherto, been the Achilles' heel of its manufacturing capability. By far the most expensive part of a television set is the picture tube, and making picture tubes is a complex and capital-intensive process. During the 1950s, Thorn had bought all its supplies of picture tubes from the main British manufacturer, Mullard. However, Mullard was a subsidiary of Philips, itself a television manufacturer and competitor. This had not mattered much when Thorn was only one of a large number of manufacturers, but once it had become the market leader, its vulnerability was more exposed. In 1960, with the television market in free fall, one of the other picture tube manufacturers – Standard Telephone and Cables – decided to sell its business to Thorn. By 1961, the third manufacturer – AEI – had also thrown in the towel and put its business into a joint company managed by Thorn. Henceforth, picture tubes were manufactured at a factory inherited from AEI, in Sunderland, in north-east England. However, the problems of manufacturing picture tubes were to bedevil Thorn in later years.

Manufacturers were not the only casualties of the slump. Britain's electrical retail trade had mushroomed during the 1950s, the majority of shops being small, owner-managed and with little capital backing. The slump left them over-stocked, short of cash and unable to pay their bills. The inventory stagnating expensively on their shelves came, of course, from manufacturers like Thorn. Ronnie Davis, Thorn's finance director, saw opportunity in this mayhem. He arranged with Thorn's merchant bankers, Hambros, to set up an investment company called Tucana to buy up distressed businesses. Thorn provided 49 per cent of the capital, the balance coming from Hambros and various institutional investors. The businesses were available cheaply and, for Thorn, there was the additional advantage that its trading debts would eventually get paid. This was the genesis of Thorn's interests in retailing, later extended to actively acquiring shops whose owners wished to retire or sell out for whatever reason. By 1968, Thorn controlled 210 electrical retail outlets in Britain.

As he had with the rental business, Jules Thorn continued to agonise about the reaction of his other retail customers to news that he was now competing with them. Considerable efforts were made to avoid having to disclose Thorn's involvement in Tucana, which was not included in the consolidated accounts of the Thorn Group. Two Thorn executives would attend Tucana board meetings, but would swap first names for the purposes of the board minutes. The camouflage was successful and few people outside the company were aware of Thorn's involvement. Even shop-owners selling their businesses to Tucana were generally unaware of its ownership, although this was revealed later when Thorn shares were used to pay for the acquisitions. Thorn had overcome its coyness about the true ownership of Tucana by 1966, by which time its shareholding had risen to 50 per cent, and it became a wholly owned subsidiary in April 1968. The rather mixed pedigree of the shops was to haunt Thorn in later years.

Thorn itself was not immune from the effects of the television slump. Although the lighting business had continued to grow, as the market for fluorescent tubes continued to expand and new types of lighting for roads and other outdoor applications were introduced, television sales and rental stagnated through the early 1960s. By 1963, however, the market had started to recover, helped by the imminent launch of the BBC's second channel, which required new receivers, and a pre-election boom engineered by the Conservative government. By the year ending in March 1964, Thorn's pre-tax profits had reached £7.5 million, a threefold increase over 1960. The company had increased its share of both the television and lighting markets and was poised to do some more inspired deal-making.

As noted in Chapter 1, one of these deals was in the area that Thorn now saw as its third leg – domestic appliances. It had entered this field in 1951 with the acquisition of Tricity. Tricity had stuck very successfully to electric cookers throughout the 1950s and was the major supplier to the state-owned electricity boards, which at the time controlled most of the retailing of cookers. By 1962, it was making about one-quarter of all electric cookers sold in Britain and was very profitable. By then it had also started branching out: the 1962 chairman's statement noted that, at the Ideal Home Exhibition in March that year, the Tricity Melodie, a cooker with a built-in transistor radio, and the Tricity Duet, a cooker and a refrigerator combined in one unit, had been introduced. The former is an interesting, if short-lived, example of synergy. The move into refrigeration was to be more enduring, but domestic refrigeration, a much more competitive market than electric cookers, was never a profitable business for Thorn.

In April 1965, Thorn moved into gas cookers by acquiring Glover and Main. Natural gas had recently been found in the North Sea and over the next decade there was to be a large switch from electricity to gas for cooking and heating. Glover and Main brought with it interests in heating, ventilating and air-conditioning, as well as gas metering and commercial catering equipment. It was also to play a bit part in a later takeover drama, to which we shall return.

The more important deal of the mid-1960s was in lighting. Thorn's partner in the manufacture of television picture tubes, AEI – or Associated Electrical Industries to give it its full name – was the result of an amalgamation of a number of long-established electrical manufacturing companies – Metropolitan Vickers, British Thomson Houston and Ediswan – most of whom had been members of the ELMA ring. Consequently, it had inherited a large share of the British lighting market and was the market leader in incandescent lamps. With Thorn's leadership in fluorescent lamps, a merger of the lighting interests of the two companies had obvious attractions. Encouraged by the success of their joint venture in picture tubes, the two companies decided to put their lighting interests together in 1964. The merged company, which was given the name of British Lighting Industries (BLI), was owned 65 per cent by Thorn and 35 per cent by AEI. The two companies had twelve factories between them, one of which was closed as a result of the merger, and most of the leading brands. Combined, they were clearly the dominant force in the industry.

One member of the original ELMA ring was, however, left outside this new grouping. GEC was another electrical manufacturer with a long history, run by an ambitious new managing director, Arnold (later Lord) Weinstock. The formation of BLI was not a cause for rejoicing on his part, but GEC and Thorn were on friendly terms and a dialogue developed between them on the future of the lighting industry. This took the form of regular meetings at GEC's head offices in London, which would be attended by Arnold Weinstock and Kenneth Bond, the GEC finance director, while

Jules Thorn would send Jack Strowger and Harold Mourgue, at the time the finance director and chief accountant, respectively, of Thorn. These meetings were the occasion for some gentle gamesmanship. By the time the Thorn pair had made the journey of a mile or so back to the Thorn head office, Arnold Weinstock would have briefed Jules Thorn, by telephone, on what had been agreed – an account that usually bore little resemblance to their recollection and which resulted in a sharp rebuke for them from Jules Thorn.

Not wishing to carry on with this unhappy experience, Jack Strowger took to sending Harold Mourgue on his own. The profitability of their respective businesses would be compared at these meetings and Harold Mourgue found to his surprise that GEC could produce detailed figures for each product, all of which seemed to show a much higher level of profit in the GEC business. Jules Thorn was too wily to be taken in by these figures, however, and he insisted that they must have been prepared in order to carry on the tradition of playful deception which had been established between the two companies. It is possible that these jolly occasions might, in time, have led to a merger of the lighting interests of the two companies, were it not for an event that was to show a new audacity in Jules Thorn.

Despite the creation of AEI, the British electrical engineering industry still remained fragmented and uncoordinated when compared with its equivalents in other major industrialised countries. There were no companies of the size of Siemens in Germany or General Electric in the US. AEI itself had sunk into the comfortable habits of its predecessors and showed little capacity for leading any further restructuring. The Labour government that came to power in 1964 had a considerable appetite for industrial intervention and it had formed the Industrial Reorganisation Corporation (IRC) as a catalyst for industrial restructuring. As another keynote of the government was the importance of participating in what it called the 'white heat of the technological revolution', it was inevitable that the muddled state of the electrical industry would be high on the IRC's agenda. Arnold Weinstock's GEC was seen as one company with the necessary drive to lead a restructuring of the industry and it received the backing of the IRC and the government when it decided to bid for AEI, in spite of being much the smaller of the two companies. The bid was hotly contested by AEI and accounts of the twists and turns of the ensuing battle dominated the business news through the summer of 1967.

Thorn, with two joint ventures with AEI, was keenly interested in the outcome of the bid. Jules Thorn did briefly consider entering the fray himself, as a white knight to rescue AEI, but his innate caution stopped him: AEI was a bigger company than Thorn and had interests in areas, such as power generation equipment, that were well outside Thorn's areas of competence. He was, however, anxious to stop GEC strengthening its position in any negotiation on the future of the British lighting industry, or indeed of British Lighting Industries. By the autumn of 1967, it appeared that AEI's last defences were crumbling. One Sunday morning that October, Jules Thorn and Jack Strowger arrived at AEI's grand Georgian head office in Grosvenor Place, behind Buckingham Palace, and negotiated a deal to buy AEI's 35 per cent stake in BLI for £12 million, paid in cash. This represented a price/earnings multiple of 14.6 times the earnings of BLI in the year to 31 March 1967. Although significantly greater than AEI's share of the net assets of BLI, the price was relatively cheap compared to Thorn's own price/earnings multiple – around 18 at the time – and the additional profit to Thorn was much less than the additional interest it had to pay on the cash. Under the London Stock Exchange's current Takeover Code, companies are not allowed to sell important assets while someone else is bidding for them, but this was before such a code existed. This did not, however, stop GEC from feeling very sore about the whole episode, and relations with Thorn became extremely frosty for a while. In the following year, the two companies engaged in a vicious battle for market share.

There was, happily, a thaw a year later when Kenneth Bond of GEC indicated that his company wished to re-establish good relations with Thorn and, as a token of goodwill, was prepared to sell GEC's interest in London Weekend Television to Thorn. This gracious gesture was acknowledged but taken no further. Although GEC and Thorn did work together in some areas – they had a number of joint ventures in making components for light bulbs which would survive till the 1990s – there would remain a sharp edge of rivalry between them. Late in 1968, there were further discussions on a merger of their lighting interests, which were again abortive, probably because the issue of who would control the merged company could not be resolved. Following these discussions, Jules Thorn took some pleasure in observing, at a board meeting, that Osram-GEC, the GEC lighting company, was making a loss and: 'BLI's policy of matching GEC's terms had had the desired effect.'

Jules Thorn's audacity would not have surprised Arnold Weinstock if he had noticed another event involving Thorn which had taken place a few months earlier, in the summer of 1967. This involved a company called Metal Industries. Metal Industries was an odd choice for Thorn to take an interest in, but at about this time the idea of diversifying preoccupied it. Metal Industries was a rambling, industrial conglomerate whose interests included electrical control equipment, meters and transformers, hydraulic pumps, an electrical wholesaler, a scrap metal merchant and a ship-breaking yard. Presiding over this collection of businesses was a blue-blooded board under the chairmanship of a former governor-general of Uganda, Sir Walter Coutts. The company had lost its way: pre-tax profits had fallen from £2.5 million in 1962/63 to £1.5 million in its 1965/66 financial year. By the mid-1960s, it was a sitting target for the newly fashionable financial whiz-kids and, sure enough, Slater Walker acquired a 16 per cent shareholding in it. In the early summer of 1967, however, Slater Walker sold its shares to Aberdare Holdings, another industrial conglomerate, which then launched a hostile bid for Metal Industries, valuing the company at around £14 million.

Thorn's interest in Metal Industries appears to have been entirely opportunistic – apart from the fact that it had a small catering equipment business, there was nothing in common between the two companies. A more important factor was that Thorn's share price had been particularly strong since the start of the year. Having stagnated, along with the rest of the stock market, since the election of the Labour government in 1964, the shares were to rise by over 50 per cent during 1967 – roughly twice as much as the FT Ordinary Share Index.

By the time Thorn made a move, however, Aberdare and its club of merchant bank supporters had, between them, acquired over 50 per cent of the shares. The directors of Metal Industries preferred Thorn to Aberdare, but their situation looked hopeless. However, the company secretary of Metal Industries came up with a suggestion that seemed to offer the possibility of escape. Metal Industries had an issued share capital of 7.5 million shares, but its authorised share capital was 12.2 million shares. Could a way be found of issuing the 4.7 million unissued shares to Thorn, thereby putting it level with Aberdare? With some equally innovative thinking, Thorn and its lawyers found the answer. Thorn would sell the Glover and Main business, which it had acquired the previous year, to Metal Industries in exchange for those 4.7 million shares, and it would then bid for the rest of the company. However, the first part of the deal would go through only if the second part was successful. By agreeing to this proposal, the directors of Metal Industries would reduce Aberdare's holding from around 53 to 32 per cent, while Thorn would end up with 39 per cent.

The deal caused an uproar, but there was nothing to stop it under the prevailing rules. A comment in an editorial in *The Times* of 17 July 1967 sums up the general view: 'The latest move by Thorn does not offend against the letter of the well-known 'Queensberry rules' of the take-over game. (These are a set of recommendations drawn up by the merchant banks themselves and endorsed last year by the Stock Exchange Council.) But, in our view, it offends against the spirit."

In the end, a settlement was found which got everyone off the hook. Aberdare and its supporters accepted a slightly higher offer from Thorn for the shares they owned, giving as their reason that Metal Industries was not worth the extra 5 per cent and they were better off taking their profit and departing the field of battle. From Thorn's point of view, everything had worked out for the best. Thorn had secured victory without actually having to complete its ingenious manoeuvre of selling Glover and Main to Metal Industries. The mere threat had been enough to scare off the opposition.

There was some mild rapping of knuckles by the Stock Exchange after the deal had been done, but it probably did no long-term harm either to the reputation of Jules Thorn or to that of the company. However, the episode had two enduring results: firstly, it hastened the introduction of a formal code on takeovers and caused the writing of Rule 21 of that code, which specifically forbids stratagems of the type used in the Metal Industries deal; secondly, and more relevant to our story, it set Thorn down a path of diversification the end result of which only time would reveal. Perhaps the real lesson of the whole episode is that the deal-making culture of the City of London can make even serious industrialists forget their original purpose and turn into financial engineers.

3

Radio Rentals

Nineteen sixty-eight was to be a landmark year for Thorn. The three preceding years had been miserable and the company's pre-tax profits had stagnated at just over £10 million. The UK market had been very difficult, as the Labour government, elected in 1964, had strangled the boom let loose by the previous Conservative administration in a futile attempt to hold the value of sterling on the foreign exchanges. By 1967, television sales and new rentals in the UK market had fallen by one-third. The chairmans statement in the annual report for that year states:

> For nearly two years the British economy has been under siege conditions and there has been virtually no growth. During this period the consumer durable sector has suffered particularly badly and Thorn Electrical Industries, with a major stake in this sector, has inevitably been under pressure.

However, the devaluation of sterling in November 1967 had allowed some easing of economic constraints and exports had, of course, become more profitable. In addition, in July 1967, the BBC had started broadcasting one of its channels in colour, and it seemed as if another television boom was in the offing. The annual report for the year ending on 31 March 1968 showed pre-tax profits up by nearly 40 per cent, helped by various acquisitions, of which the largest was Metal Industries. The most important news, however, concerned deals that would be completed after the year-end and hence were not reflected in the accounts. Two of these – Kenwood Manufacturing and KMT (Holdings) – we will return to later. The third, which was to be the most crucial deal done by Thorn under Jules Thorn's leadership, had actually been announced on 29 January but, as it had been referred to the Monopolies Commission, it would not be consummated until August 1968. This was the acquisition of Radio Rentals.

Radio Rentals had been started in 1930 by a Mr Perring-Toms, a radio dealer in Brighton, who was one of the first people to foresee the potential for renting radios. At about the same time, of course, Jules Thorn had acquired his first radio rental outlet in Twickenham. However, whereas Jules Thorn had been primarily a manufacturer with a small interest in rental, Perring-Toms's priorities had been the other way around: he was primarily a renter who had gone into manufacturing to safeguard his supply of radios. By a curious coincidence, Thorn and Radio Rentals were floated on the London Stock Exchange on the same day in 1936.

When television broadcasts were resumed after the war, Radio Rentals was one of the first companies to concentrate on renting television sets. Its radio manufacturing subsidiary started manufacturing television sets in 1949, again at about the same time as Thorn, and by the mid-1950s it had by far the largest television rental business in the UK. In 1964, it had merged with Rentaset, which had also been started in 1930 with the purpose of relaying radio signals over wire to subscribers. These systems were later converted to carrying television signals – Britain's first cable television systems – and a television set rental business was also started. The founder of Rentaset, Joseph Robinson, had intended to take a back seat after the merger, but Perring-Toms, who was to lead the merged company, died shortly after the merger was completed. As a result, Robinson became chairman of Radio Rentals in 1966.

By 1967, Radio Rentals had 615 rental outlets throughout the UK and 1.5 million television sets on rental, against Thorn's 490 outlets and 1.1 million sets on rental, together with a small number of outlets in Australia, Ireland and Italy. Its rental income amounted to £31.8 million, against Thorn's rental income of around £19 million. It was therefore a bigger force in rental than Thorn. It also owned an electrical retail chain – the Dawes group – and it manufactured television sets under the Baird name, at a factory in Bradford. It had a joint venture with the US company

RCA, which was about to start making colour picture tubes, a critical component for television manufacture. Given the overlap in activities, the rationale for the acquisition was self-evident. There was, however, a further motivation for acquiring Radio Rentals on the part of Thorn.

As noted in Chapter 1, the television broadcasting technology used by the BBC, when it resumed its service after the war, used the pre-war 405-line system rather than the higher-quality 625-line system adopted by the majority of western European countries. This had been a barrier to imports into, and exports from, the UK. However, it had been agreed in the early 1960s that when colour television was introduced, the UK would move to the 625-line system. In fact, the second BBC channel, BBC2, had started broadcasting in 1964 on a black and white 625-line system, requiring new sets and generating extra business for the manufacturers. By the late 1960s, of course, Far Eastern manufacturers had become a real force in the market for audio equipment in the UK and had established a foothold in television. Imports of radio sets, mainly from the Far East, had increased from 20,000 sets in 1958 to 2.4 million by 1967, while production by British manufacturers had fallen. Television imports in 1967 were minuscule, amounting to some 5,000 sets in a market of 1.4 million, but the experience in radio was a chilling vision for television manufacturers of what could happen once the technical barriers vanished with the full adoption of the 625-line system in the early 1970s. Clearly, scale of manufacturing and control over distribution were going to be critical for survival.

It was this which motivated Thorn to woo Radio Rentals. Its chairman was wined, dined and entertained by Jules Thorn; he was invited to visit Thorn facilities; promises were made of a seat on the Thorn board and, possibly, chairmanship of the merged rental business. Finally, towards the end of 1967, he was won over. There remained, however, the question of price. This was clearly going to be a very major acquisition for Thorn. At the time the deal – to be paid for in Thorn shares – was first agreed between the two companies, Radio Rentals was expected to earn pre-tax profits of around £8 million for the year to 28 February 1968, while Thorn was expecting to earn around £14 million in the year to 31 March – a split of 36 to 64. However, Radio Rentals demanded a premium for ceding control to Thorn, and the deal agreed and announced in January would have given the shareholders of the two companies an almost equal ownership of the combined business – a price that made some members of the Thorn board wince.

The referral of the whole matter to the Monopolies Commission, in February, gave them more time to fret about the price the company was having to pay. In the meantime, Radio Rentals' results turned out to be better than anticipated – pre-tax profits were £9.37 million and, because of an unusually low tax charge, after-tax profits were £7.09 million, an effective tax rate of only 24 per cent. This strengthened the hand of the Radio Rentals board. But other things had been going Thorn's way. Its share price had been particularly strong, rising by nearly 50 per cent in the first half of 1968, which in turn put a higher value on the offer for Radio Rentals. In addition, a flurry of small- to medium-sized acquisitions, paid for in shares, in early 1968, had enlarged Thorn's existing shareholder base. Whether or not the impending Radio Rentals merger was a consideration in making these acquisitions at this particular time has to remain a matter of speculation, but it does look as if it played a part. In any event, the terms of the deal were renegotiated following its clearance by the Monopolies Commission and the final terms gave Radio Rentals' shareholders approximately 47 per cent of the combined company for contributing 39 per cent of the pre-tax profits. The value put on Radio Rentals was approximately £180 million – equivalent in today's money to £1.6 billion – which equated to twenty-five times its previous year's earnings.

Despite the high price, it was to be a very successful acquisition. The industrial logic was impeccable and the implementation of the merger, under the supervision of Jack Strowger and Harold Mourgue, was carried out diligently and without affecting the momentum of the businesses. By keeping intact the high-street presence and identity of its two existing rental chains – DER and Multi-Broadcast – and the two inherited from Radio Rentals – Radio Rentals and Vista – Thorn suffered no loss of market share. In their submissions to the Monopolies Commission, the two companies estimated that they expected to reduce operating costs by upwards of £3 million, some of which would be passed on to customers. Thorn's total profits from the area labelled 'consumer electronics', which included both the television manufacturing and rental activities, amounted to around £6 million in 1967/68, the last year before the acquisition. The addition of Radio Rentals' profits for the same period would have increased this to a little over £15 million. By 1970/71, the combined profits had grown to £21 million.

There was, of course, growth in the market over this period, but much of the contribution from this was absorbed, at this stage, by higher depreciation and installation charges. Significant benefits do, therefore, appear to have been realised. With the market growing strongly as all the television channels switched to a colour service in 1969, consumer electronics manufacturing and rental were to provide an increasing proportion of Thorn's profits through the 1970s. By 1975/76, profits from this area were over £52 million and amounted to 70 per cent of the total. The Radio Rentals deal was probably the major contributor to Thorn's survival as an independent entity through the tough business climate of the 1970s. However, as we shall see, it was not enough to ensure Thorn's viability as a manufacturer of consumer electronic equipment, at least in the long term.

A postscript to the deal sheds some light on Jules Thorn's style and personality. The chairman of Radio Rentals was appointed to the Thorn board in August 1968 and made chairman of the combined rental business. However, by November he had been relieved of his responsibilities, and he resigned from the board later that year. As a substantial shareholder in the company in his own right – he owned 1 per cent of Thorn's shares – he was a wealthy man and, apparently, was intending to step aside in due course. However, the manner of his departure left a sour taste.

Jules Thorn's American partners from the 1940s, Sylvania Electric Products, who had helped to set him up in the fluorescent lighting business, were by this time part of General Telephone and Electronics Corporation (GTE). With lighting now a minor part of Thorn's business – it contributed only 15 per cent of the profits in 1970 – they decided to sell their shareholding, which, prior to the Radio Rentals acquisition, had amounted to a little under 20 per cent of the total. Given the impressive performance of the shares – Thorn's share price had increased tenfold over the previous ten years alone – it had been a good financial investment, but it was clear that a takeover by Sylvania – the original reason for its investment – had never really figured in Jules Thorn's thinking. Ironically, GTE was to re-enter the stage, in a minor role, much later on.

If the threat from Far Eastern imports represented one of the major concerns of the Thorn board in the late 1960s, the other was the vulnerability of the company to the discretionary income of the British consumer. In the last decade, there had been two severe slumps in demand for consumer durables – in the early 1960s and then after the Labour election victory in 1964. Credit controls – which applied to rental as well as retail sales – and changes in purchase tax, the two levers of choice for government tinkering with the economy at the time, hit consumer durables first and hardest – they were in effect the shock absorbers of the economy. There were two ways in which the company could reduce its exposure. One was to look for expansion outside the UK while sticking to the products it knew; the other, to go into new products not dependent on the consumer. In the late 1960s, Thorn was an extremely parochial company – 95 per cent of profits were earned in the UK. Although the company developed a slightly greater enthusiasm for international markets over the next decade, the position did not change significantly until the EMI acquisition – in 1979, the UK still accounted for nearly 90 per cent of the profits. The reasons for this are important and we will return to them later. However, in the late 1960s, the main focus for diversification was in the UK.

Thorn had had non-consumer interests for a long time, but these were generally related to its main, consumer-oriented businesses. Much lighting equipment was sold for industrial and commercial applications and there was a small activity in electronic components. The acquisition of Glover and Main, in 1965, although mainly undertaken for the gas cooker business, had brought in commercial catering and gas meters. However, the diversification process that started in 1967 was not related to these activities. In fact, it seems to have been a rather haphazard process, the only common theme being that most of the businesses acquired made or sold industrial rather than consumer products. Given the shrewdness with which mainstream deals such as Radio Rentals had been thought through, this random scattering of assorted seed

is particularly surprising. One consequence of it was that some
of the businesses acquired were in industries facing problems
of their own. Substantial sums were invested, for example, in
companies manufacturing and distributing cutting tools, at a
time when machined metal was being replaced, in many of its
applications, by moulded plastic. Others held out some promise
of growth but were not built upon, because the next deal would
be in some entirely different area.

The first and most notable of these diversifications was the
acquisition of Metal Industries, which, as we have seen, was an
opportunistic purchase taking advantage of the strong Thorn share
price. As the share price went on rising – it was to increase by 50
per cent against the FT All Share Index between the beginning
of 1967 and the end of 1968 – more deals followed. Keyswitch
Relays, a manufacturer of elcctro-magnetic relays, was bought in
March 1968, in a share deal for £1.9 million, which represented
fifteen times net earnings. KMT (Holdings) was acquired,
also in exchange for shares, in April for £5.6 million, which
represented nineteen times net earnings. Its diverse activities
included manufacturing and distributing cutting tools, making
garage equipment, making and hiring scaffolding, and acting as
a steel stockholder. Gothic Electrical, a component distributor,
was acquired in June, again for shares, at a price of £0.7 million.
In the twelve months before the Radio Rentals acquisition was
completed, Thorn had increased its issued share capital by 9 per
cent as a result of this string of small acquisitions. Four further
acquisitions of small engineering companies were made that year
and further businesses were added to the category labelled 'general
engineering' over the next few years. By 1973, over forty separate
companies were listed in this category in the annual report.

The mechanism of using a strong share price to acquire
assorted businesses that would enhance earnings growth and
hence further strengthen the share price was well known to the
financial conglomerates. Thorn's style in the past, however, had
been to stay in a limited number of areas that its senior managers
were familiar with. Neither its management style nor its systems
were attuned to this type of financially driven conglomerate
management. The acquired businesses were left as independent
entities within a loose grouping, headed by Sir Joseph Latham,

a former managing director of AEI, who had been instrumental in arranging the transfer of AEI's shares in BLI to Thorn and had subsequently joined the board. This arrangement neither encouraged the businesses to 'sweat the assets', as the financial conglomeraters would have done, nor did it succeed in developing a strategic core. The results were therefore disappointing – by 1973, profits from engineering were lower than they had been in 1969 and the return on sales was lower than in any other part of Thorn.

More importantly, perhaps, the exercise distracted senior management from the much more critical issues that were beginning to face the company. Surprisingly, while there was much criticism from the City in later years of the wide and haphazard spread of Thorn's interests, at the time this hectic diversification attracted no adverse comment. In the buoyant mood of the period, it seems to have escaped the stock market's notice that Thorn was using its highly priced shares to diversify away from the very businesses that its shareholders valued so highly.

Acquisitions also played a major role in the mainstream areas. Kenwood Manufacturing, which made small kitchen appliances, was acquired in 1968 for £11.7 million in shares. Kenwood's style, under its eponymous founder, Kenneth Wood, had been rather more lavish than Thorn's, and Jules Thorn was horrified to discover that his new acquisition had a four-engined executive aircraft on order and the order could not be cancelled. Needless to say, the aircraft was sold immediately after it was delivered. Kenwood was one of Thorn's most expensive acquisitions, since its net assets were only £1.8 million and the price represented a multiple of twenty-nine times its previous year's earnings. However, the Kenwood Chef had given the brand name a considerable cachet, and it was hoped that it could be used in other areas. Kenwood became part of Thorn's domestic appliances division, but it sat uneasily alongside the more mundane cookers and refrigerators. Neither Kenwood nor the other domestic appliance interests gained much benefit from their association. Further acquisitions of companies making small appliances – Goblin, Hoover, Moulinex, Braun – were contemplated, but not pursued.

However, in April 1971, Thorn made a bid that was to add

significantly to its gas cooker interests. The bid for Parkinson Cowan was in the older style of Thorn deals – based on a mixture of opportunism and industrial logic. The company made gas cookers, domestic heating equipment, gas meters and washing machines. At the time of the bid it was making no profit, but Thorn had spotted that this was due to one subsidiary, Fisher Bendix, which was losing about £1 million a year, offsetting the profit of £1 million made by the rest of the business. Thorn bid around £6.3 million for the company and took control of it in May 1971. Most of the business was quickly integrated with the complementary parts of Thorn, but Fisher Bendix proved to be a bigger challenge than expected. Since this business was to acquire some notoriety in the annals of Britain's industrial relations in the 1970s, the story of its fortunes under Thorn is worth telling.

Fisher Bendix had had a chequered history. It had originally been part of a company called Fisher and Ludlow, which had been acquired by the British Motor Corporation (which subsequently became British Leyland and, later, Rover). Its management had tried to make a succession of products – bicycles, stainless steel sinks, washing machines – with limited success. Parkinson Cowan had acquired it in 1968, when demand for its gas appliances was outstripping its ability to supply them, following the landing of gas from the North Sea. At the time, it seemed a cheap way of getting additional capacity quickly. Fisher Bendix's factory was in Kirby, near Liverpool, an area whose people had a ferocious reputation for industrial militancy. It also happened to have, as its Member of Parliament, the former and soon-to-be-again Prime Minister, Harold Wilson.

Parkinson Cowan found out, in due course, that it was impossible to manufacture anything efficiently at the factory, and by the time Thorn came on the scene it had decided to close it. A buyer for the site – a property developer – was found by Thorn in August – shortly before the annual summer shut-down – and the workforce were informed of the closure plan. They went away for their summer break, muttering dark threats. Thorn's original plan had been not to reopen the factory after the shut-down, but in the meantime it had been discovered that a particular production contract had to be completed before the factory could close. When they returned from their summer break, however, production was the last thing the workforce had in mind. A serious confrontation developed and John Richards, the personnel director of Thorn, was despatched to Kirby. A meeting was called in the boardroom, which quickly became very heated. At a pre-arranged signal, a barrage of chairs, collected from the offices, was hurled at the unfortunate management representatives, who fled the scene.

Thereafter, the half-a-million-square-foot factory became the venue for a sit-in which lasted for months, while complex negotiations, involving Harold Wilson himself, went on in London. The workforce representatives pointed out that there had never been a dispute at the factory prior to Thorn's arrival – more a reflection, perhaps, on the submissiveness of previous owners than on good industrial relations. Thorn was made to feel that it had acted hastily and should have given the workers a chance to demonstrate that they could succeed. A number of the Thorn management were inclined to wash their hands of the whole thing and leave the sit-in to its fate, but Jules Thorn insisted that a settlement had to be found. Presciently guessing that Harold Wilson would soon become Prime Minister again, he knew that it was not in the company's interests to leave him with a failed negotiation on his hands. In the end, Thorn was persuaded to keep the factory open, but attitudes were not to change.

By 1973, with the coal miners in dispute with the Conservative government, the whole country was put on a three-day week as a result of power shortages. In the middle of this, the shop stewards announced to the management that they wanted a factory holiday on a certain Wednesday, as they were organising a dance on the previous evening to celebrate the continuance of Fisher Bendix and would need a day to recover from the festivities. It was pointed out that Wednesday was one of the three days that the factory had electric power and could they not choose one of the two days when the factory would have to close anyway? It turned out that this was not possible – the workforce had decided on Wednesday and Wednesday it would be. Finally, Thorn decided that no matter what the future political price, Fisher Bendix would have to go. A buyer was found, but he was no more successful than Thorn. By 1974, Harold Wilson had become Prime Minister and his industry minister, Anthony Wedgwood Benn, saw Fisher Bendix as a test-bed for his ideas on workers' co-operatives. Vast sums of taxpayers' money were lavished on it, again to no avail, and in the end it just became a symbol of the sour state of industrial relations in the 1970s.

Notwithstanding the problems at Fisher Bendix, Thorn's domestic appliance business was at its most successful in the early 1970s. Boosted by acquisitions, its contribution to Thorn's profits increased from 12 per cent in 1971 to 23 per cent in 1975, and the return on sales regularly ran at 9 to 10 per cent, a level not seen before and never to be reached again. The expanding availability of North Sea gas had boosted demand for gas cookers and central heating equipment and, as cookers were not subject to purchase tax and credit restrictions, they were relatively immune to the stop-go tinkering of the government. Cookers also had the benefit of largely being immune from competition from Continental manufacturers which had, by then, begun to affect other consumer durable markets. They were, in the main, sold through retail showrooms run by the nationalised gas and electricity utilities, a cosy, *de facto* monopoly which kept out imports. In contrast, refrigerators, which were sold much more widely, were a miserable product line for Thorn: imports, particularly from Italy, kept down prices and margins and in spite of having a 15 per cent share of the UK market, it is unlikely that Thorn made any profit out of it. In fact, by 1972, worries about the inroads of Continental manufacturers had prompted the Thorn board to consider forming an alliance in domestic appliances with one of the other British manufacturers. Extensive discussions were held with GEC and at one point the companies came close to agreement on pooling their interests, but as with Thorn's other prospective alliances with GEC, this one broke down over the question of who would control the business. Discussions were also held with Tube Investments (now TI), which, at the time, had extensive interests in the field, but these also came to nought.

Questions of scale and the threat of international competition were an even greater concern in the lighting business. The percentage of profits contributed by lighting had fallen from 45 per cent in 1965 to 15 per cent by 1970. The incandescent lamp business had become a victim of the same forces that had prompted ELMA to form its pre-war cartel. The price of a hundred-watt light bulb in 1976 – 22.5 pence – was the same, in money terms, as it had been when Jules Thorn first started his business in 1928. After adjusting for inflation, the price had fallen by 87 per cent. Reductions of this order have become commonplace in many electronic products, but usually as a consequence of genuine reductions in manufacturing costs resulting from new designs and manufacturing processes. That had not been the case in the manufacture of light bulbs – while there had been improvements, the basic product and processes were essentially unchanged. Consequently, few British manufacturers were making a profit out of incandescent lamps by the early 1970s, but because of the sunk investment and the need to keep a full range of products, they kept going.

Fluorescent lamps had been very profitable in the 1950s and 1960s – the market had grown at 10 per cent per annum in the mid 1960s – but even they were showing signs of age by the 1970s. As with the makers of tyres and batteries, part of the manufacturers' problem was their own success: the life of a fluorescent tube was about two and a half times longer than it had been fifteen years earlier, and since two-thirds of tubes were sold as replacements, the market was inevitably reduced. Lighting was one area where Thorn had started tackling markets in Continental Europe in the 1960s: a manufacturing plant – jointly owned with Sylvania – had been set up in Italy and sales companies in Scandinavia and Germany. By 1974, a third of Lighting's profits was earned outside the UK.

It seems clear, however, that by the early 1970s, the Thorn board was having serious doubts about the company's long-term ability to remain an independent player in the lighting business. These fears were amplified when it became known that General Electric of the US, one of the largest lighting companies in the world, had begun to take an interest in Europe. In 1973, Thorn's former American partner, GTE-Sylvania, had also decided to enter the British market – they had kept out while they had owned a shareholding in Thorn. There was a flurry of discussions with both these companies and, at one stage, General Electric seriously considered buying the lighting business, but in the end decided not to. The possibility of the sale aroused considerable emotion among Thorn's senior executives – lighting had after all been Thorn's original business. The fact that Jules Thorn took the possibility as far as he did indicates that he was well aware of the looming problems. Another suggestion, however, is that he was merely trying to put a value on the business, for his own satisfaction, and never had any intention of selling. Although no deal was done at this stage, both General Electric and GTE-Sylvania were to re-emerge as potential buyers of the lighting business nearly two decades later.

It was in consumer electronics that the most important developments of the 1970s were to take place. The initial take-up of colour television was slow: only 121,000 sets were sold or rented in 1968. However, in November 1969, ITV and BBC1 also started broadcasting in colour and demand took off. Sales and new rentals jumped to 500,000 in 1970, nearly doubled to 922,000 in 1971, and then doubled again to 1.8 million in 1972. For those British television manufacturers who had survived the 1960s – Thorn, GEC, Rank, STC, Decca and the multinational Philips – it felt like a return to the boom times of the 1950s, but this time there was a spectre at the feast.

The PAL (Phase Alteration Line) technology used for British (and most European) colour television was based on patents owned by a number of European manufacturers, the most important being those owned by Telefunken of Germany. There had been great reluctance to license the Japanese to use the PAL technology and the licences eventually granted had severe constraints attached to them. These included restrictions on the size of sets they could make (Japanese consumers generally bought smaller sets than the Europeans) and on the proportion of their production they could export. On top of this, individual European governments negotiated voluntary limits with the Japanese on their exports: in the UK, they were limited to a 10 per cent market share.

As it happened, in the early years of the colour television boom, Japanese imports were the least of worries for the British manufacturers. They had grossly underestimated the rate at which colour television would take off once all three channels started broadcasting in colour: the consensus in 1969 was that demand would run at around 400,000 units per year in the early 1970s. By 1972, actual British production capacity was, at a stretch, around 1.4 million sets – of which Thorn's capacity amounted to around 600,000 sets – but this was still 400,000 sets below the actual demand. Demand for rented, as opposed to purchased, sets was particularly high – some 75 per cent of sets were being rented. Thorn's capacity was insufficient to meet its requirements and, unable to buy sets from other British manufacturers, it had to start importing sets from Japan.

By 1973, UK demand had reached 2.8 million sets but, by then, a new manufacturer had arrived in Britain. Unable to export enough to meet demand for its sets because of the voluntary restraint agreement with the British Government, Sony decided to set up a factory at Bridgend in Wales. Ironically, because of the location of its plant, it was generously subsidised and warmly welcomed by the government. In the following year, Matsushita set up its own plant in Cardiff, again heavily subsidised by the government. However, by the time the third Japanese manufacturer, Hitachi, had decided to start manufacturing in the UK, the outraged British manufacturers, with support from the trade unions, managed to force the government into an embarrassing reversal of its promise of further subsidies. Hitachi, instead, formed a joint venture with GEC and eventually took over the business completely.

In the meantime, an interesting situation had developed in the business of producing colour picture tubes. These accounted for about one-third of the cost of a colour television set and, as with black and white tubes, involved a complex and capital-intensive manufacturing process. As a result of its acquisition of Radio Rentals, Thorn had inherited an interest in a joint company with RCA, which was about to start manufacturing colour tubes in Skelmersdale in Lancashire. It had previously made arrangements with GTE-Sylvania for access to colour picture tube technology, but these were abandoned in favour of RCA and Thorn's stake in the joint company was increased to 51 per cent. Initially, the Skelmersdale plant produced good profits. However, the colour tube market was of particular interest to the Japanese as it was free from the export and licensing restrictions with which the television set market was ringed – including the freedom to make the larger sizes of tubes, popular in Europe, for which the Japanese were not licensed to make sets. Since, apart from Thorn and Philips, the other British manufacturers did not make their own tubes, they welcomed the availability of cheaper tubes from Japan. The effect on Skelmersdale of the flood of Japanese colour tubes was exacerbated by the end of the colour television boom as the government slammed the brakes on the British economy in December 1973, following the oil price hike that year. By 1975, colour television sales and rentals had fallen by nearly 40 per cent and Skelmersdale was making losses at the rate of £4 million a year. The chairman's statement in the annual report for the year to March 1975 includes the following passage:

> The reduction in colour picture tube demand for the UK market, coupled with a high level of imports from Japan at prices only marginally higher than the prime cost of manufacturing in this country, has resulted in heavy losses and raised doubts about the future of colour tube production in the UK. The colour tube is the technical heart of a television set and represents a large proportion of the total cost of the receiver. Complete dependence on imports could present a serious threat to the long-term future of the UK consumer electronics industry.

Neither a Department of Trade delegation to Japan, nor direct appeals to Harold Wilson, now Prime Minister, to take unilateral action, could stop the flood of Japanese picture tubes. In October that year, the decision was taken to close the plant, resulting in the loss of 1,400 jobs and a closure cost of £15 million, equivalent to £65 million in today's money, of which Thorn's share was one-half. It was the largest financial disaster suffered by Thorn, but its psychological impact was even greater: it raised for the first time the possibility that Thorn might not have a long-term future as a television manufacturer.

The year to March 1976 was to be Jules Thorn's last as chairman. In his final chairman's statement, he repeated what had become a frequent plea:

> The Government and the UK industry must recognise the real danger of continued unfair competition from imports spreading across the whole range of consumer electronic industries. I believe that more effective measures should be introduced to deal with this problem.

Despite dreadful economic conditions in Britain – value added tax had been increased to 25 per cent during the year as the government grappled with another sterling crisis – the company did Jules Thorn proud. Pre-tax profits were up by 14 per cent to £74.4 million – the cost of closing Skelmersdale was treated as an extraordinary item and not charged against profits – and earnings per share were up by 19 per cent. Financially, the last decade had been highly successful: pre-tax profits had increased sevenfold since 1967 – nearly threefold after allowing for inflation. Earnings per share, which took account of the large number of new shares issued during the period, had increased over threefold – or by over 30 per cent after allowing for inflation. Thorn now ranked among the ten largest companies in the country. However, the long-term outlook had never been more uncertain.

4

The Succession to Sir Jules

The question of the succession to Jules Thorn had been a matter of public discussion since shortly after his seventieth birthday in 1969. In January 1970, in what was taken by many as a move towards grooming his successor, he appointed Jack Strowger as managing director of the company. Jack Strowger had been with Thorn all his working life, having joined the accounting department in 1942, and he had been appointed to the board in 1965. During the 1960s, he had been Jules Thorn's trouble-shooter and acquisition expert and had played a major role in the integration of Radio Rentals. Following his appointment, Strowger set up a more formal organisation structure, with the company divided into product groups and divisions. He also made some moves to expand the international presence of the company, particularly in the rental business in Europe. By 1974, however, Jules Thorn had still to name a successor and in the annual report that year, he acknowledged the pressure to do so by stating:

> As far as the future of the chairmanship is concerned a suitable candidate will be found. In the meantime, at the unanimous wish of my colleagues, I am remaining Chairman.

Nowadays, in most large companies, matters of succession to the chairman are arranged by non-executive directors who are expected to be above the jockeying for position that their executive colleagues are likely to be involved in. Thorn had traditionally not had independent non-executive directors, a reflection, perhaps, on Jules Thorn's discomfort in working with people he did not know well. Retiring executive directors would stay on as non-executives, but they did not necessarily have the independent viewpoint of an outsider. This was complicating the search for a successor and became another point of criticism. In response, in 1973, Jules Thorn decided that he would invite Henry Sporborg, a director of Hambros Bank – Thorn's merchant bank at the time – to be non-executive deputy chairman. However, such was his reluctance to handle the matter himself that he asked Nigel Graham Maw, the senior partner of Thorn's law firm, to approach Sporborg, without being specific about the purpose. As a result, a very confused meeting took place between Sporborg and Graham Maw, at which neither of them was sure what the other had been told and what they were expected to do. Sporborg was eventually appointed deputy chairman of the company, but the pressure to appoint a successor to Jules Thorn continued.

By 1975, still with no successor appointed and Jules Thorn in his seventy-seventh year, there was widespread concern. In the summer of that year, John Davis, the business editor of the *Observer*, noted:

> The succession at the giant Thorn Electrical Industries, which has been exercising the mind of founder and resident chairman Jules Thorn – not to mention the City – for some time, is now causing considerable interest in Government circles.
>
> The Government is, at this delicate stage, resorting to only the very gentlest form of arm-twisting. It feels, rightly, that Sir Jules Thorn, one of the most brilliant post-war industrialists, has still a lot to offer.
>
> But Sir Jules is 76. Time is running out for a smooth transition at the top, leaving him able to enjoy fully the kudos of being Thorn's first president.

John Davis went on to report the current stock market gossip that the front runner for the job was Sir Arnold Hall, then chairman of the engineering and aerospace company Hawker Siddeley. Hawker Siddeley was about to have most of its aircraft business nationalised by the Labour government, which would leave it with a large cash balance. Davis's neat solution was for Thorn to merge with Hawker Siddeley, thus allowing Jules Thorn to 'bask comfortably in the knowledge that he had both assured Thorn of continued top flight management and done it in a way that opened up vast new commercial frontiers at the same time.'

Whether such a merger would have represented a sensible approach to the problems looming for both companies is debatable. It does, however, indicate how strongly the merits of the widely diversified company were regarded in the mid-1970s. In any event, that particular idea was not taken up, but the pressure on the succession issue intensified when Thorn's results for the year ending in March 1975 were announced. After a decade of unbroken growth, pre-tax profits were down by 12 per cent. There were specific reasons for this: the difficult economic situation in the UK, the losses at the Skelmersdale picture tube factory, and the cost of closing a television manufacturing business in Belgium, which was charged against trading profit. However, it gave further grounds for disquiet among institutional investors.

The search for a successor from outside the company was inevitably going to be a long and awkward one. Jules Thorn's private and retiring nature did not lend itself to the sort of networking among the great and the good which would throw up shoals of likely names. He still regarded the company as his own, even though his shareholding at that stage, including shares held in trust, was only around 5.5 per cent. Moreover, the company had been, literally, his life's work, and to hand it over to someone else was, understandably, not an easy task for him. One of his colleagues on the board recalls: 'No one believed the old boy would retire.' This is not to suggest that there was not a great deal of search activity. A succession of likely candidates was interviewed by Jules Thorn. Board colleagues would regularly be asked to arrange to take a customer to lunch at the Ivy restaurant, next to Thorn's head office. While there, they would spot the chairman entertaining a possible successor at a nearby table. At a suitable moment, they would be called over and introduced to the candidate, but with no warning as to why they were meeting him, and, later, they would be quizzed on what they thought of him.

The person who finally emerged from this long and tortuous process as the new chairman of Thorn was Sir Richard 'Dick' Cave. In many respects, a bigger contrast to Jules Thorn would be difficult to imagine. Physically, he was a large man, well over six feet tall, and he retained the demeanour of the tank commander he had been during the war, when he had won the Military Cross in action in Germany. With a booming voice and a brusque manner, he represented a very different style of industrialist. He had joined Smiths Industries, an engineering and aerospace components company, after the war and had risen to be a very successful chairman. The link with Thorn appears to have been Sir Joseph Lockwood, former chairman of EMI and dining partner of Jules Thorn, who was a non-executive director of Smiths Industries.

Sir Richard was appointed chairman of Thorn in August 1976, at the age of fifty-six. The task he faced was a daunting one. The organisation was heavily imbued with a distinctive culture derived from Jules Thorn's half-century of leadership; the other board members were long-standing Thorn men; and their egos had been bruised by the appointment of an outsider as chairman. Jules Thorn retained a presence in the background as president of the company – an honorific role – and he kept an office on the top floor of Thorn House. However, Sir Richard was no shrinking violet and he set about making his mark in a forthright, even occasionally brutal, manner. On one occasion, fed up with what he felt was Jules Thorn's continued meddling, he stormed into his office, ripped the telephone off the wall, and announced that his – Jules Thorn's – time was over.

The informal style that had prevailed in the past was replaced with more formal procedures; salaries and conditions of service were brought into line with other large companies and attention was given to thinking more systematically about the longer term. A number of eminent non-executive directors were appointed.

At the time Sir Richard took over as chairman, Thorn was in the paradoxical position of being, ostensibly, a very successful company yet facing serious, even fundamental, problems. The share price had weakened in the recession following the 1973 oil crisis, falling by 50 per cent against the FT All Share Index by 1974 as consumer durable stocks were severely marked down. However, by 1977 it had risen by over 60 per cent. In the year to March 1977, the first under Sir Richard's chairmanship, pre-tax profits rose by 39 per cent to £103.7 million with the performance of all parts of the company improving over the previous year. But in his statement in the annual report of that year, Cave hinted at some of the underlying concerns:

> There is one part of our business on which I must make special comment because in it we must express reservation about our ability to go for growth. This is in the manufacture of current types of television and audio products. The reason for our reservation is the aggressive world strategy followed by the Japanese in this product area. I can only express the hope that realisation of the dangers of allowing the Japanese to be successful with this strategy will come in time to allow the necessary counter measures to be taken. Although the focus is currently on consumer products and their related components the same situation could arise in the much wider fields of light electronics using modern higher technologies and affecting major parts of industry that are essential for the nation's well-being. This is a matter for Government and industry acting together.

Although he specifically referred to electronics and Japanese competition, similar threats existed in domestic appliances and lighting from international competitors other than the Japanese. At root was the fact that Thorn's strategy of being a follower rather than a leader, of not investing heavily in technology, of relying on secure distribution channels in the UK market and of being an efficient but not leading-edge manufacturer, had run its course. In the growing markets of the post-war era, it was sufficient to be able to produce adequate products at reasonable prices. By the late 1960s and 1970s, however, as the main consumer durable markets had matured, radical innovation and continuous improvement in products and production methods became the only way to stay competitive. The Thorn culture, with a heavy bias against risky but discretionary expenditure on areas such as development, was not well suited to this changed environment. The mismatch was amplified by another facet of Thorn's culture, one that it shared with many other British manufacturers.

The Japanese and the leading European manufacturers of consumer durables had realised, by the 1960s, that the higher and more risky investment that these markets now called for could only be recouped by selling on an international scale. With few exceptions, most British manufacturers in the 1960s, while paying lip service to international sales, tended to regard them as a marginal rather than an essential element of their business. Exports were promoted when economic conditions allowed good profits to be earned, but were cut back or dropped when conditions changed. Some of these attitudes stemmed from the earlier relationship with export markets in the colonies: success in these largely depended on the position in the British market and, provided this was achieved, then exports could be taken for granted. Indeed, markets in the former colonies remained of particular importance to British manufacturers, although they were generally smaller and of much less competitive importance than European markets. But by the 1960s, the large European manufacturers of volume consumer goods were operating on a Continental scale: companies such as Philips, Electrolux, AEG and Braun had moved well beyond the boundaries of their home markets and had significant market shares across western Europe in markets that generally grew faster than Britain's. This gave them a scale advantage over their British rivals which, in time, became irretrievable.

In the mid-1960s, Thorn had a joint venture in lighting in Italy and small lighting operations in Germany and Scandinavia. Its consumer goods businesses had no interests in Europe, although they did have interests in Australia, New Zealand and South Africa. By 1970, the interests in Europe in consumer goods had increased, although this was entirely as a result of the acquisition in 1968 of Kenwood, which was a particularly international company. It is significant that, by 1975, one of Kenwood's European businesses – in Germany – had actually been closed down. In consumer electronics, a small Belgian television manufacturing company, Carad, was acquired in 1971 but it was closed down in 1974, following a fraud. The experience added to the company's wariness of Europe and further constrained expansion there. Market shares in the European television market in 1977 give some idea of Thorn's singular position. While the television market had some unique features, in particular the significant level of Japanese penetration, the general picture of high market shares in the UK and negligible shares on the Continent applied to most of Thorn's manufacturing businesses.

	West Germany	United Kingdom	France	Italy	Spain
Philips	15%	19%	33%	17%	25%
Grundig	26%	1%	11%	19%	16%
Telefunken	11%	1%	4%	11%	11%
ITT	6%	7%	10%	0	5%
Thomson	11%	0	26%	0	8%
Thorn	0	27%	0	0	0
Japanese	8%	14%	7%	4%	2%
Others	23%	31%	9%	49%	33%

The Thorn board were, of course, aware of the vulnerability of Thorn to international competition well before the arrival of Sir Richard. As we have seen, in both lighting and domestic appliances they had considered the need to form alliances with other companies in order to have sufficient scale to remain competitive. In television set manufacturing, however, reliance was placed on control of distribution outlets, which was one of the motivations for acquiring Radio Rentals; on protection by the PAL licensing arrangements; and, later, on some form of action by the government to protect the industry. In the event, the main damage in terms of imports, at least in the early years, came not from imported television sets but from colour picture tubes, where there were no constraints at all. Hope of further government action to protect the domestic industry – beyond the voluntary limits initially agreed with the Japanese on television sets – were not realised. All that British government lobbying of the Japanese succeeded in doing was to speed up the arrival of Japanese transplant operations in the UK – sometimes, as we have seen, supported by government subsidies. With new British factories and Japanese work practices, they were just as much a threat from Bridgend or Cardiff as they had been from Osaka or Tokyo.

Sir Richard may have had a clearer appreciation than his predecessor of the importance of operating internationally, but he did not significantly change the direction of the consumer durable businesses. He does, however, appear to have been convinced at an early stage that Thorn's lighting business was not viable as it then was. One of his first actions on taking over as chairman was to visit the two major US manufacturers, GE and GTE-Sylvania, to resurrect the possibility of a sale. It appears that while both were interested in buying the business, neither was prepared to pay the price he wanted. Given the hostility he was likely to face from his colleagues on a sale of so important a part of Thorn's heritage so early in his chairmanship, he would have had to have obtained an exceedingly generous price to carry the day.

Sir Richard was also sceptical about the future of the rental business and wanted to divert the cash being generated by it in the late 1970s into other areas. However, the arrival of the video cassette recorder gave the business a new lease of life and rental continued to be supported.

The new element of thinking that Sir Richard brought was the idea that the company should move into high-technology areas. This somewhat vague notion was to have far-reaching consequences for the company's future direction and is worth examining further, particularly as what exactly was meant by it was never clear, even within the company. Jules Thorn himself operated on the principle of borrowing technology developed by others and does not appear to have had any interest in technology as such. The only area of the company where there was any significant expenditure on developing new technology was in lighting and, even there, his attitude to it was completely utilitarian. In a revealing incident, shortly before his retirement, Thorn Lighting was invited to present the prestigious Faraday lecture to the Institute of Electrical Engineers. When he found out that acceptance was going to cost £20,000, not a large sum for a business with sales of £200 million, he insisted it was of no value and directed that the invitation should be turned down.

Part of Sir Richard's thinking was that the company should put more emphasis on technology development in its existing businesses. But the other strand was that the company should move into new, more technologically sophisticated areas where, it was hoped, it would be less subject to international competition. In the 1970s, two areas of Britain's electrical manufacturing industry that seemed immune from the problems of international competition and fluctuating markets were those that served the Post Office – which at the time was responsible for telecommunications – and the Ministry of Defence. These were customers who required no marketing or risky development expenditure; who would buy only from a small list of British suppliers; whose budgets were unaffected by the dictates of the economy; who would place contracts lasting for years; who could even be persuaded to offer protection from the consequences of not controlling costs well enough; and who always paid their bills on time – in fact, often paid them before the work was done. They were customers from heaven, and it is not surprising that any British company with the necessary skills had turned to working for one or both of them – indeed, some had abandoned any other business they may have had.

The Thorn board had, in the past, looked at entering both these areas. In fact, Thorn had formed a joint venture with L M Ericsson, the Swedish telecommunications company, in 1973, in order to supply the new generation of electronic telephone exchanges which the Post Office would require. Jack Strowger, who had been the architect of that deal, subsequently had a much more ambitious plan. In the mid-1970s, he spotted that the shares of Plessey, a major supplier to the Post Office and the Ministry of Defence, had fallen substantially. His plan was that Thorn should buy Plessey and then sell its telecommunications business to L M Ericsson, in exchange for a share stake. This would have given Thorn ownership of a large defence equipment contractor and a stake in one of the major international telecommunications companies. Jules Thorn, however, vetoed the plan. He had been a close friend of the late Sir Alan Clark, whose two sons, John and Michael, now ran Plessey and who regarded him as an honorary uncle. He would not hear of Thorn inconveniencing 'Alan's boys' in any way. In the late 1980s, Plessey was acquired by Thorn's old rival, GEC.

By 1978, Sir Richard had come around to the view that Thorn needed to make a large acquisition of a business not exposed to the vagaries of the British consumer. Thorn's own results since he became chairman had been good – in the three years up to March 1979 earnings per share had increased by 26 per cent per annum, although some of the increase had been due to a change in the way the company accounted for taxation. However, even at the pre-tax level, profits had increased by 17 per cent per annum and the shares had maintained their strength relative to the FT All Share Index. The introduction of video recorders in 1978 – entirely imported at the time – had improved the prospects for growth in the rental business. Other consumer durable markets in the UK were recovering from the 1976 slump. But the long-term problems had not gone away and the need to start implementing the strategy of becoming more international and more technological had become even more urgent. Only a radical change in direction could maintain the value of the company.

In the summer of 1979, the Conservatives, under the leadership of Margaret Thatcher, came to power with a radical programme and a modest majority. The dollar collapsed on the foreign exchanges – with conversion to sterling reaching $2.50 to the pound – and most of Thorn's exports started losing money, while competing foreign goods in British shops became even cheaper. Just then, EMI, a company full of technology and as international as any, put itself into play. The case for looking at it seemed compelling.

5

From Gramophone to Radar
The First Half Century at EMI

The origins of EMI go back almost to the invention of sound recording. The feasibility of recording and reproducing the human voice was proven when the sound of Thomas Alva Edison reciting 'Mary had a little lamb' issued from a device designed by him. The year was 1877, two years before he went on to invent the electric light bulb. In Edison's first device, the sound signal was recorded, by a vibrating stylus, as indentations on a sheet of tin foil wrapped around a rotating cylinder. In later refinements of the device, by associates of Alexander Graham Bell – of telephone fame – the recording medium was changed to beeswax coated on paper, but the cylindrical design remained. Although developments of Edison's device, the cylindrical phonograph, were to remain in use for many years, the basic design suffered from two major drawbacks: the vertical movement of the stylus as it followed the indentations distorted the reproduced sound, and the cylindrical shape of the recording surface made it difficult to replicate in quantity. The gramophone used a flat disc rather than a cylinder, across which a stylus moved along a spiral groove. The sound signal was recorded as indentations cut into the walls of the groove, which vibrated the stylus horizontally and, suitably amplified, could be reproduced as sound. The flat disc shape leant itself to the making of a metal negative (known as a matrix), from which stampers could be derived to press records in large numbers.

The designer of the gramophone was another remarkable man, Emile Berliner. Berliner was born in Hanover, in Germany, in 1851 and emigrated to the US in 1870. In 1878, a year after Alexander Graham Bell had invented the telephone, Berliner came up with a superior design of telephone receiver and went on to make a

number of inventions in telephony. His interest in telephony led
to his studying the problems of sound recording and reproduction,
and by 1888 he had demonstrated the flat disc gramophone. By
the end of the century, he and his associates had turned the
invention into a commercial proposition, with the development of
the clockwork spring-powered gramophone, wax discs for original
recordings, new techniques for making metal negatives, and the
use of shellac as the material for gramophone records.

In 1895, he formed The Berliner Gramophone Company in the
US to manufacture gramophones and records and, in 1897, his
European agent, William Barry Owen, set up The Gramophone
Company in London. The following year, Emile Berliner and his
brother, Joseph, formed Deutsche Grammophon Gesellschaft – in
which The Gramophone Company shortly acquired a controlling
interest. A bout of frenetic international expansion followed and
by the turn of the century, The Gramophone Company had established subsidiaries in France and Italy and was operating across
central Europe and Russia. In 1901, The Berliner Gramophone
Company in the US merged with the business of a collaborator of
Berliner's to form the Victor Talking Machine Company, which
would over the next half-century have a close relationship with
The British Gramophone Company.

While Berliner and his associates provided one strand in
EMI's parentage, the other was provided by the inventors and
developers of the alternative sound recording technology, the
cylindrical phonograph. Edison's original invention, developed
into a commercial product by Alexander Graham Bell and his
associates, led to the founding of The American Graphophone
Company and its associates, The North American Phonograph
Company and the Columbia Phonograph Company. Columbia
also started its European business in 1897, dispatching Frank
Dorian to Paris to establish a European trade in American-made
Columbia cylinder records. Early in its life, the American end
of Columbia went through a financial crisis brought on by poor
management. It took over a decade to restore the fortunes of the
British and European businesses of Columbia, while the American
business never really recovered, eventually going into receivership
in 1922. The man responsible for rescuing the British end of the
Columbia business was a New Yorker called Louis (later Sir Louis)

Sterling. By the end of the First World War, the London-based Columbia Graphophone Company was on its way to becoming a major record business.

The international music industry was created by the diaspora of a remarkable group of American businessmen who had learnt their trade with Edison, Berliner or with the Columbia business. William Barry Owen, the first managing director of The Gramophone Company, was a salesman who had been hired to market Berliner's products in the US before being sent to Europe to start the business there. Alfred Clark, his successor as managing director of The Gramophone Company, had worked with Edison, and then North American Phonograph before being hired by The Berliner Gramophone Company in Philadelphia. Louis Sterling was another American who had set up a cylinder manufacturing operation in Britain before his involvement in the rescue of the Columbia business. Indeed, most of the modern international music industry can trace its origins either to the Berliner businesses or to the Columbia businesses, or to both. The Victor Talking Machine Company was acquired by the Radio Corporation of America (RCA) and became RCA Victor. It now survives as a major part of the Bertelsmann Music Group (BMG). Deutsche Grammophon Gesellschaft, the Gramophone Company's German subsidiary, was seized by the German state during the First World War, and subsequently became an important part of PolyGram. The US Columbia business became the CBS music business, now owned by Sony. And EMI itself was formed by the merger of The Gramophone Company and The Columbia Graphophone Company in 1931. EMI, Sony, PolyGram and BMG are among today's top five music companies.

Berliner, of course, has a special place as the progenitor of the industry but, having started it on its course, his own interests returned to engineering and inventing. He turned his restless genius to the new field of aviation and, by 1908, he had designed an internal combustion engine that was the basis of many early aircraft engine designs. Later, in collaboration with his son, he designed an early helicopter which was successfully flown in 1919. Although he played no significant role in the development of The Gramophone Company after its early years, his cosmopolitanism and his eclectic interest in technology seemed to survive in The Gramophone Company and its successor, EMI.

When Berliner's associate, William Barry Owen, arrived in Britain in 1897, his intention was to find a British partner. He found one the following year. Trevor Williams, a wealthy British lawyer, agreed to guarantee bank loans extended to The Gramophone Company. Offices were found in Maiden Lane, off the Strand in central London, in 1898. It was at these offices that the company acquired its famous dog and trumpet trade mark.

An artist called Francis Barraud knocked at the door of 31 Maiden Lane, some time in 1899, carrying his now famous painting of his black and white fox terrier, Nipper, listening to the horn of a sound reproducing machine. He offered to sell it to Owen, as it might be of interest to Owen's company, and told him that he had entitled it 'His Master's Voice'. Owen pointed out that he had painted a machine with a cylinder, a phonograph, whereas Owen's company sold disc gramophones. If Barraud would suitably alter his painting, however, he, Owen, would buy it. Barraud was happy to oblige and Owen bought the amended painting for fifty pounds and, for a further fifty guineas, he purchased the copyright to the title. Barraud was later employed by The Gramophone Company to paint replicas of the original Nipper painting and twenty-four are known to have been produced.

The dog and trumpet logo and the 'His Master's Voice' (HMV) label were soon adopted by The Gramophone Company. The logo and label also appealed to The Gramophone Company's US associate, the Victor Talking Machine Company, who started using it in the Americas and, later, in China and Japan. Victor acquired the trade mark along with Berliner's other assets. Victor was acquired by RCA, which came to own the trade mark in the Americas and China. However, RCA lost ownership of its Japanese affiliate, Japan Victor Company, during the Second World War and this company, which is now the electronics giant JVC, owns the trade mark in the Far East. The result of this was the current fragmentation of the ownership of the trade mark.

The title of the painting, 'His Master's Voice', suggests that Nipper's owner was a recording artist. It is more likely, however, that Barraud's original painting was of a cylindrical dictating machine and not of a phonograph. Barraud's lack of appreciation of the differences between the varieties of sound recording and reproducing machines, newly appearing on the market at the time, is understandable. Early gramophones and phonographs were sound reproduction machines, but the connection with serious music was yet to be established. In its early days, the gramophone was dismissed as a toy by serious musicians. As a result, the early repertoire of The Gramophone Company consisted of ballads, comic songs and recordings of bands. It took considerable effort, helped by gradual improvements in sound recording technology, to change attitudes.

A major breakthrough came when the Italian tenor Enrico Caruso agreed to record for The Gramophone Company. His first recordings were made in a two-hour session on the afternoon of 11 April, 1902. For recording ten songs, he received a fee of £100. The fame he achieved through the sale of his records, and the considerable fortune he earned in royalties over time, enticed other established musicians to start making records. The sopranos Adelina Patti and Nellie Melba were early Gramophone Company artists. Melba's first records – fourteen twelve-inch discs bearing a mauve label with her signature – were released in 1904, with a retail price of twenty-one shillings each. Patti's first records were released in 1906 and they carried a special pink label. By the outbreak of the First World War, The Gramophone Company had recordings by a number of international performing artists in its catalogue.

The speed of the Gramophone Company's international expansion would be remarkable even in today's environment of scheduled air travel, fast telecommunications and international banking, let alone that of the early 1900s. Within a few years of its founding, the company's salesmen and recording engineers were at work in the remoter parts of the Balkans, in the Middle East, in Africa, in India and in China. Soon the King of Montenegro, the Queen of Romania and the Shah of Persia had recorded their voices for posterity. Before the outbreak of the First World War, factories had been built in Germany, Spain, France, Russia, India and, of course, in Britain. The Gramophone Company's musical repertoire was international from the beginning, a particular strength that EMI has maintained ever since. By 1906, 60 per cent of the company's profits were earned outside Britain, with one-half coming from its Russian business.

In the early years, The Gramophone Company was dependent on its associates in the USA and Germany for pressing its records. In 1906, it acquired a large area of agricultural land in Hayes, to the west of London and just north of where Heathrow Airport was later built. Here, an enormous complex of factories, offices and laboratories was erected. In its heyday, the site covered 150 acres of land and included two million square feet of factory space, providing employment for 10,000 people. For most of the next century, it would dominate the economic life of the town of Hayes, and its enormous white-washed utilitarian buildings still loom over the place, now dark and silent reminders of a vanished age. The company responsible for starting the construction of the Hayes factories was actually called The Gramophone and Typewriter Ltd. This had been formed in 1900 to acquire The Gramophone Company and its subsidiaries and to acquire the rights to manufacture the Lambert typewriter, a short-lived diversification that seemed to prefigure the numerous ventures outside music that EMI was to be involved with in the future. The typewriter business was abandoned in 1905 and the company changed its name back to The Gramophone Company in 1907.

The period up to the start of the war was a buoyant one for disc record manufacturers, in contrast to the fortunes of cylinder manufacturers. By 1913, it was estimated that one-third of households in the UK owned a gramophone. The war, however, brought growth to a halt and most of the manufacturing capacity in Hayes was switched to making munitions. By the war's end, the company had lost its German business, Deutsche Grammophon Gesellschaft, and was never able to regain control of it. It had to re-enter the German market in 1926 with a new company, Electrola. The Russian operation was also lost in the mayhem following the Russian revolution.

In spite of these setbacks, the post-war period until 1929 was a very profitable one for The Gramophone Company, with further international expansion and a revival of the British and European markets. The manufacture of gramophones in Hayes recommenced in 1919 and, in 1923, the company started its own research and development department. The introduction of electrical microphones and amplifiers increased the quality of sound recording and this, together with an increasing repertoire of popular music, greatly enhanced the appeal of the gramophone. Nineteen-twenty also saw the renewal of the relationship with the US Victor Talking Machine Company which, in exchange for an injection of fresh capital, acquired a 45 per cent shareholding in the Gramophone Company. In 1921, The Gramophone Company opened the first outlet of what was to become the HMV music retailing operation.

In retrospect, the 1920s were a golden age for the music industry not seen again until the 1960s. Both The Gramophone Company and The Columbia Graphophone Company greatly expanded their repertoires. Columbia established a particular reputation for recording complete orchestral works by the world's leading orchestras. It had secured contracts with some of the best-known composers and conductors of the day, including Sir Thomas Beecham, Sir Henry Wood, Bruno Walter, Igor Stravinsky and Gustav Holst. Among others, The Gramophone Company secured the services of Sir Edward Elgar.

This golden period came to an end in the 1930s as the Great Depression and the spread of radio broadcasting, which provided a cheaper source of entertainment, devastated the recorded music industry. The following figures are estimates of the trend in the British market for recorded music over the 1930s.

Year	Consumer Expenditure (£ millions)	% of Disposable Income
1929	5.42	0.129
1930	5.09	0.126
1931	3.54	0.093
1932	2.60	0.070
1933	2.03	0.054
1934	1.63	0.042
1935	1.27	0.032
1936	1.04	0.024
1937	1.01	0.023
1938	1.06	0.024
1939	1.14	0.024

Source: Electric and Musical Industries Limited estimates, 1957 Annual Report.

It was this collapse of the market, repeated worldwide, which brought about the merger of The Gramophone Company and The Columbia Graphophone Company in April 1931 to form

Electric and Musical Industries (although it rapidly came to be known as EMI, the company did not officially change its name until 1971). The impetus for the merger came from the large American shareholders in the two companies, RCA in the case of The Gramophone Company and J P Morgan, the US investment bank, in the case of Columbia. RCA, a pioneer of radio broadcasting, had acquired The Victor Talking Machine Company – and its shareholding in The Gramophone Company – when the Depression, and the inroads of radio, had hit the American market. Because of the RCA and J P Morgan shareholdings, at its inception almost two-thirds of EMI was American-owned. RCA sold its shares in 1935, but EMI continued to have a significant US following during its existence as an independent company.

Alfred Clark, chairman of The Gramophone Company, became the first chairman of EMI and Louis Sterling, the saviour of Columbia, its first managing director. Its directors included the legendary David Sarnoff, founder and president of RCA. With their business plummeting – record sales, in units, were to fall by over 80 per cent between 1930 and 1938 – the management of the new company set about a ruthless rationalisation of its interests. Considerable savings were achieved but, in spite of these, EMI made a cumulative loss of over £1 million in the first three years of its existence. It is therefore all the more remarkable that this period also marked the start of EMI's efforts to become a pioneer in electronic engineering.

By the time they merged, both The Gramophone Company and Columbia had established research and development departments, primarily motivated by developments in the technology of sound recording. Columbia's had been started in 1924 under Isaac (later Sir Isaac) Shoenberg, a former engineer with Marconi, who was to play a key role in the company for the next three decades. Until the mid-1920s, discs were produced acoustically rather than electronically – the singer sang not into a microphone, but into an acoustic horn. The accompanying piano would have to be placed – with its back removed – on a platform, in order to be level with the horn. Certain instruments, such as the cello and double bass, were not suitable for recording and their parts had to be taken by the bassoon and the tuba, respectively. In 1924, Bell Laboratories in the US introduced the first practical electrical sound recording system which it licensed to most of the world's record companies. For this, it required a royalty of one old British penny per pressing, representing around 5 per cent of the price of a popular record.

Columbia had taken out a licence in 1925, but Isaac Shoenberg was determined to develop his own system to avoid paying the royalty. In 1929, he recruited an engineer of exceptional ability, Alan Dower Blumlein, from International Western Electric, the British company that held the Bell patents. By 1931, Blumlein had developed an alternative system for electrical recording which actually gave better results than Western Electric's. He then went on to consider the problems of stereophonic recording – reproducing in the ears of the listener, with a pair of loudspeakers, the same signals as they would receive if they were listening to an off-centre source of sound. He recognised that it was the slight shift in the phase of the sound signal between the two ears which gave the perception of direction and depth. His work resulted in an important patent in stereophonic recording but, given the state of electrical components available at the time, as well as the depressed state of the record industry, it was not a commercial proposition. Commercial stereophonic recording would not be introduced for another twenty-five years, but Blumlein's ideas on sound perception were applied to the problem of locating aircraft by their sound in the early years of the Second World War.

Following the formation of EMI in 1931, Shoenberg was given responsibility for advanced development for the combined group. With the problem of electrical sound recording solved, he turned his attention to a new opportunity with enormous potential. Ideas for the design of a television system had existed since the discovery of photoconductivity and photoemission – the relationship between light and electricity – in the late nineteenth century. In 1884, Paul Nipkow, a German scientist, patented a complete television system. The distinctive feature of his system was a method of scanning an image, in order to convert it into an electrical signal, by using a rotating disc with a spiral of small apertures cut into it. In 1908, a Scottish electrical engineer, A. A. Campbell Swinton, described an alternative approach to scanning the image, by using the beam of a cathode ray tube to scan the image line by line. His system could not be built at the time because of a lack of suitable components, but it was a forerunner of the first practical television system.

By the 1920s, improvements in electrical components and materials had made the construction of a system possible. The man who is credited with demonstrating the first television system, John Logie Baird, went back to the mechanical scanning approach designed by Nipkow. The system he demonstrated in 1926 displayed a picture formed of only thirty lines repeating twelve and a half times per second. The picture had poor definition and flickered badly but, while his system was not adopted for practical use, it did stimulate great interest in the development of a practical system for television broadcasting. The Gramophone Company began a television research programme in March 1929, but it was the formation of EMI in 1931, which brought in the engineering expertise of Columbia, including in particular that of Alan Blumlein, which led to the establishment of the television research group that would crack all the problems involved in developing a practical system. EMI went back to Campbell Swinton's ideas for scanning the image electronically, as Baird's system had indicated that mechanical scanning was unlikely to be capable of producing an adequate picture, while advances in cathode ray tube technology had made electronic scanning a practical proposition.

The crucial achievement of the EMI team was not so much the invention of radically new technology, but the design and integration of all of the elements – from cameras to receivers and all the complex circuits in between – necessary for a practical television system. Shoenberg saw the need to design a system that would endure for many years since, once adopted, changes in the standards would be extremely complex and expensive. The EMI system displayed a picture composed of 405 lines repeating twenty-five times per second, without flickering, and was to form the basis of British television broadcasting until the 1960s. A measure of its superiority over alternatives available at the time is the fact that the alternative Baird system under consideration by the BBC could only produce a 240-line picture. A public television service using the EMI system was started by the BBC in 1936 – the first in the world and three years ahead of the US.

It would be difficult to find a better example of excellence in product development – in British industry or elsewhere – than the story of EMI's involvement with television. Here was a company that spotted a major opportunity, concentrated its resources and risked its own money in the development, used the best of the ideas available elsewhere and produced a practical system, all in the remarkably short period – given the radically new technologies involved – of around five years. The benefit to British television broadcasting of having a working system before the rest of the world and, in particular, of having a system that was good enough to use after the Second World War, when public broadcasting really got going, must have been substantial.

From the point of view of EMI's shareholders, however, the objective of all this activity was to make profits for them. In this respect, the performance was much less glowing. EMI had hoped to profit primarily by manufacturing and selling television sets. The Gramophone Company had become a significant manufacturer of radio receivers as a result of the acquisition of Marconiphone in 1929 – thus deriving some commercial benefit from the product that was damaging its record business. By the early 1930s, EMI was a major manufacturer of gramophones, radios and radiograms and had even ventured into making domestic refrigerators. Making consumer durables in large volumes was, therefore, not a new activity for the company. It made its first batch of television receivers in 1936, for the start of the BBC's public broadcasting service. Yet, while a host of other British manufacturers, Thorn foremost among them, were to profit enormously from EMI's invention for a number of years after the war, EMI itself, as we have seen in Chapter 1, withdrew from the business in the 1950s, and it is unlikely that it ever made much profit out of manufacturing television sets. It continued to make and sell television cameras and other studio equipment until the late 1970s, but eventually withdrew from that area as well. This pattern of not realising the commercial rewards that its creativity and technical excellence seemed to justify was to be a recurring theme in EMI's history.

For the record business, the 1930s were a period of retrenchment, rationalisation and consolidation, as markets for recorded music collapsed. Paradoxically, however, they were an important period for the creation of EMI's classical repertoire. It was the market for popular music which was primarily hit by the depression. Classical music, appealing to a wealthier clientele and benefiting from improved sound reproduction, held up reasonably well. In Britain, sales of classical music, as a proportion of total record sales, increased by one-quarter during the 1930s. Profit margins on classical music were also higher than on popular music, a result of the premium prices charged and the much longer commercial life of classical recordings.

At its founding in 1931, EMI had inherited a strong classical repertoire from its two predecessor companies. It was the classical repertoire from The Gramophone Company, however, sold under the HMV label, which had enjoyed the greater commercial success, and EMI therefore concentrated its resources on the HMV label. The repertoire was built up in the 1930s through the signing of major European musicians such as the conductors Arturo Toscanini and Wilhelm Furtwangler and the soprano Lotte Lehman. EMI was also able to add to its roster a number of artists dismissed by RCA Victor, whose business in the US had been hit even harder in the depression than EMI's international business. In Britain, a new generation of conductors, including Malcolm (later Sir Malcolm) Sargent and Adrian (later Sir Adrian) Boult, were signed up. EMI's support enabled Sir Thomas Beecham, who had been a Columbia artist before the founding of EMI, to establish the London Philharmonic Orchestra. Sir Edward Elgar conducted the London Symphony Orchestra, playing a number of his own compositions, for the HMV label.

Nineteen thirty-one also saw the opening of the Abbey Road studios in London, which became the main British recording studios for EMI. The Abbey Road studios were probably the first custom-built recording studios in the world, and work on building them was started by The Gramophone Company before the merger with Columbia. Prior to their opening, recording had been undertaken at various improvised studios around London, often at rented concert halls if the recording involved a full orchestra. The studios were officially opened in November 1931 with a performance, by the London Symphony Orchestra, of Sir Edward Elgar's *Falstaff* suite, conducted by the composer. Nearly four decades later, The Beatles made Abbey Road the most famous recording studio in the world, when they named the last album they recorded together after it.

The artistically creative period of the 1930s came to an end with the outbreak of war. EMI lost many of its artists from Continental

Europe, some of whom fled to the US, where they eventually signed up with rival companies. The fledgling television business was put on ice and the company's electronic engineering skills were diverted to the war effort.

Early work on the detection of aircraft at a distance using radio waves – radar – by the British physicist Robert Watson Watt had led to the building, in 1938, of a chain of radar stations on the Thames estuary and the south coast of England, which was given the name 'Chain Home'. While these stations played a crucial role in giving early warning of attacking aircraft, they were not accurate enough to enable fighter aircraft to locate the enemy in the dark in order to shoot him down. One of the engineers working with Robert Watson Watt, Dr Edward Bowden, was given the task of developing a radar set that could be carried on night fighters for this purpose. He found that one of EMI's television receivers, suitably adjusted and installed on an aircraft, could pick up a signal bounced off another aircraft and, from this, its position and distance could be determined. This was the world's first airborne radar and with it began EMI's involvement in defence electronics.

The early night fighter radar was, in practice, almost impossible to use because of the limitations of its effective range. The radar could track only to within 1,500 feet of the enemy aircraft, while the range of the night fighter's machine-guns was less than half that distance. The pilot had to rely on his eyes for the last 1,000 feet of the attack, an impossible task on a dark night, particularly once German bombers had been fitted with shields to cover the flames from their engine exhaust ports. It was a technical development by Alan Blumlein, allowing radar sets to function to within 300 feet of the target, which finally solved the problem of intercepting enemy aircraft at night. The resulting A1 Mark IV radar was to be the principal airborne interception radar used by the RAF during the war and played a crucial role in defending Britain from the Luftwaffe.

EMI's contribution to the A1 Mark IV radar led directly to a role in the development and production of another important radar set, H2S (Home Sweet Home), which was used throughout the war by the RAF for surveillance, navigation and bombing. Alan Blumlein was heavily involved in this project, which was to cost him his life. He was flying on a Halifax bomber in early June 1942, with four

EMI colleagues, in order to test the prototype H2S radar, when the aircraft crashed into a hillside in the Wye Valley, killing all five. Although the loss was a considerable setback, EMI was able to start producing H2S sets later that summer. H2S was invaluable in helping Allied bomber crews to identify their targets, and was also extensively used in the battle against German submarines in the Atlantic.

In addition to its involvement in radar, EMI was also heavily involved in the manufacture of proximity fuses for anti-aircraft shells. These were extensively used against the V-1 flying bombs, of which two-thirds were destroyed. Perhaps the best evidence of the importance of EMI's contribution to the war effort is an aerial photograph issued by the Luftwaffe in March 1942 which shows the EMI complex at Hayes marked as a principal target, but wrongly described as the factory of Marconi Ltd, one of EMI's competitors. The site was actually hit by a V-1 in July 1944, killing thirty-seven and injuring many more.

Despite its sterling contribution, EMI emerged from the war in some disarray. Almost all of the company's manufacturing capacity had been employed in making military equipment and, while this had enabled it to establish a new business for the future, going back to making non-military products was a slow and difficult process. All contact had been lost with subsidiaries in France, Italy, Germany, Belgium, Holland, Denmark, Norway, Greece, Czechoslovakia, China and the Straits Settlements. Contact had to be re-established and the possibility of renewing activities had to be determined. In March 1945, the first chairman of the company and one of the founders of the recorded music industry, Alfred Clark, retired. He was succeeded, in a non-executive role, by Sir Alexander Aikman, who had spent most of his business career in India, prior to joining the board of EMI in 1941. With him came a new managing director, Sir Ernest Fisk, an electrical engineer who had spent much of his working life in Australia.

In the fifteen years since the founding of EMI, perceptions about the nature of the company's business had changed in subtle ways. The traumatic shrinking of the record market in the 1930s, the development of television in which EMI had played the leading role, the important contribution the company had made in the use of electronics to fight the war, had all contributed to this change.

Add to this the departure of Alfred Clark, one of the founders of the recorded music industry, and it is not surprising to find that the new management had a somewhat different vision of the future – one in which music was only one of the activities of the company, rather than the predominant one. In their first addresses to the shareholders at the EMI annual general meeting in December 1946, Sir Alexander and Sir Ernest described, at some length, both the problems facing the company and its potential. Much space was given to television – the BBC had restarted broadcasts in 1946 – and to other electronic products, but the music business was covered in one short paragraph.

To the extent that such addresses reflect the real perceptions of senior management, it would be reasonable to draw the conclusion that the business of the company was seen, primarily, as engineering and technology. This was spelt out by Sir Ernest in his address:

> We have now reached the stage of being one of the foremost electronic research and engineering organisations in the world, and that must year by year take us further into these new activities. I could not enumerate them all today, but they might be summarised by saying that our fields of activity embrace acoustics, electronics, communications and allied developments of applied physics and light electrical engineering.

Yet Sir Ernest was very conscious of the need to justify the links between the various activities of the company. As if to ward off the charge of turning EMI into the conglomerate that it was to become, he said:

> From its basic activity of recorded music to its most advanced development of electronic television, [EMI] exhibits a logical sequence not only in scientific and technical development but also in business organisation. We do not step outside our normal fields of activity, but like good farmers, we attempt to grow all crops and in proper rotation of which our fields are capable and for which they are suitable.

The problem that Sir Ernest was grappling with – how to manage a business with a diverse range of activities, requiring very different skills, and what sort of organisation to have – is one that would plague all his successors. His own solution was the somewhat extreme one of disregarding the differences between the various businesses and treating them as one homogeneous activity. In its organisation, the company seems to have taken Sir Ernest's bucolic metaphor of the farmer tending a variety of crops in rotation to its logical conclusion.

It was organised not by product line or by business area, but by department: research, engineering development, manufacturing, purchasing, sales and service, and so on. But recognising that it would be impossible for one man to control the day-to-day operations of such a complex business, each department was made into a separate company. Thus EMI Research Laboratories Ltd developed ideas that were passed on to EMI Engineering Development Ltd, who would turn them into products. Their designs were in turn passed over to EMI Factories Ltd to manufacture. EMI Factories bought its raw materials from EMI Suppliers Ltd and sold its products to EMI Sales and Service Ltd. This singular organisation allowed a slimming down of the EMI head office but brought with it certain disadvantages. Chief among these was that the company had no idea as to which of its products were profitable and which were not. Each department was required to make a profit. Generally, all did, with the exception of EMI Sales and Service – the only one which sold to the outside world.

This organisation endured for nearly a decade and was probably responsible, at least in part, for a dismal profit record until the mid-1950s. This was a period of booming consumer expenditure, in Britain and elsewhere, and a time of rich pickings for most consumer goods manufacturers. Thorn, for example, increased its pre-tax profits more than sevenfold between 1949 and 1954, with an increase in profits in every year. In contrast, EMI's pre-tax profits were £1.2 million in 1949 and £1.1 million in 1954. The two figures are not strictly comparable, because some foreign subsidiaries not included in 1949 were included in 1954. However, this probably understates the earlier figure.

It was not that EMI had failed to grow. The recorded music market in the UK doubled between 1949 and 1954 – the first period of growth since 1929. As we have seen, the market for television sets was booming – it did not reach its peak until 1959. As the BBC expanded its national coverage and commercial television broadcasting started (in 1954), the demand for EMI's television transmission and studio equipment swelled. Total sales increased by over 13 per cent per annum – from £17 million to £32 million – over the period. A rapid growth in sales accompanied by a fall in profitability is usually a lethal combination: the rising sales require more cash to be invested in working capital, but the fall in profitability means that there is less cash available to invest. By 1954, EMI was facing a cash crisis. Although by today's standards its gearing – the ratio of its borrowings from banks and others to the funds belonging to the shareholders – was not exceptionally high, much of its reserves were outside the UK, in countries that restricted its ability to transfer funds back.

In December 1954, Sir Alexander Aikman was replaced as chairman (in an executive role) by a man who had hitherto made his name as an expert in the design of flour-milling machinery, Joseph (later Sir Joseph) Lockwood. Sir Ernest Fisk had left two years earlier. Joseph Lockwood's first task was to resolve the immediate financial crisis faced by the company by securing some financial headroom. This done, he moved on to reorganise the business in the UK on a product line basis, dropping the discredited departmental companies. There was now, at last, some ability to identify which products made a profit and which did not. Equally important was the recognition that EMI was now a collection of very different businesses, requiring different skills and management styles – Sir Ernest Fisk's metaphor of one farmer tending a variety of crops in rotation was no longer relevant.

6

Sir Joseph Lockwood Makes His Mark

Sir Joseph Lockwood was a dominant figure in the post-war history of EMI. He served as chairman for twenty years and EMI in its modern form was largely his creation. He was instrumental in turning the company around from the parlous state it had fallen into since the end of the war. After years of moribund financial results, between 1954 and 1960, pre-tax profits grew at 30 per cent per annum. In 1954, profits were only 3.3 per cent of sales. By 1960, they had grown to 7.6 per cent of sales. The company had been reorganised on sensible lines and its financing had been made secure.

It was the music business which derived the greatest benefit from Sir Joseph's leadership. He was the first board member to see the potential for popular music and to make a point of taking an interest in it. Many of his colleagues tended to treat it with scant disdain, seeing their real purpose as dealing in 'serious' music. The growth of recorded music in the early 1950s was also helped by two technical developments. The first was in recording technology. In the late 1940s, magnetic tape recorders were introduced into studios. The art of recording was transformed. Whereas previously the artist had to perform a complete work to perfection before a record could be made, now it was possible to reconstruct a perfect recording by piecing together slices of separate sessions. The recording of live performances also became a real possibility. EMI played a key role in the development of magnetic recording and also entered the business of selling tape recorders and recording tape to the professional and consumer markets.

The other development was in disc format and the material used for discs. Almost from the start of the recorded music industry, until the early 1950s, gramophone records were twelve-inch shellac discs which revolved at 78 rpm and held four minutes of music. The quality of sound recording had been greatly improved by the introduction of electrical microphones in the 1920s, but the four-minute format was a frustration for anyone listening to a longer piece. Shellac discs were also expensive, heavy and fragile. The technical development that moved the gramophone out of the connoisseur's living room and into the teenager's bedroom, and vastly expanded the market in the process, was first demonstrated in 1948. In that year, the US Columbia company introduced the twelve-inch microgroove vinyl record, which could hold twenty-five minutes of music per side, had greatly improved sound quality and was much more durable. Shortly afterwards, the RCA Victor company introduced the seven-inch microgroove disc which revolved at 45 rpm. It held the same amount of music as a 78, but was smaller and more durable. It soon became the standard for single popular songs.

EMI, under the management of Sir Ernest Fisk, had been hesitant in introducing microgroove records. There was an idea that only one format – 33⅓ rpm or 45 rpm – would succeed, and therefore that the company should wait. As a result, it launched its first microgroove records in 1952, two years after its main British rival, Decca, and was at an embarrassing disadvantage, particularly in the US and Continental European markets, which took to the new records much more quickly than Britain. By 1956, for example, the old 78s still accounted for 40 per cent of the UK market, whereas in the US and in France they had fallen to around 5 per cent. Sir Joseph, however, encouraged a more enterprising approach and, by 1957, the company believed that it had largely overcome its initial disadvantage.

The introduction of microgroove records was an invaluable fillip for the recorded music market, which was showing signs of flagging in the immediate post-war period. The following figures show the size of the UK market in the eleven years to 1956.

Year	Consumer Expenditure (£ millions)	% of Disposable Income
1946	4.44	0.058
1947	5.11	0.063
1948	4.67	0.054
1949	5.40	0.060
1950	5.70	0.060
1951	6.40	0.062
1952	8.30	0.073
1953	9.80	0.081
1954	10.70	0.083
1955	14.50	0.105
1956	18.50	0.128

Source: Electric and Musical Industries Limited estimates, Annual Report 1957.

In the early 1950s, EMI faced a threat from another change in the industry. For the first half-century of its existence, the industry had followed a cosy geographical division of the world from which EMI had benefited greatly. Two of the largest US companies, Columbia and RCA Victor, had had licensing agreements – agreements to exchange masters of their recordings – with EMI. They would sell EMI's recordings in North and South America under their labels and EMI would sell theirs in the rest of the world. This stemmed, in part, from the historic links between the companies. EMI had become particularly dependent on these agreements: by 1950, over 70 per cent of its catalogue consisted of repertoire derived under them and it had no other sources of American repertoire. However, by then both American partners wanted to end the arrangements. The music industry, which had hitherto been of only slight interest to the parents of RCA Victor and Columbia, was becoming an attractive profit-earner again, and both companies had decided to start their own operations outside the Americas.

In the event, the Columbia agreement came to an end in 1952 and the RCA Victor agreement in 1953. By then, EMI had taken a number of measures to contain the damage. A matrix exchange agreement was concluded with the record division of the US entertainment company MGM, covering popular music. A US operation was started to market EMI's classical repertoire in North America. As EMI did not have the right to the HMV trade mark in the US and Canada – this had been given to its former partner, RCA Victor – it used the Angel Records mark. The Recording Angel had been The Gramophone Company's original mark until it was replaced by the HMV mark purchased from Francis Barraud.

The most important move, however, was the acquisition of Capitol Records, Inc., at the time the fourth-largest US music company, in 1955. Capitol was a relative newcomer to the industry. It had been founded in 1942 and had been floated on the stock market in 1946. It was the first major label based on the West Coast and it had a particularly strong position in what was known as 'mood music' – its repertoire of artists included Nat King Cole, Peggy Lee and Stan Kenton. Capitol was acquired for around $8.5 million and initially proved to be a good purchase for EMI. It grew strongly in the first few years of ownership and, by 1957, was generating over $35 million in sales. One of its discoveries, in the early 1960s, was the seminal West Coast group, The Beach Boys, whose first album, *Surfin' Safari*, released by Capitol in 1962, started a new genre of West Coast surf music. Capitol was to be valuable in enabling EMI to exploit its repertoire of British pop in America in the 1960s. Capitol's later problems, however, brought considerable grief to EMI in the 1970s.

The early years of Sir Joseph's chairmanship also saw the rebuilding of EMI's classical repertoire. At the war's end, EMI was faced with the major task of rebuilding its roster of classical artists, having lost most of its Continental European performers. A key figure in this was Walter Legge. He was a producer who had worked in the company's International Artistes Department before the war. He rejoined the company in 1945, after completing his war service. Early in 1946, Legge undertook a tour of Central Europe, whilst his colleague David Bicknell visited Italy. Their brief was to relocate old artists and find new ones amidst the wreckage of war. It was largely as a result of their efforts that EMI was able to sign such major post-war classical artists as the soprano Elisabeth (later Dame Elisabeth) Schwarzkopf, whom Legge later married, and the conductor Herbert von Karajan, as well as the Vienna Philharmonic Orchestra. Legge also founded the Philharmonia Orchestra in London after the war, and this orchestra, under a number of conductors, including Herbert von Karajan, Otto Klemperer, Rudolph Kempe and Sir Malcolm Sargent, made a number of important recordings for EMI. Other great classical music stars signed by EMI in the post-war period include the Spanish soprano Victoria de los Angeles, and the legendary Maria Callas.

Classical music also received a considerable boost from the introduction of the microgroove record and the use of tape recorders in the recording studio. In the late 1950s, there was a further boost from the introduction of stereophonic recording, first demonstrated by the EMI scientist Alan Blumlein before the war. An early form of stereo recording of Sir Thomas Beecham conducting Mozart's *Jupiter* symphony had been made in 1934, but commercial stereo records were first launched by EMI in September 1958.

Sir Joseph's achievement in restoring EMI's music business is indisputable. Whether he was equally successful in finding a clear direction for the electronics and manufacturing side of the company is much more debatable. Despite being one of the largest consumer electronics manufacturers in Britain, EMI was never able to master the art of large volume manufacturing and, in 1959, it pulled out of the business. It seems that the EMI board were just not comfortable with the level of investment needed to remain competitive in the industry. EMI's consumer electronics brands, HMV and Marconiphone, were put into a joint venture with Thorn but this, as we saw in Chapter 1, was not a success from EMI's viewpoint.

One might reasonably conclude from this that EMI would henceforth avoid large volume manufacturing as not in keeping with its style. Yet just three years later, in 1960, it acquired Morphy Richards, a manufacturer of household appliances – electric irons, toasters, electric blankets, hairdriers, food mixers and so forth – for around £12 million. Morphy Richards was a relatively large company – its sales in 1960 were £12 million, equivalent to about half of EMI's UK sales. The timing of the purchase was particularly unfortunate as credit control restrictions brought in by the government in the following year hit the business hard. In fact, Morphy Richards never reached the 1960 level of sales again and EMI's association with it was not a happy one.

The motivation for buying Morphy Richards appears to have been a concern about 'balance', an issue that loomed large in the

minds of industrial managers in the 1960s and which encouraged
the development of widely diversified conglomerates. We have seen
a similar thought process in operation at Thorn. The 1960 EMI
annual report contains the following statement from the chairman,
by way of explanation for the Morphy Richards acquisition:

> A problem that has engaged our attention during the year has been
> the balance of products within the Group. Last year about one
> half of Group turnover was represented by gramophone records,
> which is more than it was before the 1939–45 war. The remainder
> comprises electronic capital goods, radio and television, domestic
> electric appliances, magnetic tape and some office equipment. The
> expansion and development of existing and new products takes time
> and money; quicker results can often be obtained by purchase of
> another business which can, itself, benefit from becoming a member
> of the EMI Group.

While its strategy, at this stage, may have been questionable, EMI
remained a prolific inventor. A torrent of new products poured
forth from its development laboratories throughout the 1940s and
1950s. The company had demonstrated magnetic tape recording
in 1947. In 1950, a motorised bicycle wheel was launched under
the name 'Cyclemaster'. In the following year, an office dictating
machine – the Emidicta – was on sale. Work on detection of
atomic particles had resulted in the design of photo-multipliers
which found a ready application in the measurement of atomic
radiation. By the early 1950s, the start of the Cold War had injected
new life into the military equipment business. By the mid-1950s,
EMI was making electronic machine tool controls and had also
designed its own digital computer. In 1958, it entered the market
for photographic printing systems and, in the following year, it
launched a robotic trolley for automated factories.

The involvement with computers is an interesting example
of EMI's experience with new products. The digital computer
industry was in its infancy in 1956 when EMI introduced its first
machine. The annual report of that year explains:

> Our electronic business machines are designed to work with a wide
> variety of input and output equipment so that the basic units can

be adapted to all kinds of requirements. For example, a computer has been ordered by the British Motor Corporation for special uses in the whole BMC organisation. We are also working on designs to meet the needs of smaller firms so that production planning, costing, distribution and payroll can all be dealt with in a simple machine during the week.

In 1957, the EMIDEC range of computers was launched publicly. One of the largest launch customers was Boots, the chemist. By 1960, a number of major British companies were using EMI's computers. In 1962, however, the business was merged into International Computers and Tabulators (ICT). In his statement that year, the chairman explained:

> ... it has become increasingly clear to us that in this field companies with wide experience of office machinery have an advantage over companies like EMI whose expertise lies primarily on the technical side.

For most of the 1950s and early 1960s, EMI's electronics business – which did not include consumer electronics – was very successful. Between 1953 and 1962, just before it pulled out of the computer business, sales had grown at an average rate of 13.5 per cent per annum, without the assistance of any significant acquisitions. Music sales had grown faster over the period – at nearly 16 per cent per annum – but this was with the benefit of the Capitol acquisition. It was the consumer durable businesses – radio, television and domestic appliances – which had stagnated and which seemed to be the weakest element in the 'balance' the company was trying to achieve.

Events in the music industry in the 1960s were to further unsettle the 'balance'. Since the mid-1950s, with the introduction of the microgroove disc, the arrival of rock and roll and the emergence of the record-buying teenager, the recorded music market had been growing rapidly. In the 1950s, American artists had dominated the popular music market. Although the acquisition of Capitol strengthened EMI's own popular American repertoire, it still remained very dependent on its matrix exchange agreements with US music companies for access to American repertoire.

The company's vulnerability in this respect was demonstrated by the loss of Elvis Presley. Presley was an RCA artist who was no longer available to EMI when the licensing agreement with RCA came to an end.

The need to develop British popular artists had been recognised in the late 1940s, when EMI had appointed four new Artiste and Repertoire (A&R) managers who were given the task of finding and developing new British popular music talent. A key figure in the drive to increase the company's popular British repertoire was Leonard Wood, who had joined The Gramophone Company in 1929 and became managing director of EMI Records Ltd – the main UK music company – in 1959. By the late 1950s, considerable success in the British popular music charts had been achieved. Three new artists developed by EMI during the 1950s – Cliff (later Sir Cliff) Richard, Adam Faith and Helen Shapiro – were particularly successful and Cliff Richard, of course, remains a major EMI artist nearly four decades later.

It was, however, the advent of British pop as the dominant strand in popular music worldwide, in the mid-1960s, which transformed EMI's fortunes. In 1961, The Beatles came to London with Brian Epstein – their manager and owner of a chain of record shops in Liverpool – to find a company they could record for. They were turned down by all the major British record companies in succession – including EMI. Their rejection by Decca, with whom they had a recording session in January 1962, merits inclusion in the annals of the greatest business bloomers. As Ray Coleman describes in his biography of Brian Epstein (*Brian Epstein – The Man Who Made The Beatles*, Viking Penguin, 1989), Decca's A&R manager explained his reason for rejecting them thus:

> Not to mince words, Mr Epstein, we don't like your boys' sound. Groups are out; four piece groups with guitars particularly are finished.

The episode reflects more on the chancy nature of the A&R process than on Decca's folly, but in this case Decca's loss was to be EMI's gain. One result of the recording session with Decca was that Epstein now had a reel-to-reel tape with fifteen Beatles songs on it. Still in London, and happening to be in Oxford Street, he called in at the HMV record store to look up the store manager, whom he had met in the past. The manager advised him to have some demonstration acetate discs cut from the tape, since these would be easier to play. This was a service that was available at the HMV shop. The engineer who cut the discs for him liked the sound and suggested he go and see George (now Sir George) Martin, the A&R manager for EMI's Parlophone label. George Martin had been on holiday at the time of the Beatles' rejection by EMI. Despite having been rejected by the company in December 1961, Epstein decided to give it one more try. By October 1962 EMI had released the first Beatles single – 'Love Me Do' with 'P.S. I Love You' on the flip side. It was a modest success, reaching number 17 in the British singles charts. The next Beatles single, 'Please, Please Me', however, achieved a level of sales unheard of before and a new epoch in popular culture had begun.

Within a couple of years, Brian Epstein had introduced much of Merseyside's musical talent to EMI, including Gerry and The Pacemakers, Cilla Black and Billy J. Kramer. In 1964, eight EMI artists or groups held the top position in the British singles charts for a total of forty-one weeks. Success in the American market followed. In 1966, EMI artists held the number one position in the *Billboard* "Hot 100" singles charts for twelve weeks and, for twenty-eight weeks, EMI had at least one LP in the top three. The company also enjoyed considerable success in selling US repertoire internationally. A licensing deal struck with a small Detroit-based record company, Motown Record Corporation, in 1963, gave it access to the best of the 'Tamla Motown Sound', including the music of Diana Ross and The Supremes, Stevie Wonder and Marvin Gaye. The owners of Motown offered to sell the business to EMI for $17 million – a bargain in the light of Motown's later success – but the offer was turned down.

The financial benefit of the British pop phenomenon to EMI was immediate and considerable. After the spurt that followed Sir Joseph Lockwood's assumption of the chairmanship, pre-tax profits had stagnated at around £5 million between 1960 and 1963. In 1964, however, profits grew by 80 per cent over the previous year, to over £9 million, and reached over £11 million by 1966. Cash gushed in – between June 1963 and June 1966, the company's cash reserves increased by over £16 million, equivalent in today's money to £160 million. These figures probably understate the benefit, for while music was booming, other areas of business were stagnating. Morphy Richards, in particular, was struggling, and in July 1966 it was merged with AEI's Hotpoint domestic appliance division in a joint venture in which both partners had a 50 per cent interest. Shortly afterwards, of course, AEI itself was acquired by GEC and GEC's domestic appliance businesses were added to the venture, reducing EMI's share of the larger business to one-third. This shareholding was eventually sold to GEC in 1973 for £8.8 million – around £3 million less than the price paid for it twelve years earlier. The sale finally ended EMI's involvement in large-volume manufacturing in the UK.

The boom in the music business and the withdrawal from making consumer durables served to increase the urgency of finding new ways of achieving 'balance'. A number of investments were made in electronic engineering companies, the most important of which were SE Laboratories, which made a range of electronic instrumentation, and Associated Fire Alarms and Minerva Fire Defence, which installed security and fire alarms. More importantly, EMI decided to broaden its involvement in entertainment and leisure by acquiring The Grade Organisation.

The purchase of The Grade Organisation is one of the more controversial acquisitions made by EMI and was to have far-reaching consequences. The Grade Organisation was the creation of the three Winogradsky brothers, Lew and Leslie (who had changed their name to Grade) and Bernard (who had adopted Delfont as his surname), who were to play a dominant role in the British entertainment industry in the 1960s and 1970s. At the time that EMI acquired it, The Grade Organisation was a major artist's agency which also owned a cinema chain and was involved in the promotion of stage shows. As such, it represented an extension of EMI's interests in entertainment into areas other than music. The controversial element was the price paid for the business: the original idea had been to acquire the business for around £4 million, but as a result of a series of leaks, the eventual price paid was close to £9 million. Since the total turnover of the business was around £1 million, and it had virtually no tangible assets, it was an expensive purchase, as subsequently admitted by

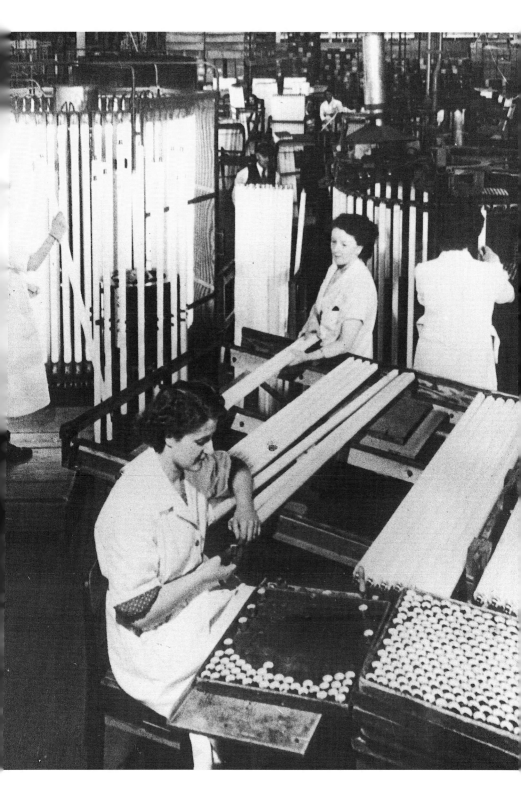

Thorn factories in Great Cambridge Road, Enfield

An early television set, 1930

A Ferguson television set, 1949

Radio Rentals, 1995

Thorn House, St. Martin's Lane, London, 1959

Tricity cooker from the early sixties

Kenwood Chef, circa 1968

Lighting fixture

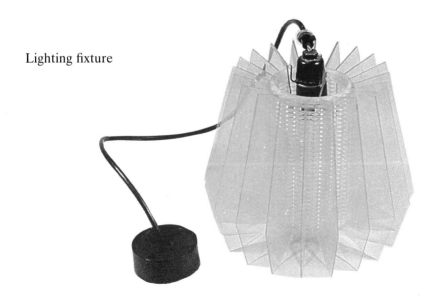

Rent-a-Center, USA, 1995

THORN

Thorn Group logo, 1996

a very satisfied Bernard (later Lord) Delfont. It also opened up entirely new pastures for diversification, under the guidance of Delfont, who joined the EMI board as a director. The original artist's agency business of The Grade Organisation was sold in 1970, but the entertainment and leisure division sprouted new interests at a remarkable rate: by the end of the 1970s, its portfolio included the Blackpool Tower, the Empire Ballroom in Leicester Square, squash clubs, dance halls, bingo clubs, film and television production and distribution, restaurants, fast-food outlets and pubs.

The most important part of this multifaceted grouping was the Associated British Picture Corporation, since it came closest to making EMI an entertainment conglomerate and prefigured a strategy that was to find many disciples in the 1980s and 1990s. ABPC was engaged in film and television production through two subsidiaries, Associated British Productions and Anglo Amalgamated. It also owned Elstree Studios, which were extensively used by other film producers. Another subsidiary, Associated British Cinemas, operated one of the largest cinema chains in the UK. And it had a controlling interest in Thames Television, which operated the commercial television weekday franchise for the London area. Twenty-five per cent of ABPC's shares were owned by Warner Brothers Seven Arts, Inc., of the US, and EMI bought these shares in January 1968 for £9.7 million. It had planned immediately to make an offer for the remaining 75 per cent, but was not prepared to accept the conditions laid down by the Independent Television Authority (ITA) – which regulated the commercial television franchises – at the time. However, towards the end of 1968, an understanding was reached with the ITA and, in January 1969, EMI bid for the remainder of the shares.

ABPC was the largest acquisition made by EMI. The total cost, including the amount paid to Warner Brothers, was £56.6 million, equivalent in today's money to £490 million, most of which was paid for in EMI shares. In 1969, ABPC made pre-tax profits of £3.5 million, which would have given post-tax profits of £1.75 million at the tax rate prevailing. The price paid for the business was therefore around thirty times net profit, considerably higher than EMI's own price-to-earnings ratio. Financially, its effect on the company was to reduce earnings per share, and it never lived up to the initial concept of allowing EMI to combine ABPC's talents with those of the music business to address the 'audio-visual' future. Culturally, the cinema and film businesses were something of a shock to the strait-laced and generally conservative gentlemen of EMI, who never quite got used either to the unorthodox methods of the cinema business, or to the amount of high-risk investment required in film-making. It is unlikely that any member of the EMI board, Lord Delfont apart, ever felt comfortable with it. Lord Delfont, however, was reputed to have an ability to smell money from a considerable distance and, while he was rarely able to explain his decisions to his colleagues, they appear to have been happy to leave him to run the business as he wished.

The acquisition of ABPC made EMI the largest British entertainment company. It had, in fact, become overwhelmingly an entertainment company, since music, cinema and television accounted for 86 per cent of profits. It had also become even more complex, its interests ranging from making sophisticated military equipment to staging live theatre in the West End of London. The problem of managing such diversity was certainly recognised by John (later Sir John) Read, who had become chief executive of the company in 1969. He and his colleagues shared a strong and explicit belief in the advantages of a large diversified company. The organisation was founded on what was known within the company as 'integrated diversity', which was seen as a way of combining all the strengths of a large company with the responsiveness and motivation of a small one. The effectiveness of 'integrated diversity' was to be rigorously tested in the years ahead.

Within a year of taking over as chief executive, Read was faced with a crisis in the American music company, Capitol, as severe as any faced by his predecessor. Capitol had maintained a tradition of independence from its British parent since its acquisition. It had, for example, at one stage refused to take on The Beatles in North America, in spite of pressure from Leonard Wood, managing director of EMI Records in the UK at the time. It was only The Beatles' later success which persuaded Capitol's management to climb on the bandwagon. The independent spirit was accentuated when, in 1968, Capitol acquired a manufacturer of magnetic tape, Audio Devices, Inc., which was listed on the

American Stock Exchange. The acquisition was effected by a reverse takeover of Capitol by Audio Devices, with an issue of shares to EMI, the end result of which was to leave Audio Devices, now renamed Capitol Industries, Inc., as a listed company of which EMI owned 72 per cent. This gave further grounds for making policy independently of the parent company.

Capitol had prospered during the 1960s when British pop music had dominated the US market. Between 1966 and 1972, Capitol sold thirty-five million albums of The Beatles alone. But the ready availability of British repertoire seems to have led to the loss of skill at nurturing home-grown talent. The high profits in the fat years had encouraged a lavish style and the running costs of the business had grown substantially. By the early 1970s, the reign of British pop was coming to an end, displaced around the world by American repertoire. At the same time, the American economy went into recession and spending on records slumped. The combined effect of these trends would have been severe enough in any business, but they were compounded by the practice in the industry of allowing retailers to return records and tapes in exchange for new stock. Faced with high interest rates and slow-moving stock, retailers found it preferable to keep rotating their inventory at the record company's expense. Capitol's sales fell by over 20 per cent in the year ending 30 June 1971 and the business made a loss of £6.2 million, wiping out most of the profits of the worldwide music business. The effect on EMI as a whole was severe – the net earnings of the company were almost halved.

The man chosen by Read to staunch the losses at Capitol was Bhaskar Menon, who had made his reputation as a music industry manager while running the Gramophone Company of India, an EMI subsidiary. He replaced much of the senior management of Capitol and, as a result of a drastic overhaul, brought the company back into the black by the following year, when it made a modest profit of £1 million on sales of £52 million. However, the lack of American repertoire would continue to be a weakness of EMI for years to come.

In the meantime, the issue of balance continued to exercise the board of EMI. The acquisition of ABPC had turned the company into an entertainment conglomerate with a smallish electronics business. It was now felt necessary to redress the balance. In his chairman's statement in 1969 – following the acquisition of ABPC – Sir Joseph said:

> . . . we must now emphasise our firm intention to continue to expand substantially our activities in the realms of technology. For half a century the people and organisations who make up the EMI Group have made important contributions to the scientific and technical progress of the nation. Now that technology in particular is being called upon to help restore our national balance of payments position, EMI is planning a more vigorous and expanding role.

The electronics businesses had had a miserable time in the late 1960s. The start of colour television broadcasting in the UK in 1968 had led to an upsurge in demand for cameras and studio equipment, but defence cutbacks had reduced orders for military equipment. In spite of a number of small acquisitions, profits from electronics fell by 13 per cent in 1968 and then again by 17 per cent in 1969. Much of the company's engineering talent was involved in doing 'cost plus' development work for the Ministry of Defence – work for which the government paid a predetermined rate of profit on the costs of the work, largely independent of what those costs turned out to be. Although it was reasonably secure work, the amount of profit that could be earned was modest. Moreover, it neither trained managers who could successfully make and sell commercial equipment, nor did it generate new products that could be sold commercially. The predominance of the government as a customer of Britain's high-technology industries for the half-century between the start of the Second World War and the end of the Cold War, affected both EMI and its peers in the electronics industry in many ways. Not least of these was the development of a culture happiest when dealing with bureaucrats, whether in Whitehall or elsewhere, but uncomfortable in the commercial world.

The company's Central Research Laboratories (CRL) had continued to do innovative work and to produce ideas of dazzling ingenuity in the heroic tradition of Isaac Shoenberg and Alan Blumlein, yet none of them had resulted in the commercial success they seemed to merit. The pioneering work in television and sound recording had not led to a profitable consumer electronics business;

technical brilliance in the design of digital computers had not
been sufficient foundation for an enduring computer business;
the innovative engineering in radar, so crucial to the war effort,
had yielded only a modest military electronics business.

By coincidence, as the directors of EMI scratched their heads
in search of ways of reinvigorating the company's technical
businesses, an engineer in the research laboratories was working
on a problem, the solution to which would change the fortunes
of EMI in ways that no one on the board could possibly have
imagined.

7

The Scanner Story

One of the casualties of EMI's decision to withdraw from making digital computers was an engineer called Godfrey (later Sir Godfrey) Hounsfield. While many of the staff went with the computer business to ICT, Hounsfield himself went to work at EMI's Central Research Laboratories in Hayes.

Some of the work that CRL did was on general areas of potential interest to the company, rather than on developing specific products or techniques. Hounsfield had expressed an interest in working on pattern recognition – designing machines that would do what the human brain does when it identifies typed or handwritten characters, voices, faces or patterns. The area was of general interest to EMI because of its interests in industrial automation, television and military equipment. The process of pattern recognition by a machine involves the transformation of information from one form to another, for example from visual to electronic, and this generally requires the object to be recognised to be scanned in many different ways to separate its essential features.

It was this chain of thought which led Hounsfield to the basic idea of the computerised axial tomography (CAT) scanner. He envisaged a scanning device in which the object to be recognised was placed at the centre of a pencil-like scanning beam, which scanned across the object at different angles. Measurements would be taken as the scanning beam circled the object and from these, in theory, a picture of the object could be mathematically reconstructed. The reconstruction of the visual image from a series of measurements was no mean task and would have been impossible without computers. The problem was somewhat analogous to being given a table of numbers in which only the totals of each row and each column were visible, and being asked to work out what the contributing numbers are. For a table with two rows and two columns, it is a simple task. For three rows and three columns, it is considerably more difficult, though matters are helped if the totals along diagonals are also available. Actual scanners work with arrays – columns and rows – of 320 x 320 or more, which gives some idea of the computational complexity involved. Many readings have to be taken at many angles through the rows and columns of the table and, from these, each element in the table has to be calculated. One of the reasons why the CAT scanner was successful so quickly was that its development coincided with the introduction of minicomputers, which made computing cheaper and more readily available.

The thought that these techniques could be applied to medical diagnosis occurred fairly early to Godfrey Hounsfield. Conventional X-ray techniques give a very confusing picture of all the organs, bones and tissues in the path of the X-ray superimposed on one another. For certain parts of the body, the head for example, conventional X-ray is of little value, because of the two layers of skull bone through which the X-rays must pass. At the core of Hounsfield's idea was the notion that most of the information collected in a conventional X-ray cannot be used. Because the X-ray photograph is the result of the rays' passage through a number of different objects, it is, again, rather like looking at a table of numbers but seeing only the totals of each column. However, if one could also collect the totals calculated in other directions – rows, diagonals and so on – one could calculate the number in each cell of the table and one could reconstruct the image of all the objects through which the X-ray had passed by calculating the density of the tissue at each point. It seemed to Godfrey Hounsfield that his method, by using all the information available from the X-rays, would even allow doctors to see soft tissue organs that could not be seen by any other method, short of cutting open the patient. Doctors would be able to see a section through the body, at any point, showing all the internal organs, rather in the way that a slice of salami shows all its constituents. If the technique could be developed into a practical device, its value would be enormous.

The idea had now reached a point where Godfrey Hounsfield felt obliged to seek the views of his superiors as to whether they were prepared to spend money on further development. In 1969, the electronics and research interests of EMI had been grouped together in an organisation called Electronic and Industrial Operations (E&IO), under the chairmanship of John Kuipers, a former colleague of John Read at Ford, who had joined the company in 1967. Another member of the E&IO board was Len Broadway, Director of the Central Research Laboratories. Both Kuipers and Broadway were in favour of taking the project further but their colleagues were not. The funds available to E&IO for speculative research of this sort were very limited; it had little knowledge of the medical equipment market; and it was far from clear that a practical device could be built. However, EMI wanted to redress the 'balance' of its businesses and was keen to encourage new technical ideas. Kuipers and Broadway eventually succeeded in persuading their colleagues to take the work further, but on a tiny budget.

By late 1968, Hounsfield had demonstrated mathematically that pictures could be reconstructed from readings of imaginary objects and had shown the extent to which a scanner could differentiate between various densities of body tissue. Since EMI was not prepared to risk any more money on the project without independent corroboration of the machine's potential as a medical device, the Department of Health and Social Security (DHSS) was asked if it would support the project. Hounsfield was able to convince it sufficiently to persuade it to contribute £5,000 towards further work, if EMI would match this amount.

Hounsfield scrounged together parts of discarded machinery – an old lathe bed and indexing machine, two photo-multiplier tubes, a radioactive source for scanning the object (later changed to an X-ray tube) and a punched tape machine for storing the results – and lashed together the first demonstration of CAT scanning. It was obvious that a powerful computer would have to be used to handle the large volume of data generated by the machine. CRL had recently acquired a time-sharing teletype terminal in order to design klystron tubes, which are used in radar sets. A young engineer, Steve Bates, at the time working on klystron tubes, was one of the few people who knew how to use it and his department would offer to do computing for other people in order to supplement its budget. Bates was told by his boss that Hounsfield had a strange idea which he wanted to test on the terminal, but since he didn't have any money, Bates should not spend much time on him. Bates was later to become the computing guru for the scanner.

At first plastic objects were scanned in the lashed-up scanner, then various diseased brains in formalin, followed by pigs' bodies. By late 1969, working with medical specialists from the National Health Service (NHS), Hounsfield had refined the machine to the point where it was able to produce a good picture of a slice of the brain of a patient who had died of a tumour. The project was now at the point where it was realistic to think about trials on living patients. The company was still reluctant to make the investment necessary to build the prototype machines required for clinical trials, but the DHSS, by now convinced of the potential of CAT scanning as a diagnostic device, agreed to buy a prototype and underwrite the cost of four more machines, in return for a 3 per cent royalty on future sales. The Atkinson Morley Hospital in Wimbledon was chosen as the site of the first clinical trials and, by the autumn of 1971, the first trial on a patient – a woman suspected of having a brain tumour – was undertaken. The scanning process was slow – it took three to four minutes – and the data had to be stored on magnetic tape and sent off elsewhere to be processed. But the picture, when it finally arrived, clearly showed the location of the brain tumour. Without the scanner, locating the tumour would have required intricate and potentially dangerous surgery. Its diagnostic value had been proven beyond doubt.

Although the scanner was now generating considerable excitement among medical collaborators, the scientists and engineers involved in it were still somewhat bemused by the turn of events. The consensus of opinion was that they would be able to build and sell half a dozen machines, recoup the money spent and forget about the scanner. Kuipers and Broadway recognised that the idea might have potential to earn significant royalties if licensed to medical equipment manufacturers, but neither saw any justification for EMI making scanners itself. Kuipers had the patents held by EMI reviewed by a firm of attorneys in New York, with a view to starting discussions on licensing. Their advice was very favourable: the patent position was strong; the idea had much potential; and there would be a number of companies anxious to buy licences. They advised starting negotiations at an extremely high royalty level of 8 per cent of sales. A team from the medical division of General Electric (GE), America's leading manufacturer of X-ray equipment, was invited to discuss terms.

It was at this point that the project passed from John Kuipers to the man who would play a crucial role in the story of the CAT scanner. In 1971, as part of its plan to revive its technology businesses, EMI had recruited John Powell, a senior executive of Texas Instruments, the American electronics company. He had joined the board of EMI as Group Technical Director. As an Englishman who had worked for one of the leading US electronics companies, he was well placed to advise the board on how to develop a cohesive technology business out of EMI's fragmented interests. His first impression, as he stated in an interview given in 1980, was that EMI was devoted to too many products and dedicated to too few.

Since John Kuipers was shortly to leave for Australia to run the EMI business there, he passed responsibility for the meeting with GE to Powell. Following the meeting, Powell told him that nothing had come out of it, since EMI was not going to license the scanner but would make and sell it itself. Years later, after the saga of the CAT scanner had unwound, the EMI board was much criticised for its decision to develop the scanner on its own. This criticism misses the point that the board never really made a decision on the issue. The company's culture was one where considerable authority was delegated to operating management and the original decision to go it alone was neither made by the board nor discussed by it at any length. It may seem surprising that a decision which was to have such far-reaching consequences for the company simply slipped past the board. Sir Joseph Lockwood – who was still a non-executive director at the time – is reported to have expressed regret at not having forced a thorough discussion. But this was after the project had gone sour. In any event, given the background and experience of the board, and the diversity of EMI's activities, it is debatable whether they were in any position to make an informed decision.

In trying to reconstruct the decision-making process, it is easy both to assume a situation where all the relevant facts are arrayed before the decision-makers and to imbue the process with a finality that it probably lacked. The reality is that in place of facts there are possibilities, prejudices, judgments. Decisions are seldom made once and for all. More often they are tentative, contingent on events taking certain courses, which either reinforce them or change them. There was indeed considerable scepticism within EMI about the merits of going it alone. But was it not the company's objective to find a large, technically advanced field in which to develop its business? The medical electronics business was full of huge, established companies. But EMI's patents on the CAT scanner were watertight. Moreover, the initial investment needed to get into the business – involving building around fifty machines – was estimated at around £6 million, large but not enormous when set alongside sums spent by EMI on recent acquisitions at the time.

Questioned in 1979 by the magazine *Management Today* about the decision to go it alone, John Powell had this to say:

> We weren't exactly coming up with world-beaters every day, so the collective view was that we should do it ourselves . . . The British have taken the soft option of selling know-how too often – the jet engine and hovercraft are examples of British inventions which have not been fully exploited here. EMI, too, had had some technological breakthroughs in the past but failed to make the most of them. With the scanner, I was convinced that we had a real opportunity to build up a worldwide business and to create wealth for Britain.

The reception accorded the scanner at its first major public display, at the annual meeting of the Radiological Society of North America in Chicago in November 1972, was enough to make it clear that the initial investment was not substantially at risk. It also made it clear that North America, with its enormous expenditure on health and its willingness to use the latest technology in the field, would be the largest market. With demand for the machines exceeding all expectations, pricing them was not easy. Peter Hayman, who was finance director of E&IO at the time, remembers a meeting to set a price for the initial batch of scanners. Someone suggested a price of £50,000, which would adequately recover the development costs and earn a good profit. He suggested doubling the price and asking for a non-returnable deposit of 30 per cent when the order was placed – a common practice in the defence equipment industry but unheard of elsewhere. The down payment would cover the manufacturing cost of the machine, so the amount of investment that had to be made in the business was minimised and EMI's cash would be conserved. Such was the demand for scanners that hospitals squirmed and paid up, even though they would not see their scanners for six months, and 30 per cent payment with order became the established practice.

For the first five years of its existence as a business, EMI Medical exceeded the most optimistic expectations of its originators. The sales and profits of the business over this period were as follows:

£ million	1972/73	1973/74	1974/75	1975/76	1976/77
Sales	0.3	5.1	20.4	42.1	93.2
Profit (a)	-0.07	1.2	9.2	12.5	14.7
% RoS	-23	24	45	30	16

(a) Before interest and tax

In the criticism that followed the demise of the business, it was often forgotten that EMI had managed to establish a major business, based on new technology, with virtually no start-up losses. It was an exceptional feat by any standards, owing much to the modest expenditure on initial development, the speed with which the business was put together and the radical nature of the benefits it delivered. For the first few years of the life of the business, John Powell's decision seemed to be vindicated. Had it decided to license, the company would never have been able to earn in royalties the sort of profits it was generating, while also building a worldwide business.

Ironically, it was the revolutionary importance of the scanner as a diagnostic tool which was partly responsible for the eventual demise of the business. The phenomenal growth stretched the organisation to breaking point and beyond. Moreover, it rapidly became such an important item of hospital equipment that the incumbent medical equipment suppliers were obliged to retaliate or lose their own businesses. As the capabilities of the scanner became widely understood by medical practitioners, hospitals started earmarking their entire X-ray equipment budgets for buying scanners. Making scanners became a matter of life and death for X-ray equipment suppliers. The speed and aggression of their response was certainly underestimated, although it was recognised at the outset that EMI would not have the market to itself for more than a couple of years. In the event, it was four years before competitors were able to deliver products. The following table shows scanners installed, both in total and by EMI, over the period:

Units	1971/72	1972/73	1973/74	1974/75	1975/76	1976/77
EMI	1	5	35	122	198	343
Total	1	5	35	124	352	613
% EMI	100	100	100	98	56	56

What was not recognised at the outset was the cavalier disregard by many American companies for the rights of the patent holder. Used to a more gentlemanly tradition in Britain, the American habit of producing a competitive product first and then discussing terms with the patent holder on the courthouse steps came as a surprise. As later payments for royalties and patent infringement were to demonstrate, it was not that EMI's patents were lacking in validity, but that the cost in time and money of enforcing them was high.

Those involved at an operational level in the business trace the start of the problems to two events: the launch of the body, as opposed to head, scanner, and the expansion of the US company from a sales and support operation to a manufacturing and engineering one. Until the end of 1975, the business had been largely based on the head scanner. This was an easier device to engineer than the body scanner, since the scanning time – during which the patient had to keep still – could be much longer. Moreover, the benefits of the head scanner, over alternative diagnostic methods, were so enormous that their use could be justified beyond question.

By 1975, scanning times had been reduced from the three to four minutes of the original prototype to twenty seconds, at which level whole-body scanning became a realistic possibility. EMI demonstrated the first body scanner at a radiologists' conference in Bermuda in March 1975 and had booked fifty orders for it by the end of that year. By then, the first competition was beginning to appear, although much of it was on paper rather than in the marketplace. Ten companies were offering scanners but only two, apart from EMI, were in a position to deliver any. The biggest potential threat came from GE, and it became apparent that GE had chosen the body scanner as its battleground and scanning speed as its weapon. In 1975, GE had demonstrated a body scanner with a scan time of under five seconds – compared to twenty seconds for the then current EMI 5000 machine – and the American market had become convinced that this was what the standard should be. In fact, GE was much further from being able to deliver its machine than everybody – including EMI – believed: it did not start deliveries until 1977. The scanning speed was the result of a complex trade-off between picture quality, cost, and other factors. Although the EMI 5000 was a very basic machine by today's standards, it was adequate for most diagnostic purposes. By choosing to emphasise scanning speed, however, GE was able to slow down EMI's sales – even before it had a machine to deliver – and force EMI to compete on scanning speed.

By 1976, the scope of EMI's US medical operation had been widened beyond its original role of sales, service and support, to include the manufacturing of scanners. With competition from American manufacturers growing, there was a fear that a foreign-built machine would be vulnerable to 'buy American' pressures on US hospitals. The decision to expand the US business at this point was partly a result of a call John Powell had received from a former colleague from Texas Instruments, Norman Provost. He had expressed interest in managing EMI's US medical operations and, with his extensive experience of the electronics industry, he was well equipped to do so. A factory was built at Northbrook, Illinois, near Chicago, which included a small engineering group. At about this time, news of GE's fast body scanner – still under development – was beginning to affect sales of the EMI 5000.

Godfrey Hounsfield and his team in CRL were working on an entirely new body scanner, with a faster scan time and much better picture quality than GE's still-to-be-launched machine. This machine, which was given the name Topaz, required an entirely new X-ray source and was inevitably going to take time to develop. As concern about the threat from GE mounted, the US management came up with a new proposal: they would design a new body scanner using existing components but with a much faster scan time than the EMI 5000, and they would have their design ready in ninety days. With a convincing presentation, John Powell was persuaded to back this proposal for what came to be known as 'the 90-day scanner'. The US now became an entirely autonomous operation, with its own engineering development, manufacturing and marketing.

In the UK, development of the Topaz machine continued at CRL. A new factory was opened in Radlett, north of London, to concentrate on head scanners, while the original factory at Hayes built the EMI 5000 body scanner. A host of other EMI companies was involved in supplying components – X-ray devices, displays, data storage units – for the scanner. In an attempt to broaden the medical equipment activity from diagnosis to treatment, a company that made cancer therapy equipment – SHM Nuclear Corporation – was acquired in California. This group of businesses operated as a loose federation, co-ordinated by a committee that met once a month.

In a move that seems surprising, given the task facing EMI Medical, John Powell had been appointed group managing director of EMI in 1974, and no one had been appointed to replace him. Steve Bates remembers being asked to attend a meeting over dinner, in January 1977, at the Selfridge Hotel in London, where John Powell had a suite of rooms, with other executives involved in developing the scanner. John Powell was late for the dinner and explained, when he arrived, that earlier that evening The Sex Pistols, a punk music group recently signed by EMI Music, had used a four-letter word during a television appearance. He, John Powell, had to convene a meeting to decide whether their contract should be terminated. During the course of the dinner, someone complained that one of the problems that EMI Medical was facing was that there was no one person responsible for co-ordinating the whole business. John Powell's reply was that he was that person. Bates left the dinner wondering how the person who had to decide on whether or not the Sex Pistols should be censured for using four-letter words could also co-ordinate EMI Medical.

The management of the US operation had suffered a severe blow when, in the summer of 1976, Norman Provost, whose availability had been instrumental in the decision to expand the US operation, suffered a fatal heart attack while on a visit to the London head office. By 1977, it was clear that the '90-day scanner' under development in the US would take very much longer. In the event, it was first shipped to customers in September 1979, more than two years later than the planned date, as the EMI 7070. In a desperate attempt to resolve the problems on it, engineers working on the Topaz machine at CRL were diverted to working on the US machine, and the computer being used for Topaz was shipped over to the US. The strains on those involved were enormous. At any time, much of the company's engineering talent was sitting on airliners between London and Chicago. In the meantime, the spanking-new US factory lay empty. Since sales of the EMI 5000 had collapsed in anticipation of the new scanner, the sales force also had little to do.

The final mishap in the EMI Medical saga was one over which it had no control. Concern about the growth in health-care costs became an issue in the 1976 US presidential election which brought Jimmy Carter to power. One result was the introduction of new regulations for capital expenditure by hospitals underwritten by the federal government. Any item costing in excess of $100,000 required a 'certificate of need'. Scanners, costing $250,000 or more, were right in the sights of the regulators. In fact, they were one of very few items that fell into this category. There was an immediate brake on further orders and, by 1977, the US market had slumped by a quarter. There is a view among those involved in the business at the time that EMI's potential American competitors had a hand in persuading the US Government to institute 'certificates of need' at this particular time. Coincidentally, the requirement was lifted when a number of competing American products came on the market.

The slump in the American market at this juncture was one blow too many for EMI Medical. In the year to 30 June 1978, sales fell by 30 per cent and, in the following year, by a further 35 per cent. In those two years, the combined losses amounted to nearly £30 million, almost wiping out the cumulative profit of £37.6 million earned by the business in the previous five years of its existence. While the collapse of the CAT scanner business was a major factor in the demise of EMI as an independent company, and despite the horrendous losses in the last two years of the existence of EMI Medical, the scanner actually made a considerable profit contribution over its life. Patent licence fees and settlements from patent infringement suits provided income of £117 million, mainly to THORN EMI after it had acquired EMI in December 1979. After taking into account the profits and losses of EMI Medical and after allowing for the costs incurred by THORN EMI in closing it down, the net profit contribution was over £70 million.

When pressed to put their finger on the one factor that was primarily responsible for the failure of EMI to establish an enduring medical business, many of those involved point to the problems inherent in growing a major international business at the speed at which EMI Medical grew. The suddenness of its growth was clearly outside the range of expectations of the decision-makers in the early 1970s. The only way it could have been accommodated was by acquiring an existing medical company, probably in the US, that had the necessary organisation and people in place. There were certainly companies that EMI could have acquired in the early 1970s which would have fitted the bill, although it seems that John Powell himself wanted to build an organisation from scratch.

It is, however, a moot point as to whether or not there is something about the diversified conglomerate, with its lack of any overriding business mission, its fragmented culture, the remoteness of corporate management from the real business issues, and the importance it attaches to 'balance' across its diverse interests, which particularly handicaps it in building a major new business. Such a task requires a level of dedication, a willingness to stick with the enterprise through thick and thin, and a thorough understanding of the underlying dynamics of the business, which sits uneasily alongside the somewhat one-dimensional, heavily financially driven, tinkering-with-portfolios approach typical of conglomerates.

8

The Fall of EMI

Losses in EMI Medical totalling nearly £30 million in two years were no small matter, even for a company the size of EMI. The damage, however, was not necessarily irreparable. What brought EMI down was a combination of events, of which the scanner débâcle was just one. The two years when the losses in EMI Medical had been mounting up, 1978 and 1979, also happened to be a particularly bad period for the music business.

Until 1978, EMI Music had enjoyed a prosperous run over some years. From a low point in 1971, when losses in North America had almost wiped out its profits, the business had staged a successful recovery. Apart from a blip in 1975, largely due to the recession in the US, profits had grown year after year. In 1977, it made operating profits of nearly £33 million, a level not approached again, after allowing for inflation, until 1990. The early 1970s were also an important creative period for EMI's British popular repertoire. Pink Floyd, one of EMI's greatest bands, began their recording career in 1967. *Dark Side Of The Moon*, their pre-eminent album, was released in 1973 and became one of EMI's most important rock albums, remaining in the British album charts for six years and still selling well more than two decades later. Queen, with the flamboyant Freddie Mercury, were signed up in 1972. Their 'Bohemian Rhapsody', released in 1975, was the best-selling single of the year in Britain. Capitol had also enjoyed creative success in the early 1970s. New artists signed in the US during this period included Linda Ronstadt, Helen Reddy, Bob Seger and the Canadian singer Anne Murray. A new black music division achieved considerable success.

By the late 1970s, however, both creativity and profits had

declined. The dominant British musical style of the late 1970s was punk. Its anarchic nihilism echoed the increasingly difficult economic situation and growing social tensions in Britain, but it had little international appeal. EMI had its own well-publicised problems with one of the leading exponents of the genre, The Sex Pistols. The incident when the group made over-liberal use of four-letter words on television was followed by an alleged bout of extravagant throwing up during a flight to Amsterdam. The resulting public outrage made the management of EMI squirm with embarrassment. The Sex Pistols' contract was swiftly terminated. Although the financial damage done to EMI was small, and the next label that The Sex Pistols signed up with also terminated their contract after they had wrecked its London offices, the publicity was damaging. The incident left an impression that EMI was not whole-heartedly committed to the music business.

In 1978, EMI Music's profits fell by nearly 50 per cent and, in 1979, they fell again, by nearly 90 per cent, to under £2 million. A downturn in most markets, particularly after the 1979 oil crisis, an upsurge in music piracy and the growth of home taping of music all played a part in slowing down music industry sales. After years of lavish profits, record companies had bid up the price of artistic talent to uneconomic heights and were now paying for it. Competition had increased, as the major music companies staked out positions in preparation for a shake-out. One in particular – PolyGram – was displaying a new-found aggression. The result of the merger of the music businesses of Philips and Siemens, PolyGram had been best known for its classical label, Deutsche Grammophon – the descendant of Berliner's German business. Rejuvenated in the late 1970s, it moved into the popular music market in the US with some shrewd acquisitions and was highly successful in the disco music field – the dominant, and commercially very successful, musical genre in the US in the late 1970s.

Some of EMI Music's difficulties were of its own making. The good years in the 1970s had led to complacency and a feeling that the business was invulnerable. As profits had grown, so had expenditure, not only on advances and royalties to artists, but also on a lavish operating style. In fact, the growth in EMI Music's profits through the 1970s masked a deterioration in its relative strength over the period. Investment in new artistic talent, the seed corn for future profitability, had fallen behind the increasingly competitive US majors, CBS Records and Warner Records, as well as PolyGram. EMI Music was increasingly reliant on its roster of established stars.

Asked what he thought had caused the decline of EMI Music at this time, a senior executive of the company summarised it as a case of hubris. In his words: 'EMI Music ceased acting as a business.' It is unlikely, however, that EMI Music's malaise was not partly a result of the mushrooming diversity of its parent's interests. With the medical and entertainment and leisure divisions demanding large amounts of EMI's cash, and the attention of its senior management, the music business is likely to have been at a disadvantage compared to its more focused competitors.

The conjunction of two unrelated disasters – in its music and in its medical businesses – had a cruel irony for EMI. One reason for the importance the company had attached to the concept of 'balance' was to avoid being too exposed to any one business or industry. It must have struck the directors of the company as the most exceptional misfortune that the two events should coincide. It is, however, arguable that, although the medical and music businesses provided the immediate triggers for EMI's downfall, a fuzziness of corporate purpose was perhaps the more fundamental reason. Looking at the larger picture of EMI's development over this period, one gets a sense that the centre of the company had so many distractions that no issue really commanded its attention.

For much of the 1970s, EMI had been spending lavishly on acquisitions. The biggest recipient of this expenditure was neither EMI Music nor EMI Medical, but the entertainment and leisure division. In total, between 1967 and 1979, over £90 million – roughly 70 per cent of total expenditure on acquisitions – was spent in this area. The biggest acquisition was ABPC. In addition, £4.7 million was spent on buying the Blackpool Tower Company, £13 million on the Golden Egg Group (a hotel and restaurant group), £6 million on a chain of bingo halls, £6.5 million on the Tower Hotel in London, and £2 million on a chain of dance halls. In contrast, total acquisition expenditure in EMI Music amounted to just £16 million – which included the cost of buying out the minority interest in Capitol. EMI Medical accounted for two acquisitions totalling under £10 million.

Possibly the most inexplicable investment of this period was the purchase of an Italian company, Voxson S.p.a., which manufactured television sets and other consumer electronics equipment. This was acquired in stages between 1971 and 1973 for a total of £5 million. Since EMI had withdrawn from consumer electronics manufacturing in the UK in 1957 and had also sold its domestic appliance business in 1966 because of its disenchantment with large-volume manufacturing, this move suggests a triumph of hope over experience. The venture was predictably short-lived: in March 1975, having owned the business for four years, EMI closed it, taking a loss of £13.5 million net of tax. This was reported as an extraordinary item in the accounts for the year to 30 June 1975 and, under the accounting conventions current at the time, was not included in the profit attributable to shareholders. Had it been included, as it would be under present rules, it would have wiped out EMI's net profit in that year. To set the figure in context, EMI Medical's annual losses in its two worst years, before tax relief, were less than this amount.

The spending on acquisitions was largely financed by issuing new shares. Between 1968 and 1977, the period of greatest acquisition activity, the number of EMI shares in issue doubled. At least on the face of it, 1977 was the best year EMI had ever had – both the music and the medical businesses made record profits in that year and the ratio of operating profits to sales, one of the common measures of profitability, was nearly 9 per cent, the highest it had ever been. Over the same period, pre-tax profits increased at a compound rate of 21 per cent per annum. Because the number of shares entitled to these profits had doubled, earnings per share had increased by a lesser figure – around 12 per cent per annum – at first sight not a bad performance. However, this was a period of high inflation – averaging 12 per cent per annum – and, allowing for this, EMI's earnings per share had not increased at all. This fact demonstrates the extent of the underlying trend of decline at EMI, even before disaster simultaneously struck EMI Music and EMI Medical.

By the summer of 1978, a serious crisis was unfolding before the directors. They would shortly have to announce a reduction in pre-tax profits of 60 per cent for the year to 30 June 1978 and the outlook for the next year was hardly reassuring. Much depended on the body scanner under development in the US being available to ship to customers early in the financial year. If available, this would allow EMI to claw back some of the market share it had started losing. The directors seem to have concluded that, on balance, things were likely to work out, as they decided to pay shareholders a dividend in excess of the profits for the year. By the autumn, however, prospects for the medical business were beginning to look very bleak: the fast scanner would not be available till March 1979 at the earliest – it was to slip by a further six months from that date – and discussions with other medical electronics companies on the possibility of a joint venture had got nowhere.

John Powell, who had been the driving force behind the medical business since its inception, took much of the blame, and he retired from the board in the summer of 1979. In December 1978, David Steadman, who had been a senior executive with Raytheon, the US electronics company, was appointed to the new post of managing director of EMI Medical, the first time the business had had a full-time head, and given a last chance to save it.

By the summer of 1979, with further deterioration at EMI Music and no sign of improvement in EMI Medical, the company looked beleaguered. The company's shareholders, led by the Prudential Assurance Company, were getting restive. Concern was mounting in the British Government, as EMI was an important supplier to the Ministry of Defence and the National Health Service, as well as being a major employer; and critical press commentary was not doing much for the company's standing or for the morale of its employees. Events over the few remaining months of EMI's independence smacked more of desperation than of a considered strategy for renewal.

As a result of the criticism, Sir John Read, who had been both chairman and chief executive of the company since 1974, decided to create a new post of managing director. Roger Brooke, a director of S. Pearson and Company (now Pearson plc), was recruited. However, even before Brooke had been able to take up his appointment, the ever-enterprising Lord Delfont sprung a surprise on him and on the EMI board. The board had been taken aback by a report in the *Sunday Telegraph* which suggested that Lord Delfont was involved, in some unspecified way, with a bid for the company. A board meeting was hastily convened for the evening of 16 May 1979. Flying in post-haste from the Cannes Film Festival, Lord Delfont dismissed the report. He then went on to spring his surprise – a memorandum, allegedly drafted on the plane by his brother Lew, which proposed that he be appointed chief executive of the company and given the job of rescuing it. His stunned colleagues adjourned to sleep on the matter. Lord Delfont knew the entertainment and leisure side of the company very well, but he had neither the breadth of experience nor the standing among the company's shareholders to suggest that he was suited to the demanding task of turning around a complex and deeply troubled company. However, when the board reconvened the following morning, it was clear that Lord Delfont's memorandum had won his colleagues over. A factor in convincing them may have been his threat to resign if he was not given the job. The last thing the board would have wanted at this stage was the defection of a high-profile executive who was not averse to expressing his views in his own colourful and idiosyncratic style. He was immediately appointed chief executive, with Sir John remaining as chairman and Roger Brooke agreeing to take on the now somewhat diminished job of managing director.

While the details of Lord Delfont's original recovery plan remain unknown, disposal of substantial chunks of the company was certainly part of it. Although the company was not facing an immediate cash crisis, the confidence of its bankers would certainly be shaken by the announcement of the results for the year to 30 June 1979, which would show a further fall in pre-tax profits of nearly 60 per cent from the already depressed level of the previous year. The company actually made a loss in the six months to June and decided not to pay a final dividend to its ordinary shareholders. By now, there was little hope of turning around the medical business and, against a deteriorating economic background, the prospects for the music business in 1980 did not look encouraging. Of particular concern to the board was that the company had £28 million of convertible loan stock, due for repayment in 1981, which could be converted into shares in 1980. However, the share price at which the stock could be converted was twice the current market price, so holders of the loan stock were hardly likely to convert. Richard Watt, the EMI finance director, felt that: 'Failure to achieve conversion, with the massive re-funding problem which would follow, must be accepted as the worst kind of financial stigma, a mark that would take many years to erase: it is submitted that everything possible must be done to avoid it.'

In any event, without additional funds, the company's room for manoeuvring out of its present quagmire would be limited. The company's merchant bankers, Lazard Brothers, estimated that EMI needed to raise £100 million in short order. The desperate mood in the boardroom now seemed akin to that of the crew of a hot-air balloon running short of fuel over a shark-infested ocean. Every business was considered as ballast for jettisoning overboard. The medical business was clearly high on the list but it would, at best, be a distress sale, so other, more valuable, parts would have to go as well. A large property development on the Tottenham Court Road in central London, which was going to house EMI's new head office, was sold to the Prudential Assurance Company and leased back, raising £33 million. The board initially took the view that the company should retain its music and military electronic interests and sell everything else – essentially going back to the businesses it had before the big wave of diversification in the 1960s.

No sooner had it arrived at this conclusion than the board was, once again, taken aback by an initiative of Lord Delfont's. In July 1979, he informed his colleagues that he had been in discussion with the American conglomerate Gulf and Western – which had been given the sobriquet Engulf and Devour by the US business press because of its predatory habits – about the purchase by its subsidiary, Paramount, of a 50 per cent stake in EMI Music for £75 million. Quite apart from the fact that EMI Music was the core of the company and the proposed deal would bring to the fore the question of its parent's continued existence, the proposed price would have been a steal for a business that had made a profit of £33 million two years earlier and had some of the most valuable music rights in the world. Although Lord Delfont was authorised to continue his discussions, the two sides failed to agree on details and, by September 1979, the idea had been dropped. By then, the board had decided that the best route would be to sell the company's entire electronics and technology-related interests, and Sir John Read was authorised to find buyers for these.

It was at this point that Thorn entered the story. Thorn and EMI were no strangers to each other. They had had a joint venture in consumer electronics in the 1950s. Sir Jules Thorn had been a regular dining companion of Sir Joseph Lockwood for many years and, no doubt, the respective merits of their companies were sometimes discussed over dinner. And the EMI board had actually twice suggested the idea of a merger to Thorn – in 1974 and, again, in 1976 – after Sir Joseph had stepped down as chief executive. Although some members of the Thorn board could see merit in the idea, it had no appeal to Sir Jules Thorn. Despite his friendship with Sir Joseph, he would have found EMI's mix of risky, high-technology and volatile entertainment businesses far too racy for his taste. He might also have been conscious of the enormous cultural gulf between the managements of the two companies and, therefore, of the difficulty of merging. At the time EMI would have been negotiating from a position of strength – both the medical and music businesses were booming – while Thorn's manufacturing businesses were finding life in recession-hit Britain increasingly difficult. The delicate issue of Sir Jules's successor had still to be decided and EMI would have provided an answer. This was, possibly, another reason why Sir Jules would have nothing to do with the proposal.

Sir Jules had, of course, retired by 1979 and his successor, Sir Richard Cave, was determined to introduce Thorn to high technology. When he was approached by Sir John Read with the proposition of acquiring EMI's electronic businesses, his interest was aroused. Thorn, however, was not the only company to express an interest in the electronics businesses. With Margaret Thatcher newly installed in Downing Street, the outlook for expenditure on military equipment was good and defence electronics companies had a glamorous allure for the stock market. Knowing that they were in a seller's market on this particular occasion, EMI and its merchant banking adviser, Lazard Brothers, were determined to drive a hard bargain.

Harold Mourgue, Thorn's finance director at the time, invited John Hignett of Lazard to a fateful lunch at Thorn House to see if they could agree terms. Hignett made an aggressive pitch on the value of the electronics business and it seemed to Harold Mourgue that the price had gone up during the course of the lunch. Realising that he would be unable to agree Hignett's terms, he decided to see if he could rattle his guest instead. He said: 'If the price goes up much higher, it will be cheaper for us to bid for the whole company.' To his surprise, Hignett seemed unfazed by the observation. Later that day, Mourgue recounted the incident to Sir Richard Cave. Sir Richard said: 'You know, bidding for the whole of EMI may not be such a bad idea. Let's think about it.' It was at this point that the original notion of buying EMI's electronic businesses was transformed into a bid for the whole company.

Once Sir Richard had made up his mind to bid, there was little EMI could do to fight him. Indeed, the idea of a bid by Thorn may well have seemed a deliverance to the EMI board, since the company's chances of retaining its independence for any length of time were small. Sir Richard had been uncharacteristically diplomatic and conciliatory in his first approach to EMI. For once, the brusque, hectoring manner was set aside – although it would reappear later. Sir John Read, Lord Delfont and Bhaskar Menon, by now head of the worldwide music business, were offered seats on the Thorn board and Sir John was offered the position of deputy chairman. It was agreed that the name of the company would be changed to THORN EMI – the institution of capital letters in the Thorn name would be an enduring source of confusion – in order to present the exercise as a merger of two equals rather than the acquisition of one by the other.

Sir John, of course, felt obliged to get the best possible price for his shareholders, but his options were limited. At such times, when a large public company has shown itself willing to entertain suitors, the chairman is besieged by merchant bankers advancing the real or imagined benefits of surrendering to their particular client. Very few of these ever progress beyond the fevered imagination of the merchant bankers. EMI soon had a list of names of potential suitors from all corners of the globe, but the only other reasonably reliable alternative was an offer from Thorn's old rival, GEC. GEC, however, had a complex proposal for buying only half the shares in EMI and then buying out the electronics business. Since its price was no higher than Thorn's and Thorn had indicated that it would keep most of EMI intact, it was the preferred suitor.

Thorn's first offer, proposed to the EMI board on the evening of 15 October, put a value of 128 pence on each EMI share, to be paid in a mixture of Thorn ordinary and preference shares. The closing price of the shares that afternoon had been 95 pence. Thorn's own shares had closed at 410 pence, but when the news broke next morning they fell by more than 10 per cent, reducing the value of the offer. Since EMI's share price had been 120 pence in June, this offer failed to excite the directors. Their recommendation of the offer was important to Thorn and they used this skilfully to get the Thorn offer up to around 150 pence per share, in spite of a further drop in Thorn's share price to around 330 pence. As a result, the number of new shares which Thorn would have to issue had risen substantially during the course of the negotiations, making it a much more expensive deal for Thorn's existing shareholders, who would be 'diluted' to a much greater extent than initially envisaged. This was partially offset by making part of the payment in convertible preference shares, which earned a fixed dividend but could be converted into ordinary shares in the future, at a price of 400 pence per share. The use of convertible preference shares has since become common, but this was one of the earliest instances of their use. The offer valued EMI at around £165 million. The net tangible assets – which did not include any value for its extensive music rights – were around £150 million, so in this sense the purchase was a bargain. Of course, Thorn also took on the task of stemming the losses in the medical business and turning around the music business, and it had no management expertise in either of these areas.

The City was sceptical about the merits of the deal, believing that Thorn had bought into bigger problems than it could handle. Sir Richard Cave and Harold Mourgue pounded the pavements of the City, visiting institutional shareholders to persuade them to support the deal. This again has since become a common feature of acquisitions, but was very unusual at the time. Most institutional shareholders of Thorn were also shareholders of EMI and they faced something of a dilemma. If EMI was not taken over, its problems might overwhelm it, leaving their shares worth very little. On the other hand, supporting the deal might permanently reduce the value of their Thorn shares. Hambros, Thorn's merchant bankers, had undertaken to buy the new Thorn ordinary shares issued as part of the deal at 330 pence per share, effectively putting a floor underneath the share price. Normally, such offers are underwritten by other institutions to spread the risk. In this case, it proved difficult to get the offer underwritten and Hambros were left having to buy a substantial number of Thorn shares. As it happened, a rebound in the share price a few months later left them with a large profit for their pains, but at the time it was a close-run thing.

On the day Thorn's offer was posted to EMI's shareholders, the *Financial Times* published an interview with Sir Richard Cave. For him, the acquisition of EMI was the crowning achievement of his chairmanship of Thorn and, in the interview, he articulates, clearly and at some length, his reasons for it. The two main reasons were to become a refrain in Thorn's proclamation of its strategy over the next few years, and Sir Richard's is probably the clearest exposition. The first was an objective he had stated in the past – the need to move the company into areas of higher technology. As he put it: 'Thorn has been marvellous at improving other people's products.' He argued that, while moving into higher technology carried some risks, 'it was at least as risky being a copier of other people's technology. He believes that on a long-term view it will be in Thorn's interests (and that of the UK) to establish itself as a technical leader. The Central Research Laboratories of EMI will support a range of carefully chosen consumer and industrial products in which Thorn can be among the world's leaders. The task is to graft an innovative capability onto Thorn's established manufacturing and marketing skills.'

The second reason was one that Thorn had hitherto neglected to articulate as being in its plans and which was seen by some commentators in the City and the press as a rationalisation after the event. This was the merger of EMI's software with Thorn's hardware. As Sir Richard put it: 'We felt we had to get the TV set of the future right: the analysis was clear that we had to get into video tape and video disc, and that meant into entertainment. It's terribly important to have recorded music and film – that's why these software companies are so very difficult to get hold of.' Irrespective of whether Sir Richard's explanation on this point was based on careful research and analysis by Thorn, or was the result of him thinking on his feet, it is interesting to note that his views were similar to those proclaimed by the Japanese consumer electronics companies who went shopping in Hollywood for film and music companies a decade later, and that they are also echoed in certain of the mergers and acquisitions among media, cable and telecommunications companies today.

It was not only the City which was sceptical about the merits of the acquisition. The reaction of the majority of executives, both in Thorn and in EMI, was decidedly mixed. Many of Thorn's senior managers were manufacturing men who could see little advantage to their businesses and had no more empathy with EMI's portfolio of activities than did Sir Jules Thorn. On the EMI side, most managers harboured the conceit that they were considerably superior to their Thorn counterparts – despite Thorn's manifestly better financial performance. In many respects, of course, EMI was the more professionally managed and more modern company and its managers saw themselves as a sophisticated, cosmopolitan group. The thought of taking second place to Thorn's humdrum, narrow-minded toilers was not appealing. Their morale was not much improved by Sir Richard's peremptory manner when he addressed their serried ranks in the Manchester Square office soon after the acquisition was completed. Notwithstanding the concessions made during the negotiations to EMI's status as a partner, for him it was still a takeover by Thorn and he was determined to drive that message home. Orders were issued to close the rather grand Manchester Square offices as soon as possible and to dismantle many of the trappings of status and prestige within EMI. One EMI director recalls coming with a colleague to Thorn's head office for his first meeting. Waiting in Thorn's spartan and draughty lobby to be summoned by the Thorn board, he whispered to his colleague: 'I now know how the Abyssinians must have felt when they were hauled into the Coliseum in Rome as slaves.'

Notwithstanding Sir Richard's efforts, in reality the acquisition resulted in little change in EMI's style and culture. The original businesses of Thorn and EMI remained unsullied by any trace of influence on each other. Even the Manchester Square office survived as the office of EMI Records (UK). Fifteen years after the merger, the Thorn staff in the company could still be easily distinguished from EMI's.

Amongst all those who were opposed to the acquisition, none felt more strongly than Thorn's founder, Sir Jules Thorn. Since he was still president of the company, as a matter of courtesy he was informed about the bid an hour before it was publicly announced. The news horrified him and led to a frantic telephone conversation with his old dining partner, Sir Joseph Lockwood, in a desperate attempt to see if it could be stopped. Sir Jules did not live long enough to see the changes that the acquisition would have on the company he had founded half a century earlier. He died almost exactly a year after EMI was acquired, on 12 December 1980, at the age of eighty-one.

9

From Home Entertainment to High Technology

Of the many tasks that Thorn – or THORN EMI as it now was – had to tackle immediately after the acquisition of EMI, the most pressing was the future of the medical business. Initially there was a notion that, with financial backing from Thorn, the business could be salvaged: Sir Richard Cave, in his interview with the *Financial Times*, had expressed the view that, 'it [medical electronics] is possible of correction.' Work on an alternative to the troubled American-designed EMI 7070 fast scanner had continued through 1979 at CRL under Godfrey Hounsfield's leadership. Hounsfield's pioneering work on the development of the scanner had been recognised by the award of the Nobel Prize for Medicine and Physiology in 1979. The idea of using the new CRL design to revive the medical business was suggested by CRL to THORN EMI's management. However, by early 1980, EMI Medical was losing nearly £2 million a month and THORN EMI did not have the stomach to absorb losses at that rate for any length of time. Anyway, in persuading his institutional shareholders to support his bid for EMI, Sir Richard had probably undertaken to stem the losses in EMI Medical quickly, even if it meant sacrificing the business. The decision to get out of it was taken within a few weeks of the acquisition of EMI.

The man who was given the task of disentangling the company from its involvement in medical equipment was THORN EMI's new managing director, Peter Laister. He had joined Thorn in the summer of 1979, to succeed the long-serving Jack Strowger – managing director of Thorn since 1974 and, at one stage, regarded as a possible successor to Jules Thorn. EMI came on the market a few months after Peter Laister had joined Thorn. He was not the instigator of the EMI deal, but he was an enthusiastic supporter of it and, as events transpired, it fell largely to him to try to find a happy conclusion to it. Laister was an engineer by training who had had a successful career at BOC, the industrial gases group, before joining Ellerman Lines, the shipping and brewing company, as managing director. In contrast to Sir Richard's autocratic, domineering style, Laister was by nature a conciliator and consensus-seeker, but he was also an independent thinker and not afraid to back his hunches against sceptical colleagues.

His first major task in the company, the sale of the medical business, was successfully accomplished within a few months of the acquisition of EMI. By April 1980, terms had been agreed for the sale of the bulk of the business outside the US to General Electric. As noted previously, the net profit to THORN EMI from the scanner, taking into account both the patent income and all the costs incurred in withdrawing from the business, was in the region of £70 million and, since the costs were largely the writing off in the accounts against assets inherited from EMI and, therefore, absorbed no cash, the cash benefit was closer to £100 million. The medical business turned out to be a net asset to THORN EMI, rather than a net liability, as many had feared.

Peter Laister's role in the affairs of the company was to become increasingly important from then on. During 1980, Sir Richard Cave was diagnosed as suffering from cancer and had to have a major operation, followed by many months of convalescence. The timing of this event could hardly have been worse from the company's point of view, since it meant that ultimate authority was obscured when decisive action was at a premium. As managing director, Peter Laister effectively became chief executive in Sir Richard's absence, but it was with less than full authority and in a company to which he was still a newcomer. As he puts it: 'He [Cave] wouldn't let go, but couldn't take control either.' Although Sir Richard remained chief executive until September 1983, his poor health meant that Peter Laister had to take responsibility for steering the company during a crucial period.

Laister's initial impression of Thorn, prior to the acquisition of EMI, was summed up by him as: '[It was] a very interesting company but it had to change. It was living in a different era – over-staffed, over-manned and in too many businesses.' Just how much it had to change was made evident by the recession in the UK and the rise in the value of sterling on the foreign exchanges which followed Margaret Thatcher's first election victory in 1979. In the year to 31 March 1981, profits from domestic appliances fell by over one-third and lighting made a loss of £10.1 million, compared to a profit of £10.6 million in the previous year, as its entire export business became uncompetitive. The motley collection of engineering companies also suffered a severe downturn. In total, the company's pre-tax profits fell by 17 per cent – including, for this purpose, a full year's contribution from the continuing EMI businesses for the previous year, to allow a fairer comparison. Even this situation was achieved only because EMI Music had recovered to contribute a profit of over £20 million, having done no better than breaking even in the previous year. In the first full year after the acquisition, the original Thorn businesses made an operating profit of £93 million, 31 per cent below the previous year, while the original EMI businesses made an operating profit of £36 million, 70 per cent above the previous year.

It was the problems in the older Thorn manufacturing businesses, rather than the opportunities offered by EMI, which occupied a great deal of Laister's time in his first couple of years in the company. In the three years to March 1983, the total number of employees in THORN EMI was reduced from 125,000 to 91,000. Some of this reduction was a result of the sale of certain businesses, but a considerable part was the result of redundancies – mainly in the Thorn manufacturing businesses. Of this time, Laister, a caring and compassionate man by nature, says: 'These were the saddest and hardest days I have had in industry.' He also feels that what was done in this period should silence those who subsequently accused him of being a visionary rather than an 'operator' – a tough, sleeves-rolled-up business manager who could master the cut and thrust of the real world.

The irony is that the real failure of the company may well have been strategic – in the sense of an inability to see the issues it faced in a broader context – rather than a lack of zeal or an excess of squeamishness. The underlying problem of Thorn Lighting – its small size in relation to the growing international competition – had been recognised under the regime of Sir Jules Thorn and, in the period since, the problem had become more acute. No amount of pruning, no matter how painful, would redress that. Domestic Appliances had seemed relatively safe in this respect, since international competition in its main profit earners – gas and electric cookers – was slower to develop. But it was heavily dependent on a cosy relationship with the nationalised gas and electricity utilities, which had a virtual monopoly on the sale of cookers. Where it was exposed to international competition – in refrigerators, for example – it had become unprofitable. By the late 1970s, with fitted kitchens all the rage, the monopoly of the utilities was on the wane, even before their privatisation put an end to their role as significant outlets for domestic appliances. The signs were that the problems in Domestic Appliances would, in time, match those in Lighting.

Although Sir Richard had suggested, in his interview with the *Financial Times*, that an important reason for acquiring EMI was 'to graft an innovative capability onto Thorn's established manufacturing and marketing skills', the reality was that nothing EMI brought with it had any relevance to the problems of Thorn's manufacturing businesses. Although CRL had an impressive record of technical innovation, there was a world of difference between the skills they had and what was required to build better cookers or refrigerators more cheaply and sell them more widely. Technology comes in specific varieties and does not have the general applicability sometimes attributed to it. Even in those businesses of Thorn's which used technologies closer to the specific ones that EMI had, such as its industrial electronics activities, there was little interchange. Technology was not sitting on the shelf, simply waiting for someone to come and use it. It would take time and money, allied to CRL's skills, to produce new products or solutions. And it was precisely their inability to see how such expenditure could be justified which had led to the Thorn businesses falling behind in technology. So the real problem for Thorn had not been access to technology but not being able to see how it could be used commercially and its costs justified, a problem that EMI's acquisition did not alleviate. The grafting of EMI's innovative capability on to Thorn's manufacturing and marketing skills was a neat idea which had little hope of turning into reality. At the working level, there was simply no mechanism to allow such grafting. While corporate strategists could lead the horse to water, it was not in their power to make it drink.

Arguably, the acquisition of EMI was not only irrelevant to the long-term problems of Thorn's manufacturing businesses, but it actually made matters worse. By holding out glittering possibilities in the glamorous new areas of home entertainment and high technology, it distracted the board from tackling the immediate problem areas. But it did not lead to what might have seemed a logical move in the circumstances: to get out of the older manufacturing businesses the better to concentrate on the new opportunities. To concentrate its time and resources on these would have seemed an eminently sensible decision at this juncture.

Peter Laister's own preference seems to have been to concentrate on home entertainment and high technology and to withdraw from the less high-tech manufacturing businesses. He canvassed deals to sell Thorn Lighting to the US company GTE, and to merge the domestic appliance business with that of Electrolux, the Swedish appliance manufacturer, in exchange for a 33 per cent shareholding. These suggestions found little support among the old Thorn men who formed the majority of the executive directors on the THORN EMI board at the time. Laister's strategy would have seemed to them to be an attempt to recreate something like the old EMI on the ashes of the old Thorn. Nor did his suggestions arouse much enthusiasm among the non-executive directors. The reality is that the vision of home entertainment and high technology as the future of the company was not shared by many on the board. There were, in fact, only a small number of genuine believers at the centre of the company. There were other reasons for not taking a more radical approach: selling businesses at the nadir of their fortunes was not going to get the best prices for them; there was a hope that new management would be able to restore them; and there was a belief that the marriage of EMI's technology with Thorn's manufacturing skills would indeed produce the results that Sir Richard Cave had predicted. The comfort of a 'balanced' portfolio of businesses still had a seductive appeal, even though the example of EMI had demonstrated that its security was questionable.

At root, there was a lack of belief among the senior management in the brave new world towards which the company was supposed to be marching. The majority of the old Thorn hands on the board would have had no sympathy with a policy of rapid withdrawal from the manufacturing businesses in an attempt to build a future in unfamiliar areas. There was considerable doubt as to whether the ingredients that had made Thorn a successful company in the past – avoiding risks by being a follower rather than an innovator, borrowing rather than inventing new technology, not making large, speculative investments in new products – could, or indeed should, be replaced by the entirely different set of skills that seemed to be needed in the fast-moving and risky world of home entertainment and high technology. The growth prospects in both home entertainment and in high technology, in the early 1980s, were, of course, significantly better than in the majority of the old Thorn businesses and, in addition, the competitive position of the old Thorn manufacturing businesses was being eroded fast. To that extent, switching the portfolio, as envisaged by Laister, made sense. It did, however, beg the question as to whether a company with the culture of THORN EMI, as it was in the early 1980s, was an appropriate starting point for Laister's vision.

In any event, Laister's more radical ideas – which also included the possible purchase of the music company PolyGram – were taken no further at this stage. Laister was a consensus-seeker and did not relish the showdown with his board colleagues – and, probably, a change of faces at the boardroom table – that would have been necessary for him to get his way. For much of this period, Laister was also subordinate to Sir Richard Cave, who was still chairman, albeit often absent, and who was himself sceptical about the home entertainment part of Laister's vision.

Laister did, however, have his way in pursuing the home entertainment strategy through organic investment, and one of his first moves was a venture that seemed an ideal opportunity to combine the hardware and software expertise of THORN EMI. In the late 1970s, three companies – Philips in the Netherlands, RCA in America and the Japanese company JVC – had separately demonstrated video disc players. Unlike video recorders, which had preceded them by a few years, video disc players could not record: they were intended to play pre-recorded discs. JVC's system – VHD – used a ten-inch disc that could hold around two hours of video programming – enough for a full-length feature film. Their advantage over video cassette recorders was that they produced pictures of higher quality and it was cheaper to replicate programme material on video disc.

THORN EMI had established a good relationship with JVC because of its role in popularising the JVC video recorder system – VHS – in the UK, through its rental outlets. This had been an important contributor to establishing the ascendancy of VHS over the technically superior Sony Betamax system. As a result of this happy co-operation, THORN EMI, JVC and JVC's parent company, Matsushita Electrical Industries, agreed to work together, worldwide, on launching the VHD system. It seemed the perfect partnership: THORN EMI with its music and film catalogue, its distribution outlets in Europe and its manufacturing capability in Britain, and JVC and Matsushita with their technology, manufacturing and marketing resources in Asia. America was to be covered by General Electric, which was also part of the consortium. The intention was to make filmed entertainment as ubiquitous in the home as pre-recorded music.

The project involved considerable investment of time and money over a period of three years but, by the summer of 1982, with the product still to be launched, General Electric got cold feet and withdrew from the US end of the consortium. RCA had launched its rival system in the US and had been disappointed by the level of interest. By late 1982, THORN EMI also decided that the prospects for video disc did not look good, and the project was mothballed. Laister would have persevered with the venture, if only to build up the relationship with the Japanese partners – which he valued greatly – but the board would not let him. The total expenditure by THORN EMI on the project was £20 million, of which £18 million was written off in the accounts for the year ending 31 March 1983. The reasons for the failure of the video disc can largely be summed up in the fact that, lacking a recording facility, it offered the consumer less than the video recorder. In the absence of the video recorder, it may well have established a habit of buying filmed entertainment on disc. Launched after the video recorder, it was merely a frivolous novelty. For THORN EMI, it was also a rude introduction to the thin line that divides commercial success from expensive failure in the fast-moving business of technological innovation.

Although the video disc project had been a failure, home entertainment continued to be a major plank in THORN EMI's strategy. At the time that the decision to axe the video disc project was being taken, both satellite and cable television were being liberalised in Britain. This again seemed to be at the centre of the home entertainment sector's interests, and THORN EMI already had a stake in cable television through its ownership of a network in the town of Swindon, a legacy of the Radio Rentals acquisition. In the 1983 annual report, it set out its intentions as follows:

> The forthcoming expansion of broadcasting by satellite and cable TV presents three separate but interrelated areas of opportunity for the Company. First, a wide range of the Company's existing products and services can be supplied to the cable industry and it will be our aim to maximise these sales. Secondly, despite uncertain financial implications we are studying with other parties the extent to which we should become involved in operating cable systems as a franchise holder. Our initial intention is to expand in Swindon and our other existing areas of cable operation. Thirdly, cable TV is a natural extension to television, video and cinema for the Company's software interests. Accordingly, the Company intends to be a major cable TV programme supplier and has already started work on the provision of a range of programming for sale to potential franchise holders.

Over the next two years, there was considerable activity in these areas. In addition to expanding the Swindon network, THORN EMI took a stake in consortia laying new cable networks in Coventry and Leicester; music and film cable and satellite channels were started; and the possibility of starting a direct satellite broadcasting service, in association with the BBC and other parties, was considered. However, THORN EMI, in common with all the other early participants in cable and satellite broadcasting, grossly underestimated both the sums involved and the time that would pass before it would see any return on its investment. Enthusiasm for cable television had been whipped up by Kenneth Baker, at the time the Minister for Information Technology, but the government's predictions for its expansion were wildly optimistic.

Even now, nearly a decade after THORN EMI pulled out of cable television in the UK, the industry is still described as an investment for the long term – by which is usually meant that no one has yet figured out how it will ever make a profit.

If the union between Thorn's hardware and EMI's software and the idea of grafting EMI's innovative capability on Thorn's manufacturing and marketing skills were two reasons for the acquisition of EMI, the third and, indeed, original reason had been entry into the steady and profitable market for professional and military electronic equipment through EMI's defence electronics business. After the war, EMI Electronics had established itself as a leading supplier of electronic equipment to the Ministry of Defence, matched only by the Marconi Company. At the time, Marconi was a subsidiary of Cable and Wireless, the telecommunications company. Cable and Wireless was nationalised by the post-war Labour Government and the stake in Marconi was put up for sale. EMI bid for it, but apparently its bid was vetoed because of the dominant position it would have gained in defence electronics. Instead, Marconi was sold to English Electric and, as a result of the restructuring of the British electrical engineering industry in the late 1960s, had become part of GEC. Over the years, EMI Electronics had fallen far behind Marconi in its importance as a defence equipment contractor. It had earned steady if unspectacular profits, but because it had restricted its activities to the safe but commercially humdrum business of being a developer of bespoke equipment for the Ministry of Defence, it had not achieved the success of its former rival.

In 1980, Sir William Barlow, the last chairman of the Post Office before its telecommunications activities were separated, joined THORN EMI as chairman of its engineering group, covering all of the company's non-consumer activities. He in turn recruited Tom Mayer from Marconi Communications to the post of managing director of THORN EMI Electronics. Tom Mayer started in his new role in early 1981. At the time, THORN EMI Electronics had around 5,000 employees and sales of around £100 million. Almost all of its business was in defence electronics and 90 per cent was with the Ministry of Defence, mainly in the field of development projects. It spent no research and development money of its own and had virtually no exportable products. It also did no marketing or selling: the men from the ministry would simply ring up and announce their requirements and THORN EMI Electronics would supply them.

One of Mayer's first actions on taking over was to provide a sum of £2 million per year to be spent on developing new products conceived by the company rather than by its principal customer. He had assumed that the company would be bursting with ideas on how the money should be spent. To his surprise, no one in the company seemed to have any suggestions, so strongly was the supine culture embedded. Over the years, THORN EMI Electronics was able to move away from this culture and considerably improved its profitability by designing its own products and selling these both to the Ministry of Defence and to governments abroad. However, given its size, on its own it was never going to be an important part of THORN EMI. Tom Mayer himself wanted to expand it into non-military electronics, possibly rebuilding the former pre-eminence in broadcasting and communications equipment, which had been lost during the 1970s. The head office of THORN EMI, however, was working independently on other plans for diversifying the company's high-technology interests and Mayer's ideas received little support.

One of these plans was to expand into information technology. The British computer company, ICL – into which EMI's computer interests had been merged in the 1960s – had been rescued by the Labour government's National Enterprise Board when it ran into difficulties in the late 1970s. The Conservative government, elected in 1979, was keen to return it to private ownership as soon as possible. THORN EMI considered acquiring the business – which would have made it the leading British computer manufacturer – but eventually decided against it. Instead, it decided to go into the computer software business, acquiring the computer software and service interests of BOC for £16.5 million. The two companies acquired from BOC, Software Sciences and Datasolve, made THORN EMI an important player in this still fragmented and rapidly growing market but, because its interests then moved on to other areas, computer software and services never became a significant business for the company. The most important outcome of their acquisition was that they brought with them Colin (later Sir Colin) Southgate, the future chairman of THORN EMI, who

had founded Software Sciences before selling it to BOC, and
who joined THORN EMI to head its newly formed information
technology division.

By 1984, THORN EMI was as diverse and complex a company
as any. There had been some tidying up of the leisure division
inherited from EMI: the hotels and restaurants had been sold in
July 1980 to Scottish and Newcastle Breweries for £23 million; the
Blackpool Tower, Empire Ballroom and other assorted assets were
sold to Trusthouse Forte in October 1980 for £16 million; and the
bingo halls had been sold to Bass Leisure for £14 million. This
disposal programme showed a profit of £12.9 million in the year to
March 1981. New interests in areas such as computer software and
services, robotics and video programming had emerged. The 1984
annual report gives an impression of this bewildering diversity:
Tina Turner and Riccardo Muti jostle for space with pictures of
hydraulic equipment and cutting tools; stills from the films *Passage
to India* and *Super Girl* alternate with pictures of soldiers crouching
beside THORN EMI night vision equipment; a photograph of a
Rumbelows store shares a page with a picture showing research
into fibre optic sensors.

This complex assortment inevitably raises a number of vital
strategic questions. Is it possible successfully to manage such
diversity within one company? Are there any benefits to being
so widely spread? Do the separate businesses benefit by being
part of this diversity?

Conglomerates were, of course, beginning to fall out of favour by
the early 1980s, but Laister himself did not regard THORN EMI
as a conglomerate. He preferred to describe it as a multi-product
company. As the 1984 chairman's statement put it: 'We have a
range of businesses that benefit from a series of relationships.'
The distinction is an important one. The financially driven British
conglomerates, of which Hanson is the best-known example, have
never sought to encourage any interrelationships between their
portfolio of businesses – although latterly there are signs that
even they might have started paying lip service to such links in a
newly adopted obsequiousness to industrial logic. Businesses are
regarded as separate, cash-generating assets to be bought, managed
and sold on purely financial criteria. The actual nature of each of
the businesses is of little importance, but the management style

rules out businesses in fast-changing industries or industries that require any specialist understanding. The role of the parent company is to trade in businesses rather than to trade in products or services – an activity that is left entirely to its subsidiaries.

In contrast to the financially driven conglomerate, the multi-product company – to use Laister's term – selects its portfolio of businesses on the basis of real or assumed links between them. It is not just the attractiveness of each business which needs to be considered, but its actual or potential relationship with other businesses in the portfolio. Laister's vision, as he explained it recently, sounds not dissimilar to that sketched out, a decade or more later, by telecommunications, media and entertainment companies in their quest for the multimedia future. His idea was to build up one of the top European groups based on an interlinked network of businesses in music and filmed entertainment and the manufacture and distribution of hardware, allied to control of new ways of distributing the software – cable, satellite, and so forth. At the time, THORN EMI referred to this clutch of businesses as home entertainment, but today they would be called multimedia. Laister also saw a need for links between home entertainment and 'high technology electronics'. As he put it: 'I believed that domestic, business and defence electronics would become diffuse in terms of technology.'

THORN EMI was, of course, not the only large company in the 1980s to have based its strategy on the perceived links between different industries. Examples of aircraft companies becoming automobile manufacturers, oil companies mining for coal and brewers running hotels spring immediately to mind. An American business academic called Theodore Levitt published an article in the *Harvard Business Review* in 1975, under the title 'Marketing Myopia', which provided the intellectual underpinnings for much diversification based on perceived interrelationships. Stated baldly, his diagnosis of the reason for the decline of companies in the face of technological change was that they defined themselves too narrowly. His much-quoted example of the buggy-whip industry, which should, apparently, have defined itself as being in the transport business in order to survive, is something of a classic, if extreme, case. Levitt must take some credit for having convinced oil companies to redefine their business as Energy;

aircraft manufacturers to redefine theirs as Transportation; and brewers theirs as Leisure – the new definitions invariably written as proper nouns to lend them a proprietary uniqueness.

While this sort of expansive definition is useful in thinking about an industry in the context of its customers, suppliers and competitors, it does not necessarily make a case for the benefits of common ownership across interlinked industries, no matter how close the links. Petroleum and motor cars are intimately connected, but there seems little strategic rationale for car manufacturers and oil companies to invade each other's turf. In other instances, there may be a case for common ownership at a particular time in the growth cycle, but only for a particular time. One example of this is the role of recorded music companies, in their early period, as manufacturers of both gramophones and of discs. Another is the role of computer hardware manufacturers as important suppliers of software at the time when the hardware was proprietary to them. At other times, common ownership may actually disadvantage one or other of the linked businesses. There is, for example, reason to believe that EMI Music was slow in launching compact discs – the players for which were designed by Sony and Philips – partly because of THORN EMI's support for JVC, its partner in the video disc project. (However, once EMI took the decision to support compact discs, it participated fully in the launch of the product in Europe and the US.)

Judging which interrelated businesses can benefit from common ownership is complex enough but, even having got that right, the multi-product company faces a further problem. How does it ensure that the separate businesses actually interrelate with each other in the way that the head office envisages? Simply assembling a hand with all the right cards, as in a game of rummy, and believing that success will follow, may be missing the point. The closer analogy may be with a game of chess: the trick is not simply to assemble the right pieces on the board, but to place them in the correct relationship to each other. And since it is the interrelationship which is important, is it necessary to have common ownership as well?

A further problem with concentrating on the search for links with fellow businesses is that it runs the risk of generating an insular, inward-looking attitude. The relationships can achieve an importance in the minds of the managers which is disproportionate to the advantage that can actually be gained in the marketplace. Arguably, this happened with the video disc venture: in concentrating on the links between its hardware and software activities, which could be used to launch the video disc, the company misread the market's appetite for the product.

Neither the benefits of merging EMI's software with Thorn's hardware, nor the benefits of grafting EMI's innovative capability on Thorn's manufacturing and marketing skills – two of the objectives set out by Sir Richard Cave at the time of the acquisition of EMI – were ever achieved by THORN EMI. The business units that were supposed to work together to achieve these benefits simply did not do so, either because they did not believe there were any, or else because they could see benefit accruing to some other part of the company, but not to themselves. An organisational structure that stressed independent accountability, rather than shared responsibility, was, in any case, not conducive to co-operation between businesses. The manufacturing businesses of Thorn either saw little advantage to be gained from EMI's technology, or were unwilling to commit the resources necessary to take advantage of it. As to the merger of entertainment hardware and software, the experiment with video disc aside, neither the hardware nor the software side saw any benefit in co-operation. The real problem for the consumer electronic manufacturing business of THORN EMI in the early 1980s was how to match the efficiency, quality and innovative capability of Far Eastern manufacturers. Collaboration with the music and film businesses was a long way from their immediate concerns.

Sir Richard Cave retired from the chairmanship of THORN EMI in March 1984, a little over four years after the acquisition of EMI and a convenient point at which to assess how successful the merged entity had been in financial terms. In 1979/80, net earnings per each THORN EMI share had been 58 pence. In 1983/1984, they were 45 pence, having been considerably lower in the intervening years. Some of the reduction can be attributed to the original Thorn businesses, which were facing a much more difficult business climate. But it is clear that the EMI businesses were also dragging the company's performance down. It would be interesting to know what Thorn's earnings would have been if EMI had not been acquired. Only an approximate answer can be given to the question, as the borrowings of the company, and the interest payments on those borrowings, were not allocated to the separate businesses inherited from Thorn and EMI. On some broad assumptions, however, the earnings per share would have been in the region of 50 pence, which means that the acquisition, rather than enhancing the earnings for the shareholders, had reduced them by 10 per cent. Since the strategic objectives of the acquisition were not achieved, the result is unsurprising.

10

Further Adventures in High Technology

As managing director of THORN EMI, Peter Laister was the obvious successor to Sir Richard Cave. The non-executive directors of the company, who had an important say in the choice of successor, were not without some reservations about Laister's management style and performance over the previous four years. The video disc venture, championed by him, had been an expensive failure and looked rash and ill-judged in retrospect. There was a feeling that the merger between Thorn and EMI had not worked, that there were still two quite distinct cultures within the company, and that the managing director and his team had failed to find and exploit the advantages that the acquisition had been based on. However, having been in effect the chief executive of the company during Sir Richard's extended period of illness, Laister had the advantage of being the incumbent. Notwithstanding any reservations the non-executive directors may have had, he was appointed chief executive in September 1983 and chairman at the end of March 1984.

It was shortly before taking over the latter role that he launched a venture that would astound most observers of the company as well as much of its management. The bid for British Aerospace was a piece of inspired opportunism clothed in a gossamer veil of strategy. By 1984, British Aerospace had had a short but unsettled history. Formed as a nationalised company in 1978 by the then Labour government, it was an amalgamation of Britain's aircraft-building heritage, put together against the fierce opposition of its previous owners, Hawker Siddeley, Vickers and GEC. No sooner had the new company got under way, however, than its architects were unseated in the 1979 general election. It was at the top of the incoming Conservative government's list of nationalised companies to be sold back into private ownership and was duly floated on the stock market in 1981, with the government retaining a 48 per cent shareholding.

Against this background of revolving ownership, the management of British Aerospace had been struggling with the task of rationalising the scattered interests it had inherited on its formation. Divided into two groups – Aircraft and Dynamics, each in turn divided into six divisions based around the factories of the original constituent companies – it was an organisational nightmare. There were too many layers of management, too many factories, too many separate businesses and too many employees. The stock market's perception of the company had been coloured by the problems facing the civil aviation industry in the early 1980s: in 1983, worldwide orders for large commercial jets amounted to 232 aircraft, compared to a peak of over 700 in 1978. British Aerospace's involvement in large jet aircraft was through its membership of the Airbus consortium, and here it faced another problem. Its French and German partners in the consortium wanted to build a new aircraft – the A320 – for which they were receiving financial support from their respective governments. If it was not to be sidelined, British Aerospace would have to find over £600 million as its contribution to this project, and it was looking to the British Government to provide the lion's share of this. Handing out subsidies for speculative industrial ventures was not, however, something for which the Thatcher government was known, and there was considerable uncertainty as to whether the money would be forthcoming. It was a combination of these factors which had caused a slump in the company's share price and created the opportunity spotted by Laister's advisers.

Although much of British Aerospace's business was in military aircraft and equipment, an area highly rated at the time by the stock market, its shares languished at a price-to-earnings multiple of six, less than half that of other large defence equipment suppliers such as GEC, Plessey and Ferranti. THORN EMI's own shares commanded a price to earnings multiple of fourteen and therein lay the opportunity for a manoeuvre well known to generations of conglomerate builders. If British Aerospace were acquired for a price even 50 per cent higher than the current

market price, its price-to-earnings multiple – which indicated
how expensive the shares were – would still only be nine, less
than the price-to-earnings multiple of THORN EMI's shares.
If THORN EMI could acquire it by issuing its own, more
expensive shares, in exchange for British Aerospace's cheaper
paper, the earnings available for THORN EMI's shareholders
would automatically be increased and they would be better off.
Also, since it was expected that, after the acquisition, THORN
EMI's shares would be rated on a par with other large defence
equipment suppliers, both sets of shareholders would benefit from
the deal. In effect, purely as a result of changing perceptions of
the business, British Aerospace would be worth more as part of
THORN EMI than it was as an independent company. The idea
that only such a deal would 'release value' in British Aerospace,
to use merchant bankers' jargon, was an important point in winning
over its management.

  The felicitous financial arithmetic of the proposed deal was
accompanied by an ambitious, if somewhat fragile, industrial
justification. One element of this was based on the company's
long-standing ambition of becoming a high-technology defence
equipment supplier, which had been one of the main reasons
for acquiring EMI. Surprisingly, THORN EMI's own defence
division, which was a significant supplier to British Aerospace,
was not consulted on the merits of the proposed deal. Another
element was based on the ambitious proposition that THORN
EMI should be able to supply every element in the distribution
chain for media and entertainment: it produced films and recorded
music; it manufactured television sets and video recorders; it sold
and rented these through its shops; it operated cable television
networks. Why not add in the capability to make and launch
satellites as well? Equally important, if less specific, were two
other motivations: the importance of size for its own sake – the
undeniable point that a combination of THORN EMI and British
Aerospace would be bigger than either company on its own – and
that this conferred some general advantage. And then there was
the hoary issue of 'balance' – British Aerospace's aeroplanes and
missiles 'balancing' THORN EMI's records and televisions.

  It seems likely that it was the financial arithmetic rather than
the attempt at industrial logic which motivated the board to

support the proposed bid. A crucial board meeting took place at THORN EMI's head office in London on 29 March 1984 to discuss the proposal. The date is important as it was two days before Sir Richard Cave retired as chairman, but he was not present at the meeting, which was chaired by Peter Laister. Sir Richard had, however, circulated a letter to the board, stating his opposition to the proposed bid, more on the grounds of a lack of management within THORN EMI to run an enlarged business than on problems with the underlying strategy. There was some discussion on this point but, in the end, Peter Laister persuaded his colleagues to support the proposal over the opposition of Sir Richard. It is clear in talking to some of those present at the meeting that there were serious reservations about the whole project, and that the strategic case was unconvincing. However, the impression was that Laister had staked his reputation on the idea and in the end it came down to a choice between backing him or casting a vote of no confidence in a man who was due to become chairman in two days' time.

The chairman of British Aerospace, Sir Austin Pearce, was approached by Peter Laister in early April and a series of cordial meetings took place between the senior managements of both companies during the month. By early May, the Ministry of Defence and the Department of Trade and Industry were informed of the discussions, the former as a major customer and the latter as custodian of the government's shareholding in British Aerospace and as the potential financier of the Airbus A320 project. Both took a neutral stance – neither opposing nor encouraging the idea. Until this point, the number of people who were aware of the proposal was small, but the British Aerospace management were getting nervous about the likelihood of leaks as the circle widened, particularly as that company was due to hold its annual general meeting of shareholders on 15 May. Reluctantly, THORN EMI agreed that an announcement would have to be made on that day, thus testing the reaction of the world at large to the idea well before it would have liked.

The world at large reacted in some astonishment to the idea of combining aircraft construction and recorded music in the same company, severely marking down THORN EMI's share price while marking up that of British Aerospace. Much effort was devoted by Laister and his colleagues to explaining the commercial logic of the proposed deal to institutional shareholders and to the financial press, but the explanations were found to be unconvincing. Ominously, the news also brought THORN EMI's rival of old, GEC, into the arena as a possible alternative buyer of British Aerospace. Its commercial case was stronger – it had, after all, been part owner of one of the companies that formed British Aerospace – and it had considerably more financial firepower than THORN EMI to do the deal. It was not, however, a welcome suitor to the British Aerospace management, who now found that, in publicising the THORN EMI approach, they had signalled their vulnerability to a bid. By early June, they had reversed their originally co-operative attitude to THORN EMI and, on the 12th, they unilaterally terminated all further discussions, rejecting the logic of the deal out of hand. Faced with this rejection, there was little more that THORN EMI could do and the whole matter was dropped.

However, GEC's interest in British Aerospace, aroused by the episode, has never abated since. Although the risky business of building commercial aircraft probably has little appeal, more than a decade later GEC is still believed to hanker after the military business. There was one happy outcome for British Aerospace: before the THORN EMI approach, its shares had stood at around 230 pence. In the course of its rejection statement, it managed to disclose that the prospective THORN EMI offer would have valued them at around 400 pence – a premium of nearly 75 per cent. This then became the benchmark and the shares settled at close to this level. British Aerospace had managed to 'release value' in its shares without being acquired.

For THORN EMI, there was no such happy outcome. In the course of a few weeks, its share price had fallen by over 15 per cent, leaving it less able to finance further expansion by issuing shares. Its inability to convince the world at large that the deal made sense had been humiliating. More importantly, it raised a question, both inside and outside the company, as to whether the strategy of the previous four years made any sense. If a company with the breadth of interests of THORN EMI had to look for entirely new areas to expand into, did that mean that the original idea of merging Thorn and EMI had been a mistake and that its management felt there was little future in its existing businesses? When Peter Laister stood up to address his executives at the company's annual senior executives' conference at a hotel near Heathrow Airport at the end of June 1984, he faced serried ranks of deeply sceptical and disillusioned people. Even the one aspect of the whole enterprise for which he was given credit – having spotted the investment opportunity in British Aerospace shares – did not bring any tangible benefit: in order to keep relations with British Aerospace as friendly as possible, THORN EMI had bought no shares in it, lest this was considered a hostile act.

As it happened, there was no time for a post-mortem on the British Aerospace episode within the company as it had embarked on another project which was, in time, to become the nemesis of THORN EMI in its existing form. The rise and fall of Inmos is an epic containing a number of parables on the relationship between business, government and high technology in Britain in the 1970s and 1980s. The genesis of Inmos lay in two cultures which now seem strange bedfellows. On the one hand, the free-wheeling, capitalist traditions of Silicon Valley where clever engineers had been known to turn an idea into a personal fortune of many millions of dollars, all in a matter of a couple of years, and, on the other, the Labour government's showpiece of industrial intervention and policy-making, the National Enterprise Board (NEB).

Richard Petritz, the main American protagonist, had a background typical of many of the engineers who had made themselves a fortune in the heady years that followed the commercialisation of the semiconductor in the mid-1960s. Originally an academic physicist, he had joined the American electronics company Texas Instruments – one of the pioneers of semiconductor development – in 1958. As a result, he had been in the industry almost from its birth. Ten years later, he left TI to set up as a venture capitalist, with financial backing from a New York stockbroking firm. His first venture was to start a semiconductor company called Mostek, heavily staffed with former colleagues from TI. Mostek was a considerable financial success and was sold a few years later to the American firm United Technologies, leaving its backers wealthy men. Petritz then spent his time investing in an assortment of other technology ventures, none of which was to prove as lucrative as Mostek. However, by the late 1970s, the semiconductor industry stood on the brink of another revolution which was to provide enormous opportunities for a whole new generation of companies. Advances in technology had made possible the manufacture of extremely complex electronic circuits on semiconductor chips – very large-scale integrated circuits – and these had made possible an entirely new generation of products, most famously the personal computer, which was in the process of being commercialised by the recently founded Apple Computer.

It was an ideal time to re-enter the semiconductor business, but unfortunately, because of high interest rates, the venture capital market in the US had dried up. It was at this point that the British element entered the story. Iann Barron was a comparative rarity among British computer scientists in having successfully started a computer company in the 1960s. His company, Computer Technology, took advantage of the growing popularity of mini-computers in the late 1960s and early 1970s and enjoyed a brief period of fortune. By the late 1970s, Barron had returned to his original speciality of computer design and research, but he retained an interest in the commercial future of the British computer industry. This was a time when news of revolutionary developments in microelectronics in the US was beginning to filter beyond the technologists and their implications were beginning to dawn on industrialists, politicians and other opinion-formers. It was apparently a BBC television programme on microelectronics, shown as part of the *Horizon* popular science series, which first drew the attention of the then British Prime Minister, James Callaghan, to the possible social and economic consequences of this new technology. At the time that Petritz, in the US, was considering the possibility of another lucrative investment in semiconductors, in Britain the Labour government was pondering the need for a national policy on microelectronics.

The NEB, which had been set up in 1975, had directed much of its effort towards providing a convalescent ward for the walking wounded of British industry – Rolls-Royce, Ferranti and British Leyland had all been patients. But it had, in addition, assumed the role of patron of Britain's technological resources, and it was in this role that it had asked Barron to advise it on what Britain should be doing in microelectronics in general and in semiconductor manufacture in particular. Britain's large electronics companies had steered clear of the business of manufacturing mass-produced commodity chips, arguing that these would always be available on world markets. There were therefore no British equivalents of American companies such as TI, which had been a breeding ground for new microelectronics entrepreneurs. Barron's advice was that it was not realistic to consider starting a new chip-making operation in the UK.

Shortly afterwards, in the summer of 1977, Barron met Petritz at a computer conference in Canada, and it was at this chance meeting that the notion of combining American semiconductor expertise with British taxpayers' money, through the NEB, took shape. Barron contacted the NEB and found they were receptive to the idea. Over the next year, business plans were prepared and discussed and the terms under which the venture, Inmos, would be launched were negotiated in London, between Petritz, Barron, the NEB and its political masters, the Department of Industry. By the summer of 1978, the project had been approved by the British Cabinet and news of it was publicly announced.

From its birth, Inmos was surrounded by controversy. Inevitably, it attracted criticism from the Conservative opposition, who were ideologically opposed to the NEB and all its works. But the established electronic manufacturers, such as GEC, Plessey and Ferranti, were not in favour of the project either. Even the Department of Industry felt that it would be wiser to put the limited resources available for the development of electronics in Britain into other areas. Ideological considerations apart, there was a genuine difference of opinion as to whether it was necessary to be involved in the sort of mass-market semiconductor manufacture that was Inmos's business to have a viable electronics industry in Britain. One side of this argument represented the position adopted by the electronic equipment manufacturers: to concentrate on making customised chips – called ASICs or application-specific integrated circuits in the trade – while buying in their requirements of standard chips. The alternative view was that the design of electronic equipment and of microchips was complementary: if you dropped out of one you would be disadvantaged in the other. Two decades into the microelectronic revolution, the whole argument has a dated feel about it. Over the period, many new electronics companies, particularly in the personal computer industry, have grown and prospered without making standard microchips themselves. On the other hand, some of the largest electronic manufacturers are also large microchip manufacturers and a close relationship between the design of equipment and of microchips undoubtedly exists. National ownership no longer attracts the sentiments it did twenty years ago and the whole idea of trying to encourage British manufacturing industry by government investment in semiconductor manufacture has been discredited.

Within a year of the formation of Inmos, the political background in Britain that had made it possible had changed radically with the sweeping victory of the Conservative Party in the 1979 general election. However, although the new government was antipathetic to the concept of using taxpayers' money to finance speculative industrial investments, it took a pragmatic view of this particular inheritance from its predecessor. The NEB had initially committed to providing £50 million of funding for Inmos, in two tranches of £25 million. The first tranche had been paid at the outset and the balance was to be paid subject to satisfactory progress. Inmos had committed itself to building its first manufacturing facility in Colorado Springs, near Denver, Colorado, and a British design office had been established in Bristol.

The first decision point for the new British Cabinet was reached in early 1980, when it was asked to stump up the second £25 million. There was much agonised discussion on whether the money should be made available but eventually, after a review of the company's prospects by Sir George Jefferson, then chairman of British Aerospace, the Cabinet was persuaded to allow it. By this time, the company had realised that the funding called for in its original plan was insufficient and an additional £35 million had to be provided by way of guarantees for equipment leases – Inmos having leased rather than purchased most of its production equipment. It was hoped that this would be the last time that Inmos would need to turn to the British taxpayer. With the funding secure, Inmos established its British manufacturing facility in Newport, South Wales, in a futuristic building designed by the eminent architect Richard Rogers, which came to be known by company wags as the 'hanging gardens of Babylon'.

By the end of 1980, the company had shipped its first products, 16k static RAM chips made in the Colorado Springs

facility. The outlook for the medium term seemed set fair and
even the Secretary of State for Industry, Sir Keith Joseph – a
leading right-wing ideologue – seemed to have been won over as
a supporter. However, the NEB and the Department of Industry,
whose ranks were unblessed by anyone with actual experience
of the semiconductor industry, were soon to realise that this
industry was prone to unpredictability of an unusually severe
form. By mid-1982, the Inmos management were back asking for
another £15 million. There had been some slippage in building
up production – not unusual in the industry – and a change in the
sterling-to-dollar exchange rate had reduced the funds available
to it. In fact, given the nature of the industry, the management
had done well to have achieved what they had, but the funding
estimates had, all along, been too optimistic. In the book *The
Inmos Saga*, Mick McLean and Tom Rowland suggest that the
original estimate of £50 million had been arrived at by taking a
figure of £12.5 million from a proposal that Petritz had prepared
for a semiconductor plant in Korea, doubling it because Inmos
would have two plants, and then doubling it again because, as they
quote Iann Barron: 'Every one knows such projects cost twice as
much as you expect.'

By early 1983, the government seems to have decided to
disentangle itself from further involvement with Inmos. Its
non-interventionist philosophy – which had required it to let
many British businesses go to the wall in the recession of the
early 1980s – sat oddly with having to fund a substantially
American business venture out of British taxpayers' money.
Merchant bankers were hired to find private-sector finance,
either from the City or from industrial companies. It soon
became clear that raising institutional funding in London for a
semiconductor company was a forlorn hope. Potential industrial
buyers had no doubt sensed the government's quandary and
wanted to take full advantage of it. They were only prepared
to invest on terms that would have required the government to
write off most of its investment. Matters were complicated by
the fact that the views of the staff and management of Inmos,
who owned about 25 per cent of the company against the NEB's
75 per cent, had an important bearing on the eventual outcome.
Among the options being canvassed, one – favoured by Inmos's

American management – was that it should be publicly floated in the US where it would receive a warmer welcome than in London. Another was that a consortium of British electronics companies should jointly invest in Inmos, and it was this proposal which first aroused THORN EMI's interest.

Although some of THORN EMI's businesses were significant users of semiconductors, there was no pressing need for any of them to own a semiconductor manufacturing operation. The interest in Inmos was therefore very much a head office affair, based on a vague notion that, without a British semiconductor capability, the company would be at the mercy of Japanese and American sources of supply, although there is no evidence that this would have increased its vulnerability. A more substantive reason was that it would be useful to have control of a silicon foundry – a manufacturing facility for customised chips. In fact, the first thought was that THORN EMI and another British electronics company should set up such a foundry and should ask Inmos to manage it for them, since it had many of the necessary skills. One of the non-executive directors on the THORN EMI board was Sir William Barlow, who had previously been chairman of its engineering group and had then gone on to become chairman of the engineering company BICC. He had also, coincidentally, been appointed a non-executive director of Inmos, a fact that may have had some bearing on later events. When the matter was first discussed, in December 1983, he advised that Inmos would have no interest in managing a facility for someone else, but that if a consortium of British companies acquired Inmos, it might be possible to set up a custom chip facility within Inmos.

Soon after this meeting, THORN EMI registered its interest in joining such a consortium with the chairman of Inmos, Sir Malcolm Wilcox. However, matters then seem to have stood still for a period: the government was investigating other possibilities and THORN EMI's management was shortly to be embroiled in the British Aerospace affair. By the following summer, with the British Aerospace deal going cold, THORN EMI submitted a formal proposal to Sir Malcolm, offering to subscribe for new shares in Inmos to give it a 10 per cent shareholding, at a price of £10 million. The proposal itself was likely to have had only modest appeal to the government, since it would still leave it as the majority shareholder. However, the good news was that it implied a much higher valuation on Inmos – at around £90 million – than other offers the government had received: the American telecommunications company AT&T had valued it at around half this figure.

Since early 1983, when the government first started actively to look for a way out of the Inmos affair, the company seemed to be coming good financially. By the summer of 1984, it was forecasting an operating profit of £20 million in that year, its first ever profitable one and twice the level projected in its business plan. It claimed to control 60 per cent of the market for static RAM chips, a particularly profitable line much in demand for military applications.

Inmos – the first six years

£ million	1979	1980	1981	1982	1983	1984
Sales	.03	.18	2.1	13.7	37.8	111
Profit/(loss)*	(2.5)	(7.4)	(16.8)	(16.8)	(10.8)	20.6

* Before interest and tax

The American investment banking firm Merrill Lynch, which had been hired to investigate the possibility of a public flotation in the US, suggested it might be worth £200 million, but did not think it was realistic to float before the summer of 1985. However, a public flotation was not the best outcome from the government's point of view. Quite apart from the delay which, as we shall see, would have been disastrous, it would not have been able to sell all its holding in one fell swoop. Much the best outcome was to find one buyer to take all its holding now.

In the course of a month, between mid-June and mid-July 1984, THORN EMI moved from buying just 10 per cent of Inmos to, in effect, buying all of it. What had started off as a way of getting access to semiconductor manufacturing expertise for THORN EMI's internal requirements now became a speculative investment in the semiconductor industry. Whether frustration at the failure of the British Aerospace bid had any role in the decision is a matter of speculation. News that Inmos seemed to have turned the corner in financial terms would have had some bearing, as would the Merrill Lynch valuation. The booming semiconductor

market and the rapid growth of the personal computer industry
had also created a sense of excitement. In this heady atmosphere,
the risky nature of the proposition was overlooked. THORN EMI
had virtually no experience or understanding of the semiconductor
industry, but the handicap this imposed was not appreciated. The
board seemed to have been persuaded that the company's general
involvement in technology would be a sufficient basis for managing
a semiconductor company. Although some members had personal
reservations, Laister was authorised to purchase the government's
stake of 75 per cent for a price of £75 million.

One factor that favourably influenced Laister's view of Inmos
was the presence of Sir William Barlow on the boards of both
that company and of THORN EMI. He took the view that if the
decision to buy it was unsound, Sir William would say so, and he
seems to have relied to a large extent on Sir William's association
with Inmos. Sir William, however, found himself in an invidious
position: owing a duty to both companies and their shareholders,
he felt compelled to stay out of any formal discussions of the
matter. He recollects that the first he knew of the THORN EMI
decision was at an Inmos board meeting at which he was told that
he would not be given any papers on a possible bid for Inmos as
he had a conflict of interest. When he found out who the bidder
was, he was astonished. He considered Inmos to be 'a bottomless
pit' and tried, as best he could in the particular circumstances, to
convey this to Laister, a recollection that is confirmed by some
of his colleagues. Laister's own recollection is very different: the
impression he received from Sir William was that because Inmos
had long-term contracts for the chips it was then selling, it was
'bomb proof'. What seems to have happened is that not only did
Sir William's informal signals not get across, but his formal silence
on the matter, which in the circumstances was unavoidable, was
read as support for the proposed deal.

Selling its stake in Inmos to a large British company was the
answer to the Conservative government's prayers. However, its
advisers were no longer content simply to recover the funds that
had been put into the company and to make a clean exit: the
turnaround in its fortunes and the Merrill Lynch valuation had
raised their ambitions. Success always has a thousand fathers
and, in the aftermath of the sale of Inmos, described by one

wag as 'the government's most successful privatisation', a number of the political figures involved claimed credit for it. Ultimate political responsibility rested with Norman Tebbit, who had taken over as Secretary of State for Trade and Industry from Sir Keith Joseph. Kenneth Baker, the Minister for Information Technology, also had a role. The senior civil servant involved was Sir Brian Hayes, the Permanent Secretary in the Department of Trade and Industry. However, the man who probably deserves most credit was Sir Jeffrey (later Lord) Sterling, chairman of the shipping and construction company P&O, ardent supporter of Mrs Thatcher and, at the time, industrial adviser to her government.

The government team, led by Sir Jeffrey, played their hand adroitly. The combination of canny commercial negotiating skills, appeals to patriotism and service to the country and the suggestion of political patronage, made for a powerful suit. It was indicated that the Prime Minister herself was taking an interest in the deal; that she attached great importance to keeping Inmos in British hands; but that she had set her heart on getting at least £100 million for the government's stake – a premium of £35 million on its investment – and, as always, she was immovable. In the end a deal was struck at £95 million – 25 per cent higher than the figure agreed by the THORN EMI board – which put a value of £125 million on the whole company, THORN EMI having undertaken to acquire the shares owned by staff and management on the same terms. In addition, it took over obligations for Inmos's leases amounting to £25 million and net borrowings of £12 million.

Announcement of the deal, on 12 July, which coincided with the company's results for the year to 3 March 1984, caused a collapse in THORN EMI's share price, already battered by speculation about the earlier British Aerospace proposal. The influential Lex column in the *Financial Times* commented on the following day:

The whirlpool which swallowed THORN EMI's shares was conspicuous even amidst yesterday's seething waters and betrayed a nasty current of market misgivings about the group prospects. At 474p, down 43p, the shares have fallen 23 per cent since the day before THORN dropped its British Aerospace merger idea on them.

This could be some measure of the City's loss of confidence in Thorn's boardroom over the period, and the same is evident in the harsh reaction to the 1983–84 preliminary statement.

Pre-tax profits of £156.8 million met most expectations, but the indications given at the same time about current trading results were apparently enough in themselves to make THORN an obvious victim of consumer spending doubts. This may have deprived THORN's proposed acquisition of Inmos of a fair hearing into the bargain.

Concern about the Inmos deal is that it might emerge, as it were, as a BAe merger writ small. Chip manufacturers are notorious cash drains and have suffered from highly volatile earnings. Were Inmos's earnings next year to swing into sizeable losses rather than a healthy advance on this year's projected profit of £13 million or so – the company will pay no tax – then THORN could find itself facing yet another pressure on its balance sheet.

Net group borrowings are already 48 per cent of shareholders' funds and look set to grow by another £20 million in 1984–85 even before taking account of the Inmos purchase funds. THORN will now have no real option but to use borrowed cash.

None the less, it seems to be paying a sharp enough price, marking an exit p/e of about 9½ for Inmos. THORN has little interest for the moment in fancy notions of vertical integration and is buying a business with exciting growth prospects where capital investment can presumably be tailored to results.

Meanwhile, nothing has happened in the consumer electronics division seriously to disrupt THORN's broad cash flow projections as both the VCR and TV rental base shrink further, but the City's pre-tax forecasts for the current year reflect acute uncertainty even on this more familiar front. It all looks a case for some urgent fence mending.

Far from mending fences, the company's next move further antagonised its shareholders. The City had initially assumed that the deal would be financed by an increase in borrowings, since it did not make sense to raise money by issuing new shares with the share price so depressed. However, a few days later, the company took the stock market by surprise by announcing a rights issue.

The already battered share price fell to 421 pence, compared to the rights issue price of 446 pence. With the share price on the stock market below the price at which the new shares were to be issued, a concerted effort to explain the deal to institutional shareholders was launched. One of THORN EMI's stockbroking advisers recalls that he found himself pounding the pavements of the City with senior executives of the company only a few weeks after undertaking a similar exercise in connection with the British Aerospace deal. Having had some partial success in explaining the strategy behind that, he now felt the company was facing an uphill struggle in trying to explain an entirely different approach. As he recalls, some investors were beginning to ask: 'Do you chaps have any idea about what you are doing?'

As it happens, the rights issue, although an expensive way of raising money at the time, probably saved the company from financial disaster in the next year as the full horror of the Inmos acquisition began to unravel. The government negotiators, as well as having extracted a very full price from THORN EMI, had stampeded it into completing the deal with inordinate haste. Very little of the investigation normally carried out when businesses are acquired – due diligence, as it is called – was undertaken in this case. There was one person in THORN EMI who had actual experience of managing a semiconductor company, but he only heard about the deal on the television news, while on an unrelated trip to Tokyo. Douglas Stevenson had been a vice-president of the American conglomerate ITT, responsible for its semiconductor and electronic component operations. After retirement, he had taken on the role of technical adviser to THORN EMI and had been closely involved in the failed VHD project. Although he was later to take on the role of chief executive of Inmos, he was not involved in any way in an investigation of the company prior to its acquisition. It seems that, during the critical period during which full due diligence could have been carried out, this aspect took second place to concern about the effect of the deal on the morale of Inmos's managers and engineers.

The final mistake made by THORN EMI in completing the deal was in the form of the agreement negotiated with the government. It is common when buying a business from a majority shareholder to ask him to underwrite the state of the business at the time it is acquired, by giving 'warranties'. The seller would, naturally, rather not give warranties but, particularly where the buyer is paying a high price and has done little due diligence, he

EMI

Alfred Clark,
Chairman until 1945

Sir Alexander
Aikman, Chairman,
1945–1954

Sir Joseph
Lockwood,
Chairman,
1954–1974

Sir John Read,
Chairman,
1974–1979

'His Master's Voice', portrait of
Nipper, by Francis Barraud, 1899

Enrico Caruso, who made his first
recording with EMI in 1902

Maria Callas, who made most of her
recordings with EMI

Sir Edward Elgar, who conducted
his own works for the HMV label

Abbey Road Studios, opened in
1931

Frank Sinatra, who still records for
Capitol

Nat 'King' Cole, who recorded for
Capitol in the forties and fifties

Aerial photograph of
Hayes site taken by
the Luftwaffe in 1942

Capitol Records,
acquired in 1955

The Beatles, who
were signed by
EMI in 1962

The Beach Boys

Pink Floyd,
who have
recorded for
EMI since
1967

ABC Cinemas, which was acquired in 1969 and sold to Alan Bond in 1986

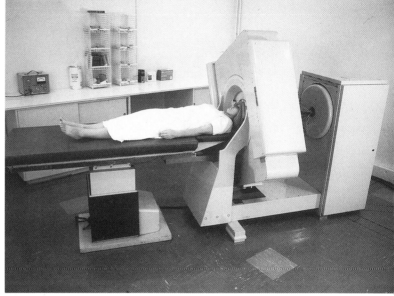

CAT Scanner, developed by EMI in the early 1970s

Nipper updated as the current HMV UK logo

Peter Laister,
Chairman,
1984–1985

Sir Graham Wilkins,
Chairman, 1985–1989

is usually compelled to do so. In this case, the government's negotiators took the rather disingenuous position that the NEB was constrained in its ability to give warranties because it was an investment institution and did not interfere in the management of Inmos, a position patently contradicted by the presence of four government-appointed directors on the board of the company. In fact, the position adopted by the government is one often taken by commercial organisations selling a business, but is usually seen through as a negotiating ploy. After all, as the seller of the business benefits from the proceeds of the sale, it seems even-handed that he should underwrite any faults in the business he is selling.

What was different in this case was that the seller was the government. Although there is no evidence that its negotiators tried to mislead THORN EMI, it seems that the fact that it was dealing with the government made the company accept a situation that would have been unacceptable if it were dealing with a commercial organisation. Laister himself recalls that there was an implied suggestion that, 'of course, the government would stand behind its moral, as well as its contractual obligations.'

The awful reality of the deal it had done dawned on THORN EMI a few months later. In the autumn of 1984, rumours of a 'sleeper' – a latent defect – in one of Inmos's most important products started circulating. Semiconductor products are prone to defects that do not show up until they have been inserted into machinery and put into use for a period. In this case, there was a defect in the best-selling 16k SRAM chip which meant that, as a result of vibrations and the effect of electric fields when in use, an electrical connection would crack – become 'open circuit' in the jargon. This particular chip had accounted for over three-quarters of Inmos's shipments and all those shipments were potentially faulty. Since many of these were now in use, in anything from computers to radar sets, the potential liability, when they failed, was enormous. Apart from any legal liability for replacing the faulty chips, an endemic fault allowed customers to break long-term contracts with the company, thus negating one feature of Inmos's business which had seemed so reassuring.

Whether there was any knowledge of this latent problem within Inmos at the time it was acquired by THORN EMI is unclear. More thorough due diligence may or may not have revealed its existence, although at that time its extent would have been very uncertain. Certainly, a better understanding of the inherent risks of the semiconductor business would have led THORN EMI to ensure that it had redress against the sellers of the business for faults that arose before the acquisition. Harold Mourgue, who had taken on the role of chairman of Inmos, first became aware of the scale of the problem in January 1985, while attending a seminar on semiconductors in New York. Also attending the seminar was a sales executive from Inmos. In talking to him about which of his customers were attending the seminar and whom he should be meeting, he discovered a very troubled man with a number of extremely unhappy customers. By the time the Inmos accounts for 1984 had been finalised, in early 1985 – accounts that showed a pre-tax profit of £14.4 million and in anticipation of which THORN EMI had valued the business – it was clear that the least one could say was that they were wide of the mark. In the six months to the end of September 1985, Inmos made a loss of £12.5 million before interest charges.

In retrospect, the government's timing in parting company with Inmos had been immaculate: any earlier and it would not have been able to set out the glittering prospects on which the business was valued; any later and it would have been unsaleable at any price. The government had made a clean getaway, as the terms of the deal left it with no liability for the latent problems. Although THORN EMI complained about the problems it had found, it received no more than sympathy. Whatever impression had been given in the original negotiations, it turned out that the government felt no obligation beyond its contractual commitments.

11

A New Regime

Even before the problems at Inmos were recognised by THORN EMI, it was clear that 1985 was going to be a miserable year. In January, the company announced its results for the six months to September 1984, which showed a 28 per cent decline in pre-tax profits. The cause of the problem was Ferguson, the television and video manufacturing business.

Ferguson had enjoyed what turned out to be its Indian summer in the early 1980s. It had successfully launched a new range of television sets, developed with government assistance and, as it turned out, the last television sets ever to be designed by a British manufacturer. By 1982, consumer spending was reviving from the first recession under the Thatcher government and much of the money was going into television and video recorders. Although the PAL television licence protection, the bulwark that had hitherto shielded British manufacturers, had ended, Far Eastern manufacturers had not sufficiently expanded their production of the larger television sets favoured by British buyers. In the year to March 1984, Ferguson earned a return on its assets of over 22 per cent.

By 1984, however, the British consumer electronics market had declined: video recorder shipments had fallen by one-third from the peak of 1982. The problem was compounded by the increased availability of Japanese sets, both imported and made in Britain. The nightmare that Sir Jules Thorn and Sir Richard Cave had dreaded had finally become real.

Ironically, the news on Inmos, which THORN EMI announced in early 1985, was upbeat: it had, ostensibly, made a pre-tax profit of £14.4 million in the year to December 1984 and even the *Financial*

Times described the news as 'one in the eye for Thorn's critic'. THORN EMI was able to say that preparations for the stock market flotation of Inmos were 'quite well advanced' and that it hoped to raise between £30 million and £50 million through an issue of new shares to finance the future growth of Inmos.

However, even as these statements were being made, the semiconductor industry was entering the most vicious down-swing of its short history. By the summer of 1985, the price of 64k DRAM chips, the most commonly used memory chip at the time, had fallen from three dollars to fifty cents in the course of six months. Although one of the reasons given by THORN EMI for the acquisition of Inmos had been 'to improve the balance of [its] spread of businesses', as its circular to Inmos's shareholders put it, it turned out that the semiconductor industry marched in time to the same cycles as the consumer electronics business, but with greater gusto. The hoary objective of 'balance' had once again proved to be a chimera. The *Financial Times*, in a long article on the plight of THORN EMI, wrote:

> The critics [of THORN EMI] charge that [it] has correctly identified a key weakness – its dependence on the UK consumer spending cycle up to now – but has opted for the wrong antidotes. Buying Inmos, the microchip manufacturer, has in this view exacerbated THORN's vulnerability to cyclicality.

In fact, a general gloom was beginning to envelop the whole of the British electronics industry. By the summer of 1985, share prices of leading companies such as GEC, Plessey and Racal had halved in value since the start of the year. Sinclair Research, the company run by the eccentric inventor Sir Clive Sinclair, which had introduced the British public to the home computer, was close to bankruptcy, owing, as it happened, a considerable amount of money to THORN EMI. Even amidst the general blood-letting, however, THORN EMI, now tarred with having jumped into the world of high technology with spectacularly bad timing, stood out as being particularly friendless.

By the early summer, Peter Laister was beleaguered. Although both the abortive British Aerospace venture and the acquisition of Inmos had been formally supported – or, at least, not opposed – by the board, they were seen as his pet projects. With the company's share price well below the level at which its shareholders had stumped up money for the rights issue that had financed the purchase of Inmos, the institutional investors were in an ugly mood. The non-executive directors of the company, there to ensure that the management did not ride rough-shod over the interests of the shareholders, were attracting criticism for not having reined in their ambitious chairman. In April, at the behest of the non-executive directors, Laister had appointed Colin Southgate to the re-created post of managing director, to manage the day-to-day affairs of the company, while Laister himself concentrated on strategy and on improving relations with the City.

It was the imminent announcement of the company's dreadful results for the year to March 1985 which finally tipped the non-executive directors from sullen displeasure to outright revolt. The move to oust Laister was apparently instigated by Peter Bennett, a former chairman of the W H Smith retailing group, who had been a non-executive director of THORN EMI since 1977. He had been most closely in touch with City opinion and apparently felt that the non-executive directors should have done more to restrain Laister and were therefore partly responsible for the problems of the company.

The move, when it came, seems to have taken Peter Laister by surprise, although Sir William Barlow, another non-executive director at the time, had warned him a few days earlier of the mood of his colleagues. Laister was summoned to Sir William Barlow's club, Brooks's, in St James's, on the evening of 13 June. A cabal of non-executive directors had met earlier in the evening to decide his fate over dinner. Laister was told that they no longer wished him to remain on the board. Sir Graham Wilkins, a non-executive director, who was not present at the dinner, was appointed chairman and chief executive and the executive directors were told of the decision at a board meeting the following day. Colin Southgate, who had been managing director since April, was to stay on in that role. Sir Graham, a former chairman of the pharmaceutical and toiletries group Beecham, was the sort of weighty industrial figure who would help to reassure the City that the company was now in safe hands. However, some of the executive directors had felt that the roles of chairman and chief executive should be separated and were surprised that this had not happened.

Interviewed during research for this book, Peter Laister acknowledged that mistakes had been made in the process of acquiring Inmos and, as chairman, he was ultimately responsible. He stressed, however, that the decision to acquire Inmos was a decision of the whole board, and not his alone. Notwithstanding Inmos, he still believes that his vision – of building a diversified company in home entertainment and high technology – was the right one for THORN EMI and, had he not lost the support of his colleagues, it would have been realised. His mistake, he believes, was in not selecting a group of board colleagues more supportive of his vision. A decade after these events, Laister remains an unreconstructed believer in the diversified company – one with a wide range of related interests. It is a point of view diametrically opposed to the one advocated in this book. Diversity, in his view, gives long-term strength and balance, and can be successfully managed. Focus, he believes, while improving company performance in the short term – hence its current popularity in the City – leads to weakness in the long term. After leaving THORN EMI, he went on to try to build a diversified multimedia group for Robert Maxwell's MCC, although that attempt was abandoned when Maxwell committed all his financial resources to buying the Macmillan publishing business.

The first task for the new chairman of THORN EMI and his managing director was the presentation – in their first week in command – of the results for the previous financial year. That the results would be dreadful was widely expected in the City. As the *Financial Times* had put it earlier in the week: 'Sir Graham Wilkins' new regime will no doubt paint as bleak a picture in this Friday's figures as it can, the better to start afresh.' In spite of this, the shares fell on the announcement to a new low point of 316 pence.

What the results showed was a fall in the pre-tax profits of just over 30 per cent as a result of the problems of Inmos and of Ferguson. This included a charge of £28 million for amounts set aside to reorganise the Ferguson business completely. However, some of the bad news was not included in these figures. The accounting conventions at the time allowed real disasters, as opposed to routine bad news, to be left out of the reported results of the company and incorporated under 'extraordinary items'. These extraordinary items included a charge of £30 million (before tax relief) to cover a major reorganisation of Inmos. Despite the collapse in profits, the company decided to pay the same dividend as it had the previous year, although the amount paid exceeded the profit attributable to shareholders.

In later years there was much debate as to whether the picture painted in July 1985 had been bleak enough. Colin Southgate, for one, felt that the company should have set aside much larger amounts to cover the problems that it had to tackle and should have halved the dividend. His contention was that, if this had been done, problems could have been addressed more aggressively and the company's eventual recovery would have been achieved sooner and at lower overall cost. The burden of paying a high dividend was particularly onerous over the next few years. Cutting the dividend paid to shareholders is, however, read as a sign of further problems ahead and of uncertainty on the part of the board as to the company's prospects of recovery. While that may be the honest position at the time, such candour can rebound to the company's disadvantage. Sir Graham was not prepared to publish a more gloomy version of the state of affairs, and Colin Southgate did not get his way on this point.

THORN EMI's plight in the summer of 1985 was certainly more desperate than a reading of the new chairman's rather terse statement, published in early July, suggests, and was probably worse than the board imagined. Along with much of the rest of British manufacturing industry, the 'metal bashing' businesses of THORN EMI – in domestic appliances, lighting and engineering – were struggling to adjust to the international competition that the 1980s had ushered in. The consumer electronics business, for long the centrepiece of the company's home entertainment strategy, was approaching its nemesis, although few within the company were prepared to recognise this fact. EMI Music had entered another of its recurrent periods of sullen unproductivity: its operating profits, having reached £36.6 million in 1982, had fallen to £10.2 million in 1985. EMI Films, also earmarked to play a major role in the home entertainment strategy, had entered into financial commitments to support future film production which its struggling parent would be hard put to meet. And Inmos, on close examination, was to prove to be an even more painful bed of nails than had been anticipated by the new regime.

In the spring of 1985, as the extent of Inmos's problems sunk in at THORN EMI's head office, Douglas Stevenson was appointed chief executive of Inmos. Stevenson, a voluble and blunt-speaking Scotsman, was the only person in THORN EMI, outside Inmos, with any real understanding of the semiconductor business and also happened to be hard-boiled enough to grapple with the task. Within a week of Peter Laister's departure, Richard Petritz, the founder of Inmos and its deputy chairman, and John Heightly, its chief operating officer, were removed from their posts and the company announced that it would be cutting its staff of 2,000 employees by one-quarter. Gallingly, THORN EMI was committed to acquiring the shares owned by Inmos's management and staff at a price at least as high as that paid to the British Government in the previous year. Not surprisingly, given the now dimmed prospects of Inmos, it had no trouble in persuading the management and staff to sell.

By 1985, THORN EMI had written off its entire investment in Inmos – amounting to a little over £130 million – even before the final payments had been made. There was, therefore, a body of opinion within THORN EMI which argued for the business to be closed down immediately: after all, as it had been recognised that Inmos had no value as a continuing business, where was the sense in continuing with it? That might, indeed, have been an attractive route in theory, but, as the pragmatists were aware, not one that the company could realistically follow. To ask your shareholders to stump up £130 million of their money and then, within a few months, to tell them that it has been lost as surely as if it had been burned on a bonfire is unlikely to win many friends. If, at the same time, you seem to be throwing away what, until very recently, had been regarded as a rare instance of British success in high technology, the opprobrium is likely to be universal. Although the City and most of the company's shareholders regarded Inmos as an unmitigated disaster, elsewhere there were many admirers of its technical achievements and there was considerable hope for its Transputer chip, which was first demonstrated to the world at the Institute of Contemporary Arts in London in October 1985.

The Transputer was not a memory chip – Inmos's staple up until that time – but a combined memory with a processor – the thinking brain of a computer – on one chip. It was a revolutionary product and, unlike the memory chips, was entirely British – designed at Inmos's Bristol site. It was felt by many to be the ideal device for embedded computing applications – uses of computer power within machinery and equipment. In *The Inmos Saga* Mick McLean and Tom Rowlands wrote:

> The Transputer, if it only achieves a fraction of its designers' goals, may well do more for the British economy than the entire £350 million Alvey research programme [a British Government funded programme], also intended to revitalise the economy through an injection of electronic wizardry.
>
> The Inmos saga should therefore give hope and encouragement to many others in Britain who believe that a thriving high-technology sector is vital to the country's future as an industrial nation.

In the face of such faith – and the authors were articulating a widely held view – it is not surprising that the new regime at THORN EMI quailed from torching Inmos immediately.

In fact, there were practical reasons as well for continuing with the business, which Stevenson described as 'problems in the pipeline'. One of these was the 'interconnect' problem on faulty SRAM chips. It was one thing to negotiate with dissatisfied buyers of these chips while there was an on-going business with which they might wish to trade in the future, but quite another if the customers knew that the supplier was going out of business. Another problem was that, in acquiring Inmos, THORN EMI had entered into commitments to supply chip-making technology to three foreign collaborators on terms that were little understood at the time. One of these agreements was with a Japanese company, NMB. This agreement covered the manufacture of 256k DRAM, at the time the next generation of memory chip. The original rationale for this deal, as far as Inmos was concerned, had been to allow it to have a presence in the market for the next generation of memory chips – it had a right to buy chips from NMB at a discount

– without itself making the enormous investment. By 1985, NMB had invested over £100 million in the project: THORN EMI had no choice but to continue to support it. Stevenson was, however, able to negotiate his way out of the other two agreements, one with the Dutch Government and another with the Korean company Hyundai.

Over the next few years, Inmos was to absorb considerable amounts of THORN EMI's money and of its senior management's time. In 1986, the company decided to cease all manufacturing in the US and the plant at Colorado Springs was closed. A further extraordinary charge of £60 million (before tax relief) was taken in the company's accounts to cover the cost of this. By 1988, all operations had been transferred to the UK and the Transputer, now a modestly successful commercial product, accounted for half the sales. However, it was not destined to achieve the success that had been hoped for and the goal of using it to entice a buyer for Inmos proved elusive. It was not until April 1989 that THORN EMI finally divested itself of its semiconductor venture, selling the business to SGS-Thomson Microelectronics BV, a Franco-Italian joint venture.

Inmos was only the most pressing of THORN EMI's problems at the time the new regime of Sir Graham Wilkins and Colin Southgate took over. At the level of broad policy, it was also a relatively simple one. By the summer of 1985, there was no one in the company who believed that its acquisition was anything other than a disastrous mistake – it was losing $2 million a month at the time – and the sooner that THORN EMI could extract itself from its involvement with it the better. It was then a matter of pragmatic management to do this in a way that minimised the damage to the company.

As with Inmos, much of the rest of the early period of restructuring of THORN EMI was grounded in pragmatic common sense rather than on a deeply considered strategic vision. Colin Southgate recalls two strong impressions of the company on being appointed managing director: firstly, an absence of discipline, and secondly, such a diversity of businesses that each could only be allowed to make tiny investments. He realised at the outset that spreading the company's resources so thinly was futile and so the idea of concentrating its efforts came naturally.

However, on which businesses should the company concentrate? A decade later, it is probably impossible for the key participants to recall their thought processes at the time uncoloured by the way events actually unfolded. Southgate recalls that, from the start, he felt that EMI Music and the rental business had a long-term future. They were, of course, both businesses that ranked alongside the largest worldwide companies in their fields. However, it would be wrong to assume from this that the final shape of THORN EMI existed as a clear vision at the time. Southgate had an eclectic range of interests, having started in the computer software industry and then been responsible for THORN EMI's high-technology interests before becoming managing director of the group. The idea of a complete withdrawal from manufacturing was not one that would have occurred to anyone at the time. The Thorn part of the company was rooted in manufacturing and, even in the mid-1980s, THORN EMI was one of Britain's largest manufacturing companies. Although there was a feeling at the time in political circles and in the City that making things was not something Britain necessarily had to do, this was not a view shared by the new regime in the company.

Southgate himself thought, at the time, that the lighting business – which still had a large share of the British market – could be built up to rank alongside Music and Rental. He also thought that Kenwood, maker of the eponymous Chef, which had some brand distinctiveness and a markedly international outlook, had considerable potential. In fact, the question of the day was not in which businesses should THORN EMI remain but rather which of its businesses had a long-term future? And that question, in turn, could not be answered without first deciding whether the problems faced by a business were a result of poor management in the past, to which a solution could be found, or a result of irretrievable strategic weakness. And this decision was not arrived at by profound analysis at the outset, but by lessons drawn from bitter experience along the way.

The remaking of THORN EMI can be divided into two phases. The first, which covers the period from 1985 to 1988, was one of managing through crises – initially, a financial crisis, as Inmos's losses threatened to drain the company of cash, and, later, the threat of hostile takeover. It was in 1988 that serious thought was first given to the long-term shape of the company, and it was over the next few years that the shape of the company evolved. Of course, by then some of the decisions taken in the crisis management period had pre-empted certain options, but these decisions were taken on their own merits, not in the context of some overall plan. In fact, in the late 1980s, the chances of THORN EMI being acquired in a hostile takeover bid were regarded as being so high that the idea of some final shape for the company would have seemed an academic distraction. The objective of the management was to get to a point where, if there was a bid for the company, they could mount a stout defence in order to extract as high a price as possible from the bidder, if not to thwart him. Sir William Barlow, who remained a non-executive director of THORN EMI until 1989, and who was not in favour of the 'break-up' of the group which took place, recalls Southgate telling him that, 'if he didn't do it, Hanson or another raider would, and he was damned if he was going to let that happen.'

That THORN EMI's management was able to reach the point where it could afford the luxury of considering the long-term shape of the company is, in itself, something of a miracle. One of the defining characteristics of business in the late 1980s, on both sides of the Atlantic, was the rise of the corporate raider at his most audacious – the Barbarian at the Gate. In many ways, THORN EMI presented an ideal prey, stuffed full of disparate, possibly under-valued businesses on which a turn could be made. At one stage, the City was full of merchant bankers busily putting together consortia of likely predators. Although share stakes in the company were built up in anticipation of a bid, no bid ever materialised. Southgate recalls that in the early years of his regime, he was not too worried about a bid: Inmos was regarded as so large and mysterious a black hole that no outsider had the nerve to bid. This is confirmed by a merchant banker who was involved in a possible consortium bid at the time. He recalls: 'We couldn't get the numbers to add up.' Indeed, given the uncertainty within the company on how to extract itself from Inmos and the cost of so doing, it is not surprising that it appeared to outsiders a sufficiently lethal poison pill to deter them.

Although the early years of THORN EMI under the new regime were characterised by pragmatic crisis management rather than by strategic vision of exceptional merit, there was one crucial change in the mind-set of the company. The concepts of synergy, of 'a range of businesses which benefit from a series of relationships', of 'values' that spanned the company and of 'balance', were jettisoned. Henceforth, each business would be looked at strictly on its own merits. This itself lifted an enormous burden from decision-making, and the first major strategic move that the new regime made bore the hallmark of this new thinking. Film-making and music were two activities that did seem to many observers to have scope for considerable 'synergy', and indeed still do, as the moves by music companies such as PolyGram testify. THORN EMI's experience suggested otherwise, and there was little hesitation in embarking on the divestment of EMI Films. Southgate himself called the decision a 'no brainer'.

12

Film Plot

THORN EMI's involvement in film production dated back to the acquisition by EMI in 1968 of The Grade Organisation, which had participated in an assortment of British films of the 1960s – Michael Caine's *Alfie* and Cliff Richard's *Summer Holiday* and *The Young Ones* being among the more memorable. It was the acquisition in the following year of the Associated British Picture Corporation (ABPC) which took EMI from being a bit player in the industry to being the largest British film producer and custodian of Britain's cinematic heritage. ABPC included among its assets the British Lion and Pathé film libraries, which owned valuable film footage going back to the start of film-making in Britain. It also owned the country's largest cinema chain, ABC Cinemas, the Elstree Studios, and a film and television distribution operation.

The acquisition of ABPC had been part of EMI's grand design to become, amongst other things, an entertainment conglomerate. In commercial terms, however, ABPC had been a disappointment. Although the cinema chain had produced steady if unspectacular profits, film production had contributed very little in the way of profits. EMI Films, as the film production business was known, had had a measure of box-office success, having participated in such late 1970s Hollywood blockbusters as *Close Encounters of the Third Kind* and *The Deer Hunter*. However, it shared a characteristic of film production companies generally, whereby success was celebrated by increased spending but there was no corresponding cutback in response to failure. Since no one had yet discovered the formula for producing successful films only, this led to an unfortunate asymmetry between the rewards of success and the penalties of failure.

In the late 1970s, there was a trend in the industry towards big-budget films based, it seems, on the evidence that most major hits were big-budget films. This view, still held in the industry today, seemed to ignore the equally valid evidence that the largest financial failures were also big-budget films, which increased the risks and raised the stakes in film-making. EMI, like many other film production companies before and since, sought to counter this by setting limits on the amount invested at any one time in film production. The mechanism for doing this was to set up a 'rolling fund' – a fund of money out of which new films were financed and into which film revenues were paid. The idea was that, by setting a limit on the size of the rolling fund, the exposure of the company would be limited. The problem is that the size of the rolling fund tends to creep up over time – when films are delayed in production, overrun their budgets or are less prolific revenue earners than expected, the fund tends to expand to accommodate the situation. But when the opposite happens, there is generally no corresponding reduction – another instance of the unfortunate asymmetry noted above. Sir John Read, the last chairman of EMI before it was acquired, spent much of his time fighting a losing battle to limit the company's investment in film production.

After the acquisition of EMI by Thorn, film production gained a central place in the home entertainment strategy. In fact, it was generally regarded as being of greater importance than EMI's music business. Although investment in film production was stepped up, the rate of commercial success remained unchanged. Films of artistic merit and some commercial potential, such as *Passage to India*, were more than offset by expensively crafted disasters such as *Honky Tonk Freeway* and *Can't Stop The Music*. As a result, EMI Films had made losses in the 1981,1982 and 1983 financial years.

If profitability in film production had proved elusive, so had the idea of synergy between films and music. For a considerable period, the headquarters of both EMI Films and EMI Music had been in Los Angeles, but the chief executives of the two businesses were more likely to meet on their occasional visits to the group head office in London. Feature films with memorable music are in a minority and subsidising loss-making films is an expensive way to get access to the occasional soundtrack rights.

With its poor profit record and risky field of operation, EMI Films was not the sort of business to appeal to the new regime at THORN EMI. What tipped them into a decision to sell it as soon as possible was the discovery of commitments it had entered into which obliged THORN EMI to take on film financing liabilities of up to $175 million. The way these liabilities had been entered into was a contributory factor in the unseating of Peter Laister. Essentially, THORN EMI Screen Entertainment (TESE), the holding company for EMI Films, had an agreement with six film producers which gave it access to all the subjects they developed for production as feature films. The making of the films would then be financed from a fund of $175 million set up by TESE. What particularly incensed Sir Graham Wilkins and Colin Southgate was that this commitment had been entered into after the end of March 1985, at a time when the full horrors of Inmos were known within the company, and without the approval or knowledge of the board. Although the money to set up the fund was to be provided by a syndicate of banks, THORN EMI, by providing guarantees to the banks, had accepted liability for the money. In its weakened financial state, an additional commitment of over £100 million was a serious matter.

By the early autumn of 1985 the news that THORN EMI was considering selling TESE was beginning to leak out. TESE had a patchy financial record, as the following figures show:

£ million	1982/83	1983/84	1984/85
Sales	91	97	127
Pre-tax profit/(loss)	(14.1)	3.4	7.8

As the largest British film business with a valuable film archive, however, it was hoped that the sale would arouse considerable interest, particularly in an industry driven more by egotism than commercial acumen. These hopes were amply fulfilled, as the company was soon inundated with enquiries from potential buyers.

The negotiations that followed soon took on the character of a passable film plot. One of the first negotiators to arrive on THORN EMI's doorstep was Gerald Ronson, chairman of Heron International and, at the time, unblemished by his subsequent entanglement in the Guinness affair. On a Monday morning, he swept into THORN EMI's head office, accompanied by a bevy of lawyers and advisers. There had been considerable speculation in the Sunday papers about the possible sale of TESE which had whetted appetites. Gerald Ronson announced that he was there to do a quick deal and was prepared to write a cheque at the meeting – indeed, at one point he reached into his jacket and pulled out a cheque book which was waved about. A quick deal was exactly what THORN EMI wanted. The new regime was anxious to complete a significant and highly visible disposal by the end of the first year under their management to show that the process of reconstruction was under way. Heron was an ideal buyer: as it had no existing film interests, the deal would not attract the attention of the Monopolies and Mergers Commission and, as it was a privately owned company, Gerald Ronson could make the decisions himself.

Alas, Ronson's enthusiasm was soon curbed by his lawyers and accountants. TESE was an immensely complex business and prodigious amounts of paperwork had to be studied first. Each film in which TESE had been involved had unique arrangements for the ownership of various rights: TESE may, for example, have owned the screen rights to a particular film in Japan but not the music rights, whereas in Indonesia it may have owned both screen and music rights but have sold the video rights to someone else. As Ronson's lawyers got to work on the mountains of paper, the chances of a quick deal with him began to recede.

In the meantime, another favoured contender for the business had emerged. TESE's chief executive, Gary Dartnall, had indicated that he and his colleagues wanted to buy it themselves. With their knowledge of the business, much of the complex investigation could be avoided. However, the omens for raising the odd £100 million in the City of London to finance the deal were not propitious. The City, where the appetite for investing in film-making had never been great, had been disillusioned by the problems of the film production company, Goldcrest. In the early 1980s, Goldcrest seemed to signal a renaissance in British film-making with a string of successes such as *Chariots of Fire, Gandhi* and *The Killing Fields*. By 1985, however, it had found that it was no less prone than the rest of the industry to the unfortunate asymmetry between profits from successes and losses from disasters which was such an enduring feature of the industry. In its case, involvement in two expensive disasters – *Revolution* and *Absolute Beginners* – had almost put it out of business.

In addition to the price of over £100 million which THORN EMI was demanding for the business, Gary Dartnall also had to find a further £100 million or more to finance the future film-making commitments that TESE had so recently and so controversially entered into. It was a major task but, undaunted, he and his merchant banking advisers, County Bank, set about trying to raise the money. The US seemed to be a more promising source of highly leveraged finance, and the US firm Bear Stearns, who understood the market for junk bonds intimately, were hired to help. Dartnall and his team worked feverishly through November to try and raise the necessary funds. The sale soon developed into a race between Dartnall's team and Ronson who, by now, had teamed up with the US Cannon Group, which owned the Classic cinema chain in Britain. Rank, the owner of the other major British cinema chain, was also in the running, but since a sale to it was certain to draw the attention of the Monopolies and Mergers Commission, it was a good deal less attractive.

By November, THORN EMI wanted to draw the bidding war to a conclusion. Anxious not to get egg on its face in such a high-profile negotiation, it insisted that the successful bidder would have to put a non-returnable cheque for £10 million on the table in order to carry on negotiations. This was clearly not something the management team could do until their financing was secured and their chances now appeared to be fading. It seemed likely that the business would go either to the Ronson/Cannon consortium or to Rank. The prospect was not one which the British film industry welcomed. As the *Sunday Times'* correspondent put it: 'The British film industry felt last week that it was being forced to choose between the devil and the deep blue sea.' The opposition to Rank stemmed from the control over British cinema outlets which the deal would give it – its own Odeon chain was the second biggest after TESE's ABC chain – but Rank was still preferable to the alternative. It was the Cannon part of the Ronson/Cannon consortium which terrified the film industry. As the same *Sunday Times* article put it:

> Cannon is the film industry's least popular success story, a giant international company, involved in every stage of the film business from production to distribution and exhibition, it has come from nowhere in the past decade by building on the premise that nobody ever got poor by underestimating public taste.

The ogres behind Cannon were two Israeli-born cousins – Menahem Golan and Yoram Globus. Menaham, who had taken his last name from the eponymous Heights which Israel had captured from Syria in the Six Day War, had trained as a theatre director and provided the artistic element of the duo, while his cousin handled the finances. They had established themselves in the film business in a remarkably short time, having started in 1979 with a loan for $350,000 to buy the defunct Cannon Group. Through inspired deal-making and some adventurous accounting, by 1984 Cannon was able to report net profits of over $12 million.

By the first week of December, Dartnall and his team were close to exhaustion after two months of travelling around the world, trying to raise money. Facing a deadline from THORN EMI to put up or shut up, he conceded defeat, going to bed and sleeping right through the following day. However, in the best tradition of movie cliff-hangers, help was on its way. Alan Bond, the Australian financier, had read about Dartnall's predicament on his flight to London on other business and phoned him up when he arrived. Bond spent the weekend in discussions with Dartnall and his team, visiting the studios at Elstree and some of TESE's cinemas. On the following Monday morning, he called Southgate to say that he was prepared to pay the deposit of £10 million and back the management's bid.

That Monday was to be a memorable one for Southgate. Both Rank and the Ronson/Cannon consortium had assumed that the management buy-out idea was finished, since Dartnall had announced as much to the press the previous week. When they heard that not only was Dartnall back in the running but that he was likely to win, a ferocious bidding war was waged through the day. While Bond, Dartnall and his advisers plotted their moves on the fifth floor of THORN EMI's head office, which was occupied by TESE, late into the evening, Southgate, on the twelfth floor, was in heated telephone conversations with them and with the two other bidders. With nothing to choose on price, which had risen to £110 million during the course of the day, he decided to accept the management's offer. The deciding factor was that both the alternatives ran a high risk of a Monopolies Commission investigation, which would have set them back by many months and might even have stopped the deal. Late that night, he collected Bond's cheque for £10 million.

There was general relief in the British film industry at the outcome, not least from Dartnall and his team. The *Financial Times*, reporting on a press conference called by Dartnall, captures his elation at the turn of events:

> Mr Gary Dartnall, chairman and chief executive of THORN EMI Screen Entertainment, held up a copy of the *Hollywood Reporter* with a front page headline explaining how his attempts to stage a management buy out had failed. Fifteen minutes earlier he had signed an unconditional agreement to buy the division from THORN EMI for £110 million sterling.
>
> It's just like 'Dewey wins Presidency' said Mr Dartnall, referring to the blackest hour in the history of the *Chicago Tribune* which on its front page announced that Thomas Dewey had won the 1948 US presidential election when in fact President Truman was the victor.

Although the Bond/Dartnall team had signed an unconditional agreement with THORN EMI and Bond had agreed to put £15 to 20 million of his own money into the deal, the buyers still had to raise the rest of the funds they needed. The agreement gave them until the end of February 1986 to do so, and Dartnall and his bankers returned once more to the task. Most of January and February was spent in talking to potential investors in the US. While the money to buy the business was raised by the deadline, they were unable to arrange bank facilities to finance future productions. Faced with the prospect of pocketing the Bond deposit and restarting the sale process, THORN EMI decided to extend the deadline by a month. When that date arrived without bank finance arranged, Bond decided he would buy the business himself rather than lose his deposit. The price actually paid to THORN EMI was £128 million, reflecting an increase in net assets over the previously agreed figure. Dartnall's elation at the apparent rescue of his management buy-out by Bond in December and his disparagement of the *Hollywood Reporter* had been premature. Rather than being a company controlled by its management, TESE, or Screen Entertainment as it was renamed, simply became part of the Bond empire.

However, in the best traditions of a horror movie, the biggest shock was kept to the end. It emerged subsequently that soon after he had entered the picture, Bond had been approached by the cousins Golan and Globus, suggesting that they take a 50 per cent interest in TESE. Since, at the time, the purchase was a management buy-out, it was not possible to accommodate them. When Bond found he had to buy the whole business himself, bringing in a partner became more attractive. However, he seems to have been advised that the Cannon cousins would be difficult partners to live with and again turned them down. They then offered to buy the whole of the business from him, to which he consented. What was particularly strange was that he had, ostensibly, sold the business for £178 million, having reluctantly bought it a few days earlier for £128 million – a gain of £50 million in a week.

For THORN EMI, the media publicity given to this second deal was painfully embarrassing, suggesting as it did that the company had left money on the table. In fact, a detailed analysis of what Bond sold the business for suggests that the real difference between what Bond paid THORN EMI and what he received, or should have received – the distinction is important – from Cannon was £18 million. The rest of the difference is explained by bank guarantees taken over by Cannon, which were not included in the figure for the previous deal. Nevertheless, one aspect of the whole affair which has never been satisfactorily explained is why Cannon, who had been negotiating with THORN EMI earlier, should have paid Bond a price significantly higher than they were prepared to pay THORN EMI. A possible explanation, which must remain speculative, is that Cannon simply made a mistake. An analysis of the documents that Cannon filed with the US Securities and Exchange Commission shows that Bond's deal with Cannon involved the sale of a company called Screen

Entertainment, Inc. to Cannon for £146 million, £18 million more than he had paid THORN EMI. Cannon also took responsibility for a film finance loan of £50 million from the Standard Chartered Bank to Screen Entertainment, Inc. Eighteen million pounds of the cash made available from this loan had been put into a company called Screen Entertainment (Jersey), which was retained by Bond as part of the deal. Cannon therefore took over the liability for the whole of the loan but left behind some of the associated cash. Is it possible that, in the rush of the deal, Cannon left the £18 million with Bond inadvertently?

As it happened, THORN EMI's embarrassment over the price was short-lived. It had received £128 million from Bond in cash, but Cannon had paid Bond only a small proportion of his price in cash, the rest being due for payment at the end of 1986. However, by the summer of 1986, Cannon was in severe financial difficulty, leading eventually to bankruptcy, and it is uncertain as to how much of his cash Bond actually received. Cannon was broken up and sold off by its creditors and, of course, Bond had his own, well-publicised, financial embarrassments not long after. For Dartnall, his management team and employees, the outcome could not have been worse. Many of them lost their jobs and were dealt with fairly brutally by the new owners, the Cannon cousins even claiming that the Mossad had brought to their attention evidence of fraud within the business.

For all its hair-raising moments, the sale of TESE was a significant landmark on the road to recovery for the new regime at THORN EMI. It also marked the end of the attempt to build a multifaceted entertainment business. It was followed by the disposal of a number of other peripheral interests which, together with the sale of TESE, raised £200 million of cash in the year to March 1986. There had been failures and disappointments, most notably the blocking by the Independent Broadcasting Authority (IBA) of Carlton Communications' bid for Thames Television, which held the weekday commercial television franchise for London and in which THORN EMI had a 46 per cent holding. Instead, Thames Television was floated on the stock market and THORN EMI was able to sell some of its shareholding by that route.

By March 1986, THORN EMI's borrowings had been reduced to under £200 million, from over £350 million a year earlier. The share price had increased to over 500 pence from the low point of just over 300 pence a year earlier. Although much remained to be done, Sir Graham and Colin Southgate could take some satisfaction from their first year in control.

13

The Last British Television
Manufacturer

The decision to sell TESE had been a comparatively easy one
to make. Although it had been a central part of the home
entertainment strategy of the previous regime, it had always
been regarded as something of an oddball, even within THORN
EMI's ill-assorted collection of businesses. It seemed to belong in
a world altogether too glamorous to inspire much camaraderie in
other parts of the company. Apart from the singular Lord Delfont,
none of the other directors had ever felt comfortable with its culture
and style. Its history within EMI had been comparatively short and,
while there was some sympathy for the plight of its management
under the Cannon cousins, its demise was little mourned. TESE
was not a sacred cow.

Tackling the next major issue facing the new regime was an
altogether more tortuous and painful process. Ferguson, THORN
EMI's television manufacturing company, had been a contributor
to the dreadful results that Sir Graham Wilkins had announced
on assuming the chairmanship in 1985. It had also been one of Sir
Jules Thorn's greatest success stories. He had taken it from being a
tiny, nearly bankrupt radio set manufacturer to being the dominant
force in British consumer electronics in the 1960s and 1970s. It
could trace its origins back to the start of television broadcasting
in Britain and it had grown and prospered through the violent
swings in the British consumer's appetite for durable goods,
mopping up its competitors in the downswings to emerge even
stronger in the next upturn. With the acquisition of Radio Rentals
in 1968, it had as secure an outlet for its products as any consumer
electronics manufacturer in the world. By the early 1980s, as all the
other British television manufacturers threw in the towel and

closed down, or sold out to the Japanese, Ferguson continued to
hold a large share of the UK television market. However, in 1984
the UK market for televisions and video recorders took a steep
downturn, just as the Japanese had increased their production.
Unsold television sets piled up in the factories and profit margins
disappeared as prices were cut.

After Peter Laister's departure, the new team at THORN EMI
reviewed the business and decided that it needed considerable
restructuring and an infusion of new management. Jim Maxmin,
who also headed up the company's rental and retail activities,
was given responsibility for it and a restructuring plan, involving
considerable rearrangement of its manufacturing facilities and
fresh investment in production equipment, was prepared. In their
first report to shareholders, Sir Graham and Colin Southgate
reported that they were setting aside £28 million to pay for the
restructuring of Ferguson. Yet, within two years of that decision,
the business had been sold to the French electronics company
Thomson Grand Public.

It is pertinent to ask whether THORN EMI could not have saved
a substantial amount of its shareholders' money by deciding to sell
Ferguson two years earlier. After all, the likely fate of the British
consumer electronics industry, once it was exposed to unfettered
foreign competition, had been foretold by Sir Jules Thorn and Sir
Richard Cave a decade earlier. Richard 'Dickie' Norman, the last
chief executive of Ferguson under THORN EMI ownership, has
a unique perspective on the British television industry. He started
working in it as a young engineer in the 1940s, and retired when
the business was sold by THORN EMI – a career that spans the
entire history of British-owned television manufacturing. In his
opinion, by the mid 1980s there was nothing that could have
preserved Ferguson as an independent television manufacturer.
Why, then, did the management of THORN EMI persist in
throwing precious cash at a hopeless cause?

Part of the reason could be put down to hubris – to the conceit
of a new management team. Much that had happened in the past
could be blamed on bad management. With a new management
team and a fresh approach, it should be possible to work wonders.
That, however, was only part of the story. Ferguson was the last
surviving British consumer electronics manufacturer and part of

THORN EMI's heritage. It employed 6,000 people in the UK. To close it or sell it off peremptorily to a foreign company, and only foreign companies were likely to buy into the consumer electronics industry, seemed a sacrilege. It was almost obligatory to try to make it work, however hopeless the odds.

The most frequently heard criticism of Sir Colin Southgate and his management team's achievements over the last decade is their withdrawal from manufacturing. Sir William Barlow, who was a non-executive director of THORN EMI and is an admirer of Sir Colin's says: 'He has done an excellent job for the shareholders but he hasn't done the job he was put in to do.' It is a view shared by others. Indeed, for anyone who was familiar with the company's manufacturing interests a decade ago – and the old Thorn was primarily a manufacturing company – it is difficult to contemplate the extent of change without feeling that something of value has been lost. The passing of control of much of THORN EMI's – and, indeed, of Britain's – manufacturing capacity into foreign ownership, the loss of jobs, the shrinking of the country's technological potential, arouse a sense of failure and regret. The supermarkets and shopping malls that now stand on the sites of THORN EMI's factories in Enfield seem to serve a much less noble purpose. However, the opposite point of view – that the new management team should have pulled out of many of its manufacturing businesses much sooner – also has some validity. In the case of Ferguson, the attempt to salvage the business against what, admittedly with the benefit of hindsight, can be seen as hopeless odds was motivated by factors other than the naked interests of the company's shareholders.

Although the British television manufacturing industry had been aware since the mid-1960s of the potential threat from Far Eastern competitors, it seems to have done little, in the time it had, to prepare itself to face it. As more and more functions were built into the electronic components that went into a television, the business of assembling sets became simpler and more capable of automation. Yet British manufacturers were increasingly shying away from the risky and capital-intensive business of making components – as demonstrated by Thorn's decision to withdraw from colour picture tube production in 1975 – or of encouraging a domestic component industry. This left them even more exposed to the nexus of Far Eastern set and component manufacturers, who were often the only source of certain components.

The level of automation in manufacturing equipment also remained woefully inadequate in comparison with Far Eastern competitors. An analysis by Michael Porter, a professor at the Harvard Business School, of differences in manufacturing costs between various countries in 1977 showed that the average man-hours needed to assemble a television set in the UK were over three times higher than in Japan. The cost of components, which accounted for 80 per cent of total manufacturing costs, was 25 per cent higher in the UK than in Japan. These disadvantages were not unique to British manufacturers. The study found that US and West German manufacturers were also significantly disadvantaged compared to Far Eastern ones, although not by as much as the British. The Japanese and, increasingly, South Korean manufacturers were simply building more reliable sets more cheaply and the gaps were growing.

Much of this is well known and should come as no surprise. What does seem curious, though, is the lack of any meaningful response by THORN EMI in the late 1970s and early 1980s. That the outlook for the company as an independent television manufacturer was bleak was certainly recognised. But that threat seems to have paralysed decision-making. Television manufacturing was seen as an integral part of the company's consumer electronics activity which, even after the acquisition of EMI, accounted for over half the company's profits. The real choices facing the company were too stark to be confronted. Much of what happened over this period now appears to be simply displacement activity. The idea of combining Thorn's hardware and EMI's software, the core of the home entertainment strategy articulated after the acquisition of EMI, is seen in this light as a subconscious effort to avoid facing the real problem. By committing to this idea, any possibility of tackling the real problem was removed. Making consumer electronics hardware became a central piece of the home entertainment strategy and the crucial question – could THORN EMI continue efficiently to manufacture hardware for the foreseeable future – was buried.

Elements of displacement activity also appear to have played a part in the decision to acquire Inmos. In an interview that he gave to the magazine *International Management* after the acquisition of Inmos, Peter Laister explained that the design of TV sets in the future was going to be fashioned around the microchip. 'We couldn't stand by and see our destiny being taken from us by makers of semiconductor items,' he said. To the extent that he was pointing to the increasing importance of electronic components in television set manufacture, Laister had a point. But Inmos had no relevance at all to the problems that Ferguson faced in 1985.

What enabled the new regime, eventually, to see the true extent of Ferguson's problems was their rejection of the idea of interrelationships between it and other parts of the company. Once it was no longer regarded as an essential supplier of television sets and video recorders to the rental business, nor as having anything to do with music and other entertainment software, the question of whether it could survive as an independent consumer electronics manufacturer was the only relevant one. By early 1987, it was clear that it could not. Despite the heavy expenditure on restructuring to reduce its cost base, in the twelve months to March 1987 it lost £12 million before interest charges, on sales of £290 million. It was turning into a disaster on the scale of Inmos. By good fortune, just then, one of the very few companies with the resources to take it over had developed an appetite for expanding into the UK.

The French response, in the 1980s, to the Far Eastern threat to their consumer electronics industry was very different to the British one. It was seen as a crucial industry for the future, one in which survival was a matter of national prestige. Unlike Britain, where the government welcomed Japanese television and video manufacturers with open arms, France spared no effort in making life difficult for them. The approach was exemplified by the decision to require imported Japanese video recorders to be sent to Poitiers, in the middle of France, for customs inspection in a branch of the French customs that was manned by one inspector. Symbolically, Poitiers happened to be the place where Charles Martel defeated the invading Moors in the year 732.

The chosen vehicle for the French national effort in consumer electronics was Thomson Grand Public, owned and heavily backed by the French Government. Thomson's position in the television market in France in the late 1970s was actually weaker than Thorn's in Britain, as it was the second-largest player in the market behind

Philips. But the French market had a much lower level of import penetration because France used a colour television system, called SECAM, almost unique to itself. Thomson also had significant market shares in Germany and Spain, although it had no presence in the UK. In spite of their protectionist instincts, the French understood that survival in the industry meant operating on a world scale. The prospect of acquiring THORN EMI's market share in the UK – amongst the largest markets in Europe – was therefore of considerable interest to them.

The deal that Southgate negotiated with Thomson was a remarkable one. Ferguson was making losses of over £2 million a month in the spring of 1987, just before it was sold to Thomson for £90 million, £10 million more than the net assets of the company. The deal was probably the most critical one in the remaking of THORN EMI and one of Southgate's greatest personal coups. Philips, the only other significant European player, was already well established in the UK and the Japanese had an aversion to acquiring, preferring instead to start from scratch on a greenfield site. The alternative for THORN EMI would have been to close the business down, at a likely cost of perhaps £100 million or more, a burden that would have severely limited its freedom of action and may well have proved fatal. The difference between the two alternatives, of close to £200 million in cash terms, would have been beyond the company's ability to finance at that stage in its recovery. To set it in context, the deal with Thomson effectively offset the financial damage suffered as a result of acquiring Inmos. THORN EMI's shareholders, having had to bear the expense of rescuing the British taxpayer from the liabilities of Inmos, now had the consolation of being rescued from the liabilities of Ferguson at the expense of the French taxpayer.

Television manufacturing is now as global an industry as it is possible to imagine. Three giant companies – Sony, Matsushita and Philips – each make over four million sets a year in factories around the world, and it is unlikely that any of them makes any money out of this endeavour. Even taking into account the profits from their other activities, their recent financial performance has been dismal. Thomson, number four in the league, also operates internationally, with factories in France, Germany, Spain, the US and the Far East. In 1994, its total sales were 38 billion French francs (roughly £5 billion) and it made a loss of nearly 600 million French francs (roughly £80 million), having made even larger losses in each of the previous three years. Were it not for the French taxpayers' support, it is unlikely that it would be viable.

The Ferguson factory in Enfield was closed soon after Thomson bought the business and the factory in Gosport, on the south coast, was closed in 1991. From being an independent television manufacturer employing 6,000 people ten years ago, Ferguson is now simply a brand name. Yet the UK now manufactures more television sets – around four million a year – than it has ever done, and the number of manufacturers in the UK is greater than it has been for the last twenty years. All of them, however, are Far Eastern. They contribute a substantial positive trade balance to the UK and their businesses here are not, by any means, all low-skill 'screwdriver operations'. Sony and Sharp do important research and development work in Wales and Oxford while Hitachi develops software in Ireland. Employment in the industry is, of course, significantly lower than it was a decade ago, but that would have been the case irrespective of the nationality of the manufacturers.

France, having taken a very different approach to Britain over the last decade, is most unlikely to have generated more jobs in the industry. It does, however, have a 'national champion' in consumer electronics, for what that is worth. Whereas policy for Britain's consumer electronic industry is decided in Tokyo, Osaka, Seoul or Taipei, policy for the French consumer electronics industry is made in Paris. In an age of global businesses, does that matter? It is an issue for politicians rather than businessmen to ponder.

14

Consolidation

The summer of 1988 marked the third year of the new regime at THORN EMI. Colin Southgate had moved up from managing director to chief executive in July 1987, while Sir Graham Wilkins stayed on as chairman. In his statement in the 1988 annual report, Colin Southgate commented:

> THORN EMI is a radically changed business. Last year marked a fundamental shift away from the past. Three years of tough restructuring have made our company lean, strong and international in outlook. We have increased profits – and more importantly profitability – and will continue to do so. THORN EMI is intent on further growth.

In three years, THORN EMI had shed most of its problem businesses together with a hoard of small, peripheral enterprises acquired over the previous three decades. In total, between April 1985 and March 1988, more than fifty separate businesses were sold, raising over £500 million in badly needed cash. Alongside the divestment of businesses, the culture of the company had been substantially changed, to the point where it would have been unrecognisable to someone from Sir Jules Thorn's era. Over 70 per cent of the top managers in the company had been replaced. Most of the senior management who had been with Thorn prior to the acquisition of EMI had left. Harold Mourgue, the last Thorn man on the THORN EMI board, retired in September 1987.

The dated, lumbering style of Sir Jules Thorn's head office, which had persisted under the regimes of both Sir Richard Cave and Peter Laister, was swept away. The 1950s concrete tower on Upper St Martin's Lane, which had been an architectural landmark in its time, was sold and a smaller, more modern head office was set up in Hanover Square. Bob Nellist, who had been finance director since 1985, had thrown out the outdated financial reporting systems and replaced them with new ones. In 1985, the legal and fiscal organisation of the company had the appearance of a maze devised for a horror film: over 1,000 separate entities were linked to each other in ways that could only be discerned from a large-scale map complete with grid references. This structure was simplified and altered, reaping considerable tax advantages in the process. From being a laggard in its management style, organisation and systems three years earlier, THORN EMI was now ahead of most large British companies.

For Colin Southgate, it had been a considerable achievement. He was a relative newcomer to the company, having joined it in 1982 as chief executive of the information technology division – a relatively insignificant element in THORN EMI's portfolio. When he was appointed managing director of the group, he had no experience of management at the centre of a large public company. By both background and instinct, he was a self-made entrepreneur rather than a large-company man. His strengths were a boundless self-confidence, an immense capacity to absorb detail, and an almost insolent disregard for long-established routine and practice. His iconoclastic approach, however, was precisely what the company needed at the time. In a sense, he was the boy in the crowd who was prepared to shout: 'But the Emperor has no clothes!'

By 1988, the board of THORN EMI could take some comfort from the knowledge that gross financial disaster had been averted. The company's gearing – the ratio of its borrowings to its shareholders' equity – had been reduced from 57 per cent in March 1985 to 9 per cent in March 1988. Earnings per share, after charging extraordinary items, had nearly trebled, from 16 pence a share in 1985 to 47 pence a share in 1988. However, what had been achieved was, arguably, the simpler part of the task. Although the restructuring that took place before 1988 required many tough decisions, the route the company had to follow, if it was to survive, was fairly clear from the outset. However, once it had overcome the immediate dangers and reached a level of stability, the intellectual problem of where it went next began to loom larger.

Despite the enormous number of divestments, THORN EMI was still a conglomerate, albeit a less diversified one than it had been. In his 1988 statement, Colin Southgate talked about 'our major businesses – Rental and Retail, Music, Lighting and our three main Technology activities, Software, Security and Electronics'. Of these, Rental and Retail was by far the biggest, contributing 60 per cent of the group's profits. The second-biggest was, surprisingly, Technology, which contributed 16 per cent of profits, ahead of Music, which contributed 12 per cent. Lighting and the Kenwood appliance business contributed 8 per cent. The task the new regime had set itself in 1985 was, in Sir Graham's words: 'to improve returns from businesses which are insufficiently profitable and to develop the Company's stronger businesses.' It was not to change the conglomerate nature of the company. In fact, the new regime had declared early on that THORN EMI should recognise that it was a conglomerate – a fact denied under previous regimes. Acknowledgment of that fact was, in itself, liberating. As one former director of the company put it: 'We could stop the futile pursuit of common values and, instead, celebrate our cultural diversity.'

However, the debate about the pros and cons of being a conglomerate was one that would increasingly occupy the board in the years ahead. By the late 1980s, conglomerates were becoming an unpopular form of industrial organisation with investors. There was and, of course, remains a growing preference for investing in single-industry, or very focused, companies. Investors want to do the job of allocating their portfolio themselves, believing they can do it more cheaply and no less adroitly than industrial managers. Management gurus advise companies to 'stick to your knitting'. There is, in all of this, something of a self-reinforcing circle: companies are urged to focus, focused companies become more popular, popularity leads to a higher share price, and so a trend is established. This is not to suggest that the preference for focused companies is simply a transient fad: there is much empirical evidence, not least the story of THORN EMI itself, suggesting that unrelated diversification can seriously damage shareholders' wealth.

There was some reflection of the growing unpopularity of conglomerates in THORN EMI's share price in 1988. Between 1983 and 1985, the share price, relative to the FT All Share Index, had fallen by 60 per cent. By 1988, despite the considerable improvement in its performance and its prospects since 1985, recovery in the share price had been modest – it still remained some 50 per cent below the 1983 level. Apart from the fact that the stock market did not seem to recognise the increased value of the company, to the detriment of its shareholders, it also meant that a predator would, in time, recognise that the sum of the parts was worth more than the whole and make a bid to break up the company. While these considerations did not lead, at the time, to a decision to become a single-industry company, they did form a backcloth to thinking in the future.

The businesses that remained in THORN EMI in 1988 were united only by the fact that – with one exception – none was a drain on the company, in the sense of making losses or absorbing large amounts of cash. The exception was the electrical retail chain Rumbelows, to which we shall return. Even Inmos, which remained part of THORN EMI until April 1989, made an operating profit of £10 million in its last year in the group. However, all faced operational or strategic problems of varying degrees of severity, and none could be regarded as secure. Apart from Music, all were heavily dependent on the UK economy – THORN EMI still derived 57 per cent of its profits from the UK. Rental faced a long-term decline in the traditional business of renting televisions and video recorders in the UK; Music had had a run of poor profitability since 1985; Technology consisted of a number of relatively small businesses with little in common; and Lighting faced all the problems of scale and competition that had raised a question mark over its long-term future in the mind of Sir Jules Thorn in the mid-1970s.

It was in 1988 that Colin Southgate and his team were able, for the first time, to consider the long-term shape of THORN EMI. A review of its businesses that year recommended that the company should set two criteria for the businesses it retained: they should have the potential of earning profits of at least £50 million a year, and they should be, or should be capable of becoming, global businesses. On these criteria, Rental and Music were naturally regarded as the core of THORN EMI, Rental simply because of its size, although it was still predominantly a UK business, and Music because it was among the leaders in its industry, albeit well behind in terms of its profitability. We will return to Rental and Music in later chapters.

The third-favourite business in 1988 was Lighting. This may seem surprising, both in view of the reservations about its viability that had existed for many years and of the withdrawal from large-scale manufacturing in other areas. However, Lighting consisted of two different, though related, businesses: the manufacture of light bulbs and tubes, a capital-intensive and very competitive business; and the manufacture of fixtures and fittings – the mountings into which the bulbs and tubes fit – which was a profitable business. The old Thorn management, with their roots in the manufacture of light bulbs, had refused to consider them as separable businesses, an attitude that certainly frustrated earlier attempts by Sir Richard Cave to disengage from making light bulbs. Colin Southgate recalls: 'I felt that Lighting could succeed if the fixtures side was built on.'

An important component of the motivation to stay in lighting was a wish to see the new THORN EMI succeed in at least one of its traditional manufacturing businesses. The charge that the new regime was engaged in a large-scale withdrawal from manufacturing could not easily be brushed off. Indeed, for critics of THORN EMI's withdrawal from manufacturing, the considerable investment in Lighting after 1985 contradicts the view that a risk-averse, anti-manufacturing attitude prevailed. Over £40 million was spent on restructuring the manufacturing and distribution systems of the business and on new capital equipment for its factories; £125 million was spent on acquiring complementary fittings companies in Continental Europe and Australasia, of which £87 million went on acquiring the French company Holophane, in a takeover fiercely contested by Emess, the British lighting manufacturer.

Perhaps the more accurate criticism is that THORN EMI took too rosy a view of the prospects of arresting the decline in the lamp manufacturing business. By the late 1980s, the major global lighting companies were manufacturing incandescent light bulbs at half of what it cost Thorn Lighting and, because of past under-investment, the difference was growing. It misjudged both the rate at which its competitiveness was being eroded and also the ability of the fittings business to support a loss-making lamp production activity. In the past, lighting had been a conservative industry where developments occurred at a sedate pace. Although Thorn Lighting's vulnerability had been apparent for some time, the view was that it had time to adjust. Hamish Bryce, who was appointed chief executive of the business in 1986, recalls: 'There were seven significant lamp manufacturing companies (excluding the Far Eastern ones). I believed they would reduce to three in twenty years; in fact, it happened in three.' His initial strategy was to concentrate on new, higher-technology light sources, where higher margins could be earned. However, a rate of change that had previously been associated only with the electronics industry was starting to afflict these areas: new types of spotlights – mirror lamps – saw their prices halve within two years, causing an £8 million swing in the profits of the business.

Hamish Bryce recalls: 'I phoned Colin in July '89 to say that the position in light sources could not be sustained and we had to find a partner. Colin regarded this as a very negative attitude, but I felt we were trying to push water uphill.' The idea of withdrawing from lighting proved to be an enormous psychological hurdle for THORN EMI's senior management, and the process of withdrawal was one of the most painful and tortuous of the company's many divestments. A considerable amount of cash and credibility had been sunk into the business since 1985. Initially, it was hoped that THORN EMI could retain an interest in it by forming a joint venture with a major foreign company. Informal discussions were held with US General Electric (GE) and with GTE-Sylvania. Both sets of discussions foundered on the issue of who was to control a joint venture.

By early 1990, with most of Lighting's markets going into recession, THORN EMI resolved that the business would have to be sold. A deal was struck with GTE-Sylvania which would have allowed THORN EMI to recover its investment in the business, including the premium paid in the recent acquisitions. An extensive due diligence exercise followed and, by the summer of 1990, both parties appeared to be ready to sign a binding agreement. This, however, was not to be. GTE, which was primarily a telephone company with a large lighting business, suddenly decided that it wished to get out of lighting itself and the deal was called off. By the time discussions with GTE were broken off, Thorn Lighting's demotivated management had spent over six months trying to secure its sale. Trade had suffered as news of the possible sale became widely known. Profits had declined sharply – in the twelve months to March 1991, the business made a loss of £1.9 million, having made a profit of nearly £33 million in the previous year. There was no alternative plan to hand. It seemed as if THORN EMI would have to grit its teeth and carry on as before.

There was only one other possible buyer of the business – the US GE – since both of the other large European lighting companies, Philips and Osram, would have had problems with the monopolies authorities if they had considered buying it. GE, a relative newcomer to the European market, had recently bought the Tungsram lamp manufacturing business in Hungary and was seeking to consolidate its position in Europe. However, it had no interest in buying the fittings and fixtures side of THORN EMI's business, as it had chosen to concentrate on making lamps, so a sale to it would involve a lengthy disentanglement of the two sides of the business. Moreover, after the experience with GTE, THORN EMI had no stomach for another lengthy due diligence and negotiation which may have, once again, proved fruitless. The deal struck with GE was a most unusual one, as GE had been given no access to the business. It was agreed, largely in GE's European head office in Hammersmith, in an almost continuous negotiating session over six days and nights. The deal, which resulted in a loss of £40 million for THORN EMI, was not one to occasion much celebration, but it was considerably better than the alternative of closing the lamp manufacturing business down. It left THORN EMI with a profitable fittings and fixtures business which was eventually sold to a financial investor, with significant management participation, in 1994.

Arguably, Colin Southgate's initial instinct to try to develop the lighting business was wrong, and the shareholders would have been better served if the business had been sold much earlier. In another area, defence electronics, his instinct to sell the business had been right but opposition within the board delayed a decision to do so. THORN EMI Electronics (TEE) had been a successful business throughout the early and mid-1980s, benefiting from increased defence expenditure in the early years of the Thatcher government following the Falklands War and from booming markets for military hardware in the Middle East. It had, however, been little developed beyond its original base, and Southgate had picked it out for divestment in his 1988 review. However, TEE was also something of a 'heritage' business: it had been part of EMI since before the Second World War; it had been a major reason for Thorn's decision to acquire EMI; it had able management and a good record of profitability, having contributed over £80 million of cash to its parent in the previous three years. The matter was much debated and it was only after Southgate became chairman, in February 1989, on Sir Graham Wilkins's retirement, that he got his way. The delay was to prove critical.

By the time the decision to sell TEE was taken, peace was breaking out around the world. By the spring of 1989, the outlook for defence expenditure seemed far from rosy and the industry's high-tech, star image was a fast-fading memory. TEE made profits of £27 million in the twelve months to March 1990, and THORN EMI had hoped to get over £250 million for the business. However, following the dismantling of the Berlin Wall in September 1989, sellers of defence companies vastly outnumbered buyers. Selling the business in this environment was made more difficult by the scandal that erupted around Ferranti, the British defence electronics company, following its disastrous acquisition of International Signal and Control. It is possible that, had THORN EMI been prepared to accept a lower price, the business might have attracted a buyer at the time. In the event, some aerospace and defence interests in California were sold in 1990, but TEE remained part of the group. What would have happened had THORN EMI managed to sell TEE a year earlier is a matter of speculation. If the business could have been sold for close to £250 million, its parent would have had considerably more freedom to develop its other interests. However, this might have been a double-edged sword. TEE's activities in the arcane world of defence equipment were regarded as something of a poison pill by potential bidders for THORN EMI. Had these been sold at a time when THORN EMI's share price was still relatively weak, a bid for the company might well have been triggered.

TEE was not the only business THORN EMI tried but failed to sell in 1989. The other was its electrical retail chain, Rumbelows. Rumbelows traced its origins to the Tucana operation which, it will be remembered, had been put together by Sir Jules Thorn by buying up financially distressed retailers. This inauspicious conception was to haunt the business for the rest of its life. With an inheritance of small, poorly sited stores and a less than sparkling brand image, Rumbelows was the weakest of the national electrical retail chains. It had never been particularly profitable. While THORN EMI was a manufacturer of the sort of products sold by Rumbelows, it had been regarded as a window on the market. However, little investment was made in it and the revolution in electrical retailing in the 1980s seemed to have largely passed it by.

In the mid-1980s, the television and video rental business of Rumbelows – the most profitable part of the company – was transferred to the rental division, further depressing its profitability. Attempts to catch up with the rest of the retail trade – by, for example, opening modern, out-of-town superstores under the Atlantis brand – and to increase its coverage by acquiring the Valance retail chain, came too late to make much difference in an increasingly competitive market. By 1989, THORN EMI had decided to get out of electrical retailing, but finding a way out proved more difficult than had been supposed. Discussions with Kingfisher, which owned the Comet electrical chain, came to nothing, largely because the value THORN EMI had set on the business was considerably greater than the price Kingfisher was prepared to pay. This over-valuation proved to be an expensive mistake: with the downturn in electrical retailing and the collapse in high-street property rents in the early 1990s, THORN EMI would have done well to have got out on Kingfisher's terms in 1989.

In the following year, the electrical retailing market in the UK declined by nearly 8 per cent. With little hope of finding a buyer, THORN EMI changed tack and decided to invest in the business, considerably expanding the number of out-of-town superstores and refreshing the product range. The 1991 annual report gave Rumbelows a prominence that had been absent for some years. This strategy was, however, soon abandoned. In 1992, the company announced that it was setting aside £42.5 million to cover the cost of withdrawal from general electrical retailing. This amount was charged as an extraordinary item in the accounts for the twelve months to March 1992.

If there is a general lesson to be drawn from the Rumbelows experience – and, indeed, from THORN EMI's other withdrawals from businesses – it is that allowing tactical considerations to overrule the strategic case for withdrawal is almost invariably a mistake. Where the company was distracted by considerations of the cost of withdrawal, or the siren song of reinvesting to get a better price in the future, the end result was usually (although not always) worse. The legacy of failing to sell Rumbelows and TEE in 1989 was to haunt THORN EMI for the next five years.

One long-running problem was, however, finally solved in 1989, when Inmos was sold. Although it was no longer making trading losses, the 'problems in the pipeline', problems that had been inherited when Inmos was acquired, were not finally resolved until 1988. By then, it was a purely British business, making SRAMs and Transputers at its facility in Newport, South Wales. A plan to bring in Philips, Siemens and the Franco–Italian firm SGS-Thomson as shareholders failed when Philips and Siemens changed their minds. Eventually, Inmos was sold to SGS-Thomson in a deal that also involved THORN EMI in subscribing $10 million in cash in return for a 10 per cent stake in SGS-Thomson. This arrangement caused the *Financial Times* to comment, somewhat acidly, that THORN EMI had had to pay someone to take the business off its hands.

What the *Financial Times* was not to know was that Inmos had a hitherto unrecognised asset of considerable value. Shortly before the sale to SGS-Thomson, THORN EMI had been approached by two Texans, George Mahr and Dave Leonard, who had formed a patent licensing firm, Mahr Leonard. George Mahr had previously headed the licensing department of SGS-Thomson's US subsidiary, and Dave Leonard was a patent lawyer who had begun his career as a semiconductor engineer. In Mahr Leonard's view, technology covered by certain Inmos patents was being used by most of the major chip manufacturers, a view they verified by 'reverse engineering' a variety of chips. They believed that THORN EMI could get substantial royalties for the Inmos patents. As a result, THORN EMI retained the patents and simply licensed SGS-Thompson to use them. Mahr Leonard were hired to negotiate commercial licences and the result was a stream of royalties, in many instances from the settlement of law suits initiated when negotiations broke down. In the years following the sale of Inmos, these royalties contributed around £70 million to THORN EMI's net profits. There was further good news in 1995 when there was a public offering of the shares of SGS-Thomson, which by then had turned into one of the very few successful European semiconductor companies. THORN EMI's shareholding was sold for £96 million. Over the years, Inmos had cost THORN EMI over £250 million: what it received from patent litigation and from the sale of its shares in SGS-Thomson was a significant, if incomplete, recompense.

15

Making Music

One business that Colin Southgate did not consider putting on his steadily growing list of disposals was EMI Music. That might, with the benefit of hindsight, seem a 'no brainer', but in the mid-1980s, the decision owed more to gut feel and a belief in the potential of the business than to its recent performance. EMI Music had been in the doldrums since the acquisition of EMI by Thorn, as is illustrated by its financial record in the five years to March 1986:

£ million	1981/82	1982/83	1983/84	1984/85	1985/86
Sales	487	501	488	582	564
Profit (a)	36.7	21.0	16.3	10.2	2.1
RoS	7.5%	4.2%	3.3%	1.8%	0.4%

(a) Before interest and tax

For almost a decade, from the late 1970s to the mid-1980s, the music division had been something of a Cinderella in the EMI and, later, THORN EMI households. In the last years of EMI as an independent company, the need for cash to sustain the scanner and to develop Lord Delfont's growing entertainment and leisure empire had meant that there was little left over to invest in Music. Its problems had been compounded by the downturn in the music markets of the world in the late 1970s and early 1980s. In 1979, as we have seen, EMI had actually negotiated to sell a 50 per cent stake in EMI Music to Paramount for what now appears a laughable sum of £75 million.

Arguably, of all THORN EMI's businesses, Music was both potentially the strongest, but also the most affected by the lack of focus in the 1970s and early 1980s. The successful management of an international music company requires a unique blend of skills. On the one hand, it requires the inspiration and sensitivity to harness the often fleeting talents of some of the most capricious and egotistical individuals on earth. On the other, it requires the discipline to run a manufacturing and distribution machine that must produce and deliver a product, with a shelf life shorter than many grocery items, anywhere on a continent within twenty-four hours, all at a minimum cost. And all of this takes place in an industry more than usually sensitive to the consumer's spending power; influenced as it is by unpredictable artistic trends; and faced with regular technological upheavals that completely transform the economics of the industry.

It is these three factors – spending power, artistic trends and technology – which have largely driven the fortunes of the industry since the war. The first post-war boom in the industry, in the second half of the 1950s, was the result of the felicitous conjunction of the birth of rock and roll and the spread of microgroove record players and records – the vinyl 33s and 45s that replaced the old 78s. In the five years up to 1958, EMI's record sales more than trebled and then levelled out until the mid-1960s. The next boom, which lasted from the mid-1960s till the early 1970s, was driven both by the music of The Beatles and New Rock and by the introduction of the cassette. EMI was particularly rich in the dominant genre, which had strong British roots, and prospered greatly. In the ten years to 1971, the British record market grew by a factor of three and a half. The roster of artists signed up by EMI's British labels included, apart from The Beatles themselves, a large proportion of Britain's best popular music talent. Bands from this period, such as The Beatles, Queen and Pink Floyd, and individual artists such as John Lennon and Paul McCartney, have continued to generate considerable income for EMI into the 1990s, with The Beatles' *Anthology 2* going to a high position in the US album charts in 1996.

The growth of recorded music slowed in the mid-1970s, with economic recession following the 1973 oil crisis and a dearth of commercially acceptable styles to stimulate record-buying. The defining musical style of that period in Britain was punk which, as we have seen, was one that sat even less easily alongside the commercial instincts of the major record companies. In the second half of the 1970s, disco music provided a stimulus for renewed growth, but disco had strong American roots and EMI's long-standing weakness in American repertoire meant that it fell behind its major competitors. In 1978/79, as we have seen, EMI Music made an operating profit of just £1.8 million on sales of £430 million.

The early 1980s were a particularly difficult period for the whole industry, with economic recession in the major Western markets. There had been no major technological innovation since the launch of the cassette over a decade earlier, so there was no incentive for music consumers to upgrade their libraries. The cassette itself had been a mixed blessing, since it had encouraged a boom in piracy and home taping. Commercially organised piracy wreaked havoc on the music industry in certain parts of the world. In the Middle East and much of Asia, EMI's once thriving music business simply collapsed. In the developed world, home taping took its toll, although there is disagreement about the extent of damage it caused. More importantly, for the consumer in the West, music had lost its excitement and new entertainment products, such as movies on video and electronic games, were taking a growing share of his or her budget.

EMI Music was not alone in suffering in the downturn, which affected all of the major music companies. PolyGram, which had been an aggressive high-flyer in the late 1970s and had overtaken EMI Music in size, made losses in the US totalling over $200 million between 1980 and 1982. Its parents, Philips and Siemens, considered merging it with Warner's music business, a deal that would have created the largest music company in the world, with 25 per cent of the US market. That deal was dropped because of the opposition of the US Justice Department, but for which it is possible that EMI Music itself may have been merged into one of the other majors.

EMI Music sat awkwardly in the home entertainment and high-technology strategy announced by THORN EMI after the acquisition of EMI. The home entertainment element of this, as we have seen, was founded on the marriage of hardware and software. However, the software that the company saw as playing the leading role was audio-visual software – films and television – rather than recorded music. EMI Music had dropped into the second tier of music companies, together with RCA, which was shortly to be sold to the Bertelsmann Group, and behind the three majors, Warner, CBS and PolyGram. The strategy that THORN EMI was then following left precious little financial resource to allow it to fight its way back into the first tier, and selling it would have provided funds for THORN EMI's ambitions in other areas of home entertainment and in high technology.

One reason for the decline in EMI's market share was a decision taken in the early 1980s to reduce the dependence on licensing repertoire from other music companies. Music companies regularly license repertoire to each other to sell in countries where the licensor does not have a business. Such licences are usually granted for a limited period. EMI's abiding problem had been a shortage of American artists who would sell internationally, which was one reason why it licensed American repertoire to sell in Europe and elsewhere. In 1974, for example, it struck licensing deals with MCA and Elektra, giving it access to artists such as Cher, Judy Collins, Carly Simon and Bread as well as an impressive back catalogue which included the recordings of Buddy Holly, Louis Armstrong, Bing Crosby and Judy Garland.

But the solution had become part of the problem. Licensed repertoire had generated work for EMI's extensive manufacturing and distribution system around the world, but had also created a culture in which finding and nurturing new musical talent was given less importance. EMI's US subsidiary, Capitol, on which the rest of EMI relied to find and develop American repertoire, had a poor record of creating megastars, as we have seen. In the early 1980s, its roster of artists included well-known names such as Kenny Rogers, Bob Seger, Anne Murray, Kim Carnes, Glen Campbell and Carole King, but lacked the sort of international superstars EMI needed. In the early 1970s, this weakness had been masked by the strong appeal that British artists had internationally, which allowed EMI to exploit its glittering array of British superstars around the world. However, international success was often preceded by success in the US market, and new British artists of the 1980s were no longer as successful in the American market as their predecessors of the 1960s and 1970s had been. Even in the mid-1990s, the best-selling British artists in the US are the now middle-aged superstars – The Beatles, The Rolling Stones, Paul McCartney, Elton John, Rod Stewart – whose careers started in the 1960s and 1970s. As a result, the share of US sales taken by British acts has fallen steadily, from over 20 per cent at the end of the 1980s to around 15 per cent now.

Capitol's own performance was, once again, a major contributor to EMI Music's depressed profits. Having made pre-tax profits of $32 million in 1980/81, it made a loss of $4 million in 1984/85. The weakness of its repertoire had made it particularly dependent on the occasional hit. In 1981, for example, John Lennon's assassination had resulted in a boom in the sale of Beatles albums. The Beatles, together with Kenny Rogers and the album of the film *Jazz Singer*, contributed 50 per cent of Capitol's record sales in the year. By 1984/85, these three contributed 5 per cent. Incidentally, although the music from *Jazz Singer* sold well, the film itself had been a flop. Bhaskar Menon had put in place a number of measures to try to strengthen Capitol's repertoire. These included the launch of the Manhattan label to concentrate on black music and revitalising the EMI America label, alongside the main Capitol label and the Angel label for classical music. However, with its market share down to 8 per cent by 1985, EMI was becoming a minor player in the US.

The early 1980s recession in the music industry had created opportunities to acquire mid-sized US companies such as Motown, A&M and Island, as well as the music publishing businesses of CBS and Chappell. However, with all its other interests, THORN EMI had an ambivalent attitude to investing in EMI Music, and the division appears to have been consigned to the role of generating cash to be deployed elsewhere. A mature music company is particularly amenable to generating cash. Much of the cost of selling recorded music is only incurred at the time a sale is made. With most manufactured products, cash has to be sunk into building inventory before a product can be sold. With recorded music, however, the major element of cost, apart from advances, is the royalties and fees to the artists, which are not incurred until a cassette or disc is sold and may not actually be paid over until some months later. With an adequate back catalogue, a music company can continue to generate considerable cash for some years, without need for significant reinvestment. This process, however, can only be taken so far: more than half a major recorded music company's sales come from new repertoire, so it cannot afford to stand still for very long.

The extent to which EMI Music's consignment to the role of cash cow was a result of a deliberate decision by THORN EMI, as opposed to simply reflecting a lack of clear purpose within the business, is difficult to disentangle. Jim Fifield, who took over as head of EMI Music in the late 1980s, believes that it had simply 'quit asking for investment'. The relationship between EMI Music and its parent does, however, illustrate some of the pitfalls inherent in the workings of conglomerate management. The parent's doubts about the attractiveness of the business, compared to its other glittering opportunities, translates into a hesitancy on the part of the business managers to ask for investment. This results in further depressing the performance and prospects of the business, justifying the parent's original doubts.

When the home entertainment and high-technology strategy was jettisoned by the new regime that took over in 1985, EMI Music's role within THORN EMI changed significantly. Colin Southgate had taken to the business from the outset. He says: 'It was people-driven, like computer software [the business he started in] and the people were larger than life. I feel more at home with such businesses.'

At the time that Sir Graham Wilkins and Colin Southgate took over at THORN EMI, by a lucky coincidence the outlook for the music industry had also started to look rosier than it had for over a decade. The main reason for this was the growing popularity of the compact disc, the first significant technological improvement in sound reproduction since the launch of the cassette in the early 1970s. The compact disc was to be an even more significant event then the cassette, comparable, in its impact on the industry, to the launch of the microgroove vinyl record in the mid-1950s. The improvement in sound quality and convenience it brought was so apparent that it immediately found acceptance with the consumer. Compact discs were launched in 1982 by Sony and Philips, but EMI did not announce its support for the product until April 1983, later than all the other music majors. Its hesitation, which was reminiscent of its delay in supporting the vinyl disc in the 1950s, appears to be consistent with a lack of appetite for playing a leading role in the industry. The first EMI compact discs were on the market later in 1983, although EMI did not start manufacturing compact discs itself until May 1986.

Interestingly, these were made in a factory in England which had originally been built to make VHD video discs, THORN EMI's support for which was another possible reason for EMI's tardiness in supporting the Sony/Philips compact disc standard.

It was not until the late 1980s that sufficient CD players had been sold to allow the sales of CDs to take off. When they did, they not only displaced vinyl records but also significantly expanded the market. The first generation of heavy music buyers from the 1950s and 1960s, now in middle age, began to buy music again, replenishing their libraries on CD. Music-buying no longer stopped at twenty-five and the industry had recaptured its magic. It received a further stimulus from the growth of music television channels, in particular MTV. By exposing audiences to an aggressive, visual image of popular music, they had an impact altogether different from radio, with its much lower-key style.

In May 1988, Bhaskar Menon, who had worked for EMI for thirty years and had been chief executive of EMI Music since 1978, handed over responsibility for day-to-day management to Jim Fifield, who was designated to take over as chief executive in due course. Fifield, an American, had spent much of his business career with the US food and consumer products group General Mills. In 1981, he was appointed vice president of its toy division, which gave him experience of managing entertainment products. From there, he moved to CBS Fox Video before being recruited by THORN EMI.

Jim Fifield credits Colin Southgate with three crucial decisions that led to the turnaround of EMI Music. As he puts it:

> Firstly, Southgate recognised that it was an under-performing asset but also chose it as a vehicle with which to build a world-class company. Secondly, he was willing to spend the money and take the risks to achieve this. Thirdly, he ignored the advice of his advisers by going outside the music industry to find a new CEO.

Southgate himself regards the turnaround of EMI Music as one of his proudest achievements and the appointment of Jim Fifield as the key event in it. Fifield believes that, at the time, the business needed an outsider to take a fresh look at it – someone with a solid business background and empathy with the entertainment business, but not a music industry professional. In accepting the job, he was particularly keen to ensure that he would get Colin Southgate's support in doing what needed to be done to build a truly world-class company. He says:

> I told him that we would make mistakes, but they would not be mistakes of omission. They would be the result of being too aggressive. Colin was prepared to accept this and has backed it all the way. I spent six months talking to people about what was good in the business and what was wrong. What I found was a business that had allowed itself to run down. It did not have the look of a winner: it was asking what was wrong rather than what was right, or could be got right. Culturally, it was in the second tier: it had a culture which believed that it was OK to finish fourth.

Many of the specific problems were the result of under-investment over many years. Fifield says: 'Factories were outdated and offices needed refurbishment. To be a winner you need to look like a winner and shabby offices do not make you look like a winner.' There were other problems. Fifield felt that 'it had reverted back from being an international company to being a series of multi-territorial companies'. It also had, of course, the long-standing problem of a lack of American repertoire. Despite its problems, however, it had some major strengths. In Fifield's words: 'It had worldwide representation, although it didn't think globally. It had a strong UK base. It had good local repertoire and it had a very strong catalogue, because of its history.'

Fifield believes that the single most important action he took was to write a letter to all the employees on what it took to have a winning culture. He particularly stressed the importance of allowing people the 'freedom to fail'. He said:

> We must be aggressive about making decisions, execute them with energy and perseverance, and accept responsibility for the results. The music business has a strong risk element, and we must be supportive of new ideas, acts and artists, recognizing that all will not succeed. These attitudes are essential for success, and imply a need for what I call the 'freedom to fail'. Risking a failure is often superior to no action, which guarantees mediocrity. Winners

do fail on occasion, but winners also acknowledge and learn from their mistakes. When things go wrong, we must avoid pointing fingers, own up, and learn from events. That way, our mistakes serve as investments in learning more about our business and the marketplace. If we don't have an occasional failure, we aren't taking enough risks.

This statement of Fifield's suggests a decisive move away from a conglomerate culture. Allowing its people the 'freedom to fail' is something that the diversified conglomerate seems to be particularly bad at. Because the centre of a conglomerate is so far removed from the underlying issues confronting its businesses, failures tend to be judged in narrow, often purely financial, terms. To paraphrase Fifield's terms, the conglomerate is particularly prone to pointing fingers and not learning from events. As a result, risk-taking at the sharp end of the business is minimised. This is not to say that diversified conglomerates do not take risks: acquiring businesses in unfamiliar industries is, perhaps, one of the most risky forms of investment, as is evidenced by the experience of THORN EMI. However, these risks are usually taken by people at the head office of the conglomerate, who are generally the furthest removed from real business activity, and hence the least suited to assessing the risks. So, perversely, risk-taking is greatest where the business issues are least understood and is discouraged where it is most necessary.

Fifield's next action was to prepare a five-year plan that included a complete inventory of the state of the company – its strengths and weaknesses, what was good and what needed to be made good, where the business was and where it needed to get to – with a thoroughness never attempted before. This plan, updated annually, still forms the basic doctrine for running the business. Fifield calls it 'the CEO's manifesto of what to do – the road map out'.

Fifields major achievement has been successfully to combine the 'hard' and 'soft' sides of music management – on the one hand, running an efficient industrial machine while, on the other, creating an atmosphere conducive to generating the new artistic creations that are the lifeblood of the industry. The first part of this involved a considerable investment in 'state of the art' compact disc manufacturing facilities, while at the same time managing a complex withdrawal from vinyl disc manufacture and a consolidation of cassette manufacture, both of which were in decline. New information systems and streamlined delivery systems were put in to give better service to retailers, to control inventory and to reduce obsolescence and scrapping of unwanted product.

At the same time, the EMI Music organisation across the world was reconfigured to allow a global approach to marketing artistic repertoire. One of the trends in the music market over the last decade has been a blurring of the convenient distinction between national and international repertoire. Whereas in the 1970s, international artists were almost invariably either British or American, the situation now is considerably more complex. Some of EMI's most successful recent international artists have originated elsewhere – the Swedish duo Roxette being a good example. At the same time, superstar status in Britain or America no longer automatically translates into international stardom. One of EMI's, and the world's, top-selling stars, Garth Brooks, has made a fraction of his sales outside the US. All of this has made the process of managing and exploiting successful stars considerably more complex. What Fifield has been able to do is to get EMI's worldwide network of companies to act as a global organisation in this process, rather than as a series of regional or national businesses.

Much effort also went into improving the creation of new artistic repertoire. This was an area in which EMI had slipped behind in the late 1970s and early 1980s. As Fifield puts it: 'There is a period for which new repertoire is missing.' Finding new artists has always been a risky process: the industry's rule of thumb is that out of every ten new artists taken on, eight or nine will be commercial failures. But unless a record company spends money at odds of five to one or worse to find the ones that will succeed, it is doomed to long-term decline.

Finding new megastars with the sales potential of The Beatles or The Rolling Stones has also become more unlikely. The evidence suggests that, while the number of artists achieving some commercial success – what the industry refers to as mid-range acts – has increased, the number of artists in the very top-selling categories has declined. This is partly a result of an increasing fragmentation of musical tastes, not only internationally but also within each market, with the result that new acts appeal to narrower sectors. Music retailers, for example, recognise more than ten different types of music in the rock category, including rock-pop, rock-rap, heavy metal, grunge, hard rock, garage, groove, thrash and trash. Reggae comes as straight reggae, ragga, jungle and ska. And then there are the categories of dance (at least seven varieties), Latin (eleven varieties) and rap (two main varieties), not to mention classical, country, folk, jazz, blues and a host of other specialist genres. One result of fragmentation is that the number of new albums on sale at any one time is vastly greater than it used to be. In a submission to the Monopolies and Mergers Commission, EMI estimated that the number of UK album releases had doubled between 1987 and 1994. This, of course, has meant that the effort going into generating new repertoire is also much greater than it used to be.

In some ways, fragmentation should be a helpful trend from the music industry's point of view, since it means that companies are less reliant on big acts. This has not, however, reduced the bargaining power of the established superstars. A top act such as U2 generates enough sales to make it a medium-sized international business in its own right, and leading international artists now surround themselves with large teams of lawyers and business managers to negotiate with record companies on their behalf. Competition among music companies has undoubtedly led to an escalation in advances paid to the very top artists. Fifield does not believe, however, that this trend has increased the risks in the business. He says: 'The deals are bigger but the volumes are also up.'

The effort and investment made by EMI Music in generating new artists has paid off. The company has been particularly successful in developing new artists in growing markets outside the US, and has had a sustained creative renaissance in the UK with the emergence of Britpop. The internal effort has been supplemented by a series of acquisitions of independent labels which have brought their own sources of A&R and catalogues with them. Independent labels have been a feature of the music industry since the 1950s, when sources of popular music repertoire exploded. Often more closely in touch with nascent trends and more fleet-footed than the majors, and often more willing to take risks, they have played an important role in finding new talent, which is then sometimes exploited in conjunction with a major. Some of the independent labels started in the 1960s and 1970s grew to become substantial music companies in their own right – labels such as Virgin, Chrysalis, Island and A&M fall into this category. Success, however, takes them to a threshold where they have to invest heavily to set up their own worldwide manufacturing and distribution to exploit their repertoire efficiently. As the independents of the 1960s and 1970s reached the status of 'mini-majors', some of them sold out to the majors. PolyGram, for example, acquired Island, A&M, Motown and Def Jam, and EMI acquired Chrysalis, Virgin, Intercord and several smaller labels.

Another important element in EMI's strategy over the last decade has been the increased importance given to music publishing, an arcane but highly profitable business, with characteristics rather different to those of selling recorded music. In most countries in the West, a new musical work is protected by copyright as soon as it is created. The initial copyright owner is usually the writer and the work is protected for his lifetime and for fifty years after his death (seventy years in the European Union). He may, however, sell it to someone else or assign it to a music publisher in exchange for a share of future royalties.

The music publisher makes it his job to find writers and composers with work that can be published. He takes on the role of promoting the work and collecting royalties and licence fees for its use. What has made the business particularly valuable in recent years is that the users of copyrighted music have mushroomed. The largest source of income is what is known as mechanical royalties, which arise when a song or a piece of music is reproduced on cassette or disc. As the recorded music market grows, so also does the income from mechanical royalties. The second largest source, performance royalties, arise when the musical work is played or performed in public – on radio, television or in a live performance. With an explosion in the number of television and radio channels around the world, this source has also been growing rapidly.

The third important source is what is known as synchronisation. This is the use of music as soundtracks on film and television, including its use in advertisements. The same piece of music can be used in a number of films and advertisements, so the potential income can be enormous. For example, one of EMI's songs, 'Wild Thing', created thirty years ago, has been used in three feature films and in advertisements for products from companies as diverse as Kodak, Volvo, Reebok, Kleenex, Sears and Heinz, earning well over a million dollars from synchronisation deals in North America alone. The fourth, and original, source of income for music publishers, publishing sheet music, is now of little commercial importance.

EMI Music has had a long involvement with music publishing but, until comparatively recently, it was simply an accidental by-product of its involvement in recorded music. A lack of real interest is suggested by its failure to secure the publishing rights for The Beatles' music. Their first two recorded songs, 'Please Please Me' and 'Love Me Do', were published by Ardmore & Beechwood, EMI's publishing arm at the time. However, Brian Epstein, The Beatles' promoter, was unhappy with EMI's marketing and so George Martin, the producer, introduced him to an independent publisher, Dick James. Rights to later Lennon and McCartney songs went into a company called Northern Songs, the shareholders in which were Lennon and McCartney, Dick James and Brian Epstein. That company was floated on the London Stock Exchange in 1965, but was not a great success. In 1969, after Brian Epstein's death, Dick James agreed to sell it to the television company ATV, for £10 million, much to the anger of Lennon and McCartney.

The recent history of ATV Music, as Northern Songs was renamed, shows how rapidly the value of publishing rights has escalated. In 1985, the singer Michael Jackson bought ATV Music for $48 million (£30 million) – no more, when adjusted for inflation, than its value in 1969. It seemed, at the time, like an expensive trophy for a super-rich pop star with eccentric tastes. It turned out, however, to be a shrewd investment. In 1995, he sold 50 per cent of ATV Music to his record company, Sony Music, for $500 million. Another deal that shows how recently music publishing has emerged from the backwaters was the sale in 1984 by PolyGram, at the time in financial difficulty, of its Chappell publishing business to Warner. PolyGram has since been scrambling to rebuild its publishing business.

EMI had begun to realise the value of music publishing in

the 1970s, earlier than its competitors. Its first significant move was the acquisition of Affiliated Music Publishers in the UK, for £3.3 million, in 1972. This was followed by the acquisition of the music publishing division of Columbia Pictures, in 1976, for $23.5 million (£13.7 million), making it the largest publisher in the world. However, for a long time, the US and British operations worked quite separately and they were not unified until 1986.

The event that made EMI's music publishing activities pre-eminent was the acquisition, in 1989, of SBK Entertainment World, Inc. This company had acquired the publishing business of CBS, Inc. in 1986, suggesting that the management of CBS, now owned by Sony, had not recognised the value of music publishing either. SBK was owned by three individuals, Stephen Swid, Martin Bandier and Charles Koppelman, who had originally approached THORN EMI with the intention of buying its publishing business. In the course of discussions, the deal was reversed and THORN EMI bought the SBK business for $337 million (£187 million). Its 250,000 compositions included such durable numbers as 'Singin In The Rain', 'Wizard Of Oz', 'Windmills Of Your Mind', 'The Shadow Of Your Smile' and 'Santa Claus Is Coming To Town'. It also brought with it Martin Bandier, who took over the running of the combined EMI and SBK publishing business, and Charles Koppelman, who set up the SBK record label for EMI and has since gone on to run EMI's North American business.

EMI's music publishing business, further boosted by the acquisition of the Filmtrax catalogue in 1990, is now the world's largest, with over a million titles. Its revenues and profits are a closely guarded secret, but the documents published at the time of the SBK acquisition disclosed that SBK's gross royalty income less royalty expense (known as Net Publishers' Share or NPS) was expected to be $37 million (£20 million) in 1988. It also indicated that EMI's own publishing business had a similar level of income. Since the income will have grown very substantially since 1988, and its costs – the overheads involved in running the business – will have remained broadly stable, it is likely that music publishing contributes a sizeable, and relatively secure, portion of EMI Music's profits.

By 1991, the benefits of Fifield's recovery plan were beginning to come through in the results of EMI Music:

£ million	1986/87	1987/88	1988/89	1989/90	1990/91
Sales	637	650	766	884	1016
Profit (a)	19.4	30.0	44.8	92	109
RoS	3.0%	4.6%	5.8%	10.4%	10.7%

(a) Before interest and tax

Sales had risen at a compound growth rate of 12 per cent per annum from the low point of 1985/86. Operating profits had risen at a compound growth rate of 120 per cent per annum. Profitability, as measured by the ratio of operating profits to sales, had risen from 1 per cent in 1985/86 to 10.7 per cent. EMI Music was in the top tier of recorded music companies and was the largest music publisher.

Although this was a considerable achievement, Colin Southgate felt that it needed one major record company acquisition to push EMI higher up the ranks of the world's leading music companies. There were few independent record companies of sufficient size to meet his criteria and those that did were likely to be hotly pursued, since the music industry had recovered its glamour by this time. PolyGram, by now restored to health, had bought Island and A&M. The other majors, Warner, Sony and BMG, were also looking at expansion, and non-music entertainment companies, such as Disney and Paramount, were showing interest in entering the industry.

In 1990, an opportunity arose to buy the Geffen label, owned by the famed Los Angeles-based music entrepreneur David Geffen. Geffen had a strong roster of current American artists and bands, including Guns 'n' Roses, then at the peak of their popularity, and was particularly noted for his creative skills. The acquisition would have done wonders for EMI's still relatively weak American repertoire, and Southgate was eager to do a deal. However, David Geffen wanted a deal that would have given him equity in a merged music business, and no satisfactory way of accommodating his wish within the THORN EMI structure could be found. Eventually, he sold his business to the American entertainment group MCA, for over $700 million in shares. Shortly thereafter, MCA was acquired by the Japanese consumer electronics group Matsushita, thus giving Geffen a further premium on the price he had received. Matsushita, it will be noted, had embarked on a search for the elusive holy grail of synergy between software and hardware, a mission on which THORN EMI had embarked a decade earlier, and it enjoyed no greater success, eventually selling 80 per cent of MCA to the Canadian drinks company Seagram.

Colin Southgate had a second chance in 1992, when Richard Branson decided to put his Virgin Music business up for sale. Virgin Music had been started in 1972 by Branson and Nik Powell. It had a colourful early history and, by the early 1990s, had an impressive roster of artists including Phil Collins, Bryan Ferry, UB40, Janet Jackson and The Rolling Stones. It had operations in North America, Continental Europe and the Far East, as well as in the UK, and had come closest, of the independents, to breaking into the ranks of the majors. In fact, as Tim Jackson reveals in his book *Virgin King*, Branson had made an attempt to acquire THORN EMI in 1987, shortly after his Virgin Group had been floated on the London Stock Exchange. It was an audacious plan, since THORN EMI was ten times the size of Branson's Virgin Group and vastly more complex. However, similar feats had been achieved by others, and the bid would have been in keeping with Branson's now established image of a swashbuckling David taking on Goliath.

As his partner in the bid for THORN EMI, Branson had enlisted the property company Mountleigh, led by Tony Clegg. According to Jackson, Virgin and Mountleigh agreed jointly to mount a hostile bid for THORN EMI and then to break it up, with Virgin taking the music business, Mountleigh the rental business and the rest to be sold off. What scuppered this plan was the stock market collapse of 1987, which caused Clegg to pull out of the enterprise. Branson was persuaded that for Virgin to attempt a hostile bid for THORN EMI on its own was too fraught with risk. Instead, he approached Sir Graham Wilkins, then chairman of THORN EMI, with the idea of pooling their respective music and retailing businesses in a joint venture, which would give Virgin control of the music venture and THORN EMI control of the retailing venture. Not surprisingly, in view of the central place occupied by music in THORN EMI's plans by this time, the idea was rejected by Sir Graham Wilkins and was taken no further by Branson.

By 1988, mutual disenchantment between Richard Branson and the stock market led to the Virgin Group reverting to being a private company. That, together with the money needed to

finance other parts of the Branson empire, in particular Virgin
Airlines, put increasing pressure on the finances of the Virgin
Group. In 1989, the Japanese media group Fujisankei bought a
25 per cent stake in Virgin Music for $150 million (£96 million),
which eased the financial pressure temporarily. However, within
two years, it was again under pressure and Branson had to take
the unpalatable decision to sell Virgin Music in its entirety. From
Colin Southgate's point of view, the timing of Branson's decision
was perfect. EMI Music was now a successful company and its
value had been recognised by the stock market. Virgin Music,
which had sales of £330 million in 1991, was large enough to
fit Southgate's requirements. It was also a bigger business than
Geffen, and included a valuable music publishing library.

The negotiations surrounding the sale of Virgin Music are
graphically described in Tim Jackson's book. He reveals that the
price of £510 million in cash, together with the assumption of
£50 million of debt, which THORN EMI eventually agreed to
pay, was substantially higher than the price that the alternative
bidder, MCA, had offered. However, as Jackson reveals, like
any good poker player, Branson had neglected to tell even his
investment banking adviser, John Thornton of Goldman Sachs,
the minimum price for which he was prepared to sell Virgin
Music. The deal was actually struck between John Thornton
and Colin Southgate when both found themselves on the same
flight to New York. However, a last-minute bid by the German
group BMG, together with Fujisankei, came close to trumping
THORN EMI. Although THORN EMI's price seemed high in
relation to Virgin Music's operating profit of £21 million in the
year to July 1991, the savings and benefits that EMI realised
from the deal meant that, financially, the purchase justified itself
while also substantially strengthening EMI's position in the music
industry. By 1995, Virgin Music was probably contributing over
£100 million to THORN EMI's profits.

Fifield believes that, 'Virgin had a more creative style. It brought
an entrepreneurial culture to EMI Music.' As a result, he says,
'EMI now marches with a more lively step.' There was a fear that
the cultures would clash – the jeans and trainers of Virgin would be
swamped by the suits of EMI. This has not happened and while
activities such as manufacturing, logistics and procurement have

been combined to yield large savings, the Virgin spirit has been kept intact. Fifield says with some pride: 'I went to great pains to preserve the Virgin culture.'

EMI Music's financial performance since the acquisition of Virgin Music speaks for itself.

£ million	1991/92	1992/93	1993/94	1994/95	1995/96
Sales	1,129	1,507	1,761	2,189	2,705
Profit (a)	125	197	246	295	365
RoS	11.1%	13.1%	14.0%	13.5%	13.5%

(a) Before interest and tax

In a ten-year period, EMI Music's sales have grown at a compound rate of 16 per cent per annum and its profits at a compound rate of 67 per cent per annum. All of this has not come cheaply. Fifield estimates that 'we invested $2 billion [£1.3 billion] over eight years in building the business'. This amounts to over one and a half times the amount raised by THORN EMI in selling off nearly eighty of its other businesses. Five hundred million pounds of the total amount invested was raised by asking the shareholders for new money, by a rights issue, for the acquisition of Virgin Music. But it is unlikely that even this would have been forthcoming if THORN EMI had not chosen to focus on a very few businesses and disengage from the rest. Nothing better illustrates the advantage of focus as a business strategy than the revival of EMI Music.

16

Rental Revival

One source of stability for THORN EMI through the tumult of the 1980s had been the steady stream of profits from its rental businesses – now known as Thorn Group. In fact, the rental business was also the major source of stability, and profit, for Thorn in the decade before it acquired EMI. In 1971/72, the first year for which the company specifically identified its profits from Rental, these contributed 38 per cent of Thorn's operating profits. Two decades later, in 1991/92, Rental again contributed 38 per cent of THORN EMI's operating profits. In between, the proportion had risen as high as 67 per cent, in 1986/87, when the company's manufacturing businesses had fallen into losses. Lacking the glamour of the music business or the excitement of high technology, Rental was, for much of this period, a massive flywheel whose sheer momentum ensured a dependable contribution to its parent. Yet its original market was also in steady decline for much of this period.

The long-term rental of television sets and video recorders by a large proportion of households was a peculiarly British phenomenon, replicated only in Australia and New Zealand. Why it flourished in the UK but never achieved the same level of popularity elsewhere in the West would make an interesting subject for socio-economic and cultural cross-comparisons. Possible reasons include the earlier launch of television in the UK, compared to Continental Europe, when television sets were unreliable; the frequent changes in British television standards referred to in Chapter 1, which made rental preferable to purchase; and the greater popularity of television viewing, particularly after the launch of commercial television in the UK in 1954. In 1968, for example, soon after colour television broadcasting started in the UK, 96 per cent of households either owned or rented a television set of some sort. In West Germany, the comparable figure was 69 per cent and in France 56 per cent. The growth of television broadcasting and of television rental probably formed a mutually beneficial circle in the UK in the 1950s and 1960s: rental expanded the base of viewers much faster than it would otherwise have grown, while good-quality, popular television expanded the demand for rented television sets.

In addition to concerns about reliability and technological obsolescence, the popularity of the traditional British television rental habit was also a result of the cost of television sets in relation to disposable income. When colour television was first introduced, in 1967, a twenty-five-inch Ferguson set retailed at £350. In terms of today's money, that would equate to £3,400. In 1996, a significantly better and much more reliable twenty-five-inch Ferguson set still costs £350. The near tenfold reduction in real price, accompanied by the disappearance of 'technological fear', illustrates most starkly the challenge faced by the British television rental industry over the last two decades or more. In 1972, over 70 per cent of colour television sets in Britain were rented; by 1992, that figure had fallen to under 30 per cent.

By the late 1970s, with the proportion of rented television sets in decline, the rental industry rested its hopes on the arrival of the next expensive consumer electronics product. This duly appeared, in the form of the video recorder, and gave the industry a new lease of life. In 1980, some 70 per cent of video recorders in Britain were rented but, as with television sets, this proportion fell steadily and was down to around 20 per cent by 1992. The video recorder was, nevertheless, a crucial product for THORN EMI's rental business in the early 1980s, and the rental industry was equally important in speeding the introduction of video recorders in the UK. In 1977/78, the segment defined in Thorn's annual report as Consumer Electronics, which included both Rental and the Ferguson television manufacturing business, contributed £65 million in operating profit and showed little sign of growth. Five years later, this figure had grown to £83 million, a compound growth rate of 5 per cent per annum. A better measure of the underlying trend is the growth in the value of television sets and video recorders on rental, since in the early years of introducing a new rental product, heavy depreciation charges eat into profit. These products on rental to customers had a net book value of £183 million in 1978. By 1983, they had grown to £462 million, an average increase of 20 per cent per annum over five years. Although Rental continued to contribute increasing profits to THORN EMI through the difficult years of the late 1980s, its underlying growth slowed sharply after the end of the video boom in the mid-1980s. In 1984, the value of rental assets had amounted to £483 million; by 1987, this figure had fallen to £441 million.

Concern about the long-term future of the traditional rental business was very much in the mind of the THORN EMI board in the early 1980s and was partly responsible for motivating diversification into areas such as video software rental and cable television. Television and video rental subscribers were, it was believed, an obvious customer base for renting video cassettes and a Video at Home Club was started to cater for them. The link with cable television sprang from the ownership, by Radio Rentals, THORN EMI's main rental business, of cable networks originally laid down to relay radio and terrestrial television broadcasting signals. The largest of these, in Swindon, was one of the early pilot sites selected to test the public's appetite for cable television in the early 1980s, enthusiastically cheered on by Mrs Thatcher's Minister for Information Technology, Kenneth Baker. Further franchises, to expand the Swindon network and to develop cable television in Coventry and, as part of a consortium, in Ulster, were won. A company called THORN EMI Cable Television was started to provide a range of services to other cable television operators in the UK and the rental business offered its invoicing and cash collection services to the cable television industry.

As we have seen, THORN EMI's attempts to build a cable television business were short-lived. The capital requirements of the business, and the time scales over which a return could be expected, were outside the company's area of experience and ability to accommodate. Nor did video software rental make much contribution. Although that business grew rapidly in the 1980s, it was not one that Rental's high-street outlets were particularly equipped to handle, and success went to a new type of specialist video rental shop. In fact, one of the lessons from this period of diversification was that THORN EMI's rental business was very good at performing a very narrow range of functions and, by the same token, was not very good at doing new things. Answers to the question of what competencies the traditional rental business could deploy into other areas – what its real strengths were – proved to be elusive. Was it the more than 1,000 outlets on high streets throughout the country? Was it the database of more than three million customers? Was it the efficient invoicing and cash collection system? Or was it the ability to repair or replace electronic equipment throughout the country?

An important figure in the move to revive Rental was Jim Maxmin, who joined the company in September 1983 and was appointed chairman of THORN EMI's rental and retail businesses. Maxmin had previously worked for the Lex Service Group and had been head of its Volvo franchise. A creative and iconoclastic marketer, Maxmin's task was to shake up a hitherto successful but conservative organisation which was in danger of losing its sense of direction. Although the underlying trend in the traditional rental business was recognised by the incumbent management, there was little appetite for any radical change in strategy in response. Maxmin and his new team of heretical outsiders, which included Stuart McAllister, who would later head THORN EMI's successful HMV retail group, were often at loggerheads with the old-timers.

In the mid-1980s, THORN EMI had four rental chains in the UK. The largest of these was Radio Rentals, with over 500 outlets across the country. DER, which had been the original Thorn business, was also a national chain, with over 400 outlets. MultiBroadcast was a smaller regional chain, with 150 outlets in the south of England, and Focus was another regional operation, concentrating on northern England and Scotland, with around thirty outlets. In addition to these, Rumbelows also ran a rental business, with over 375,000 accounts, from its retail outlets. Maxmin's first reorganisation, in 1986/87, was intended to give each of these operations a sharper focus and distinctive image, while also rationalising activities and reducing costs. Radio Rentals and DER remained as separate, specialist rental chains, with Radio Rentals being given a premium image, while DER catered to a wider public. Focus and MultiBroadcast were combined into an operation called THORN EMI TV and Video Centres, which combined renting with retailing and was aimed at a younger audience. Rumbelows was given the role of concentrating on retailing. The reorganisation resulted in significant cost savings. Having shed 1,350 jobs, the combined Focus/MultiBroadcast operation greatly improved its profitability. However, the new management team quailed from the much larger, and more risky, task of combining the two major rental chains, Radio Rentals and DER, although this would have to be tackled later. And Rumbelows, as we have seen in Chapter 14, remained a weak player in the highly competitive electrical retailing arena.

Alongside rationalisation and sharper focus, Maxmin and his team had to look for new directions for growth, if they were to do more than preside over profitable decline. One development was a renewed interest in promoting the rental business outside the UK, both organically and by acquisition. THORN EMI had conducted international rental operations for many years, and Radio Rentals had had a small number of outlets in Australia, Ireland and Italy before it was acquired by Thorn. By 1984, there were rental operations in thirteen countries, including most of western Europe (with the notable exception of Germany), Hong Kong, Singapore, Australia and New Zealand. However, Australia and New Zealand apart, rental in these countries was aimed at particular niches rather than at the mass market. In 1986/87, Granada's Swedish Telerent business was acquired, the first acquisition under the new regime of Sir Graham Wilkins and Colin Southgate and a mark of confidence in the future of Rental. In the following year, there were more acquisitions in Denmark, France, Spain, Italy, Switzerland and Ireland, and in 1988/89, in Australia and Hong Kong.

Maxmin himself appears to have wanted the rental business to address a more upmarket clientele. One venture with this aim was a shop called 'Le Set', in the smarter end of the Fulham Road in London, crammed full of exotic electronic devices. 'Le Set' was not a success and the venture was abandoned soon after. However, whether Rental's future lay upmarket or downmarket was a question much debated between Maxmin and Colin Southgate. In Southgate's view, it was the less affluent, rather than the wealthy, who would be Rental's

future customers. This belief was reflected in the acquisition of
the US company Rent-A-Center (RAC) in 1987. In its effect on
the future development of Rental, this acquisition compared in
importance to the 1968 acquisition of Radio Rentals by Thorn.
The Radio Rentals acquisition had changed the perception of
rental from being an outlet for television sets to being a business
in its own right and Thorn's most important profit-earner. RAC
brought, in time, a new perspective to the rental business. It was no
longer constrained by the tried and tested format of the traditional
UK rental business, but could be envisaged as a range of ways of
giving customers access to a wide collection of products. It was
this shift in perception, unlikely to have been achieved without
the acquisition of RAC, which gave a new lease of life to Rental
in the 1990s.

RAC was in the business of rent to own as opposed to the
traditional UK business of 'rent to rent'. It rented a range of
household durable goods, including televisions and video recorders, but extending to household appliances and furniture. These
were rented, usually on a weekly basis, with the renter having the
option to buy the product outright after a certain number of rental
payments, typically between twelve and twenty-four months. In
essence, it provided 'liquidity constrained' consumers – those
without cash or unable to get credit – with immediate access to
goods. RAC had opened its first store in 1973 and had grown
rapidly in the years before THORN EMI acquired it. Revenues
had grown at over 40 per cent per annum in the four years before the
acquisition, and net earnings had grown at just under 40 per cent
per annum. Based in Wichita, Kansas, it had 270 company-owned
stores and a further 168 franchised stores across the US.

The price paid for RAC was $600 million, hefty for a business
that had net earnings of just under $10 million in the year immedi-
ately prior to the acquisition. Representing a price-to-earnings
multiple of sixty, it was an expensive purchase by any standards.
However, because of large tax losses in the US arising out of the
Inmos business and other US operations, THORN EMI was in
the position of being able to shelter RAC's earnings from income
tax for a number of years, and this reduced the price-to-earnings
multiple for THORN EMI to a more manageable level of around
thirty-three. It was, nevertheless, an expensive purchase judged

on strictly financial parameters, particularly as there were no immediate cost savings to be made. However, judged on its broader impact on the rest of THORN EMI's rental business over a number of years, RAC has proved its worth, and Sir Colin ranks it, alongside the acquisition of Virgin Music and SBK, as one of the three deals that transformed THORN EMI. Its acquisition was also an important milestone in the restoration of confidence in THORN EMI. The acquisition was funded by a rights issue – an issue of new shares to existing shareholders and the first call to shareholders for cash since the disastrous 1984 rights issue to fund the purchase of Inmos. The fact that the board were prepared to bid for the business, and go to their shareholders for the funds to back it, suggests that they could see their way out of the problems of the recent past and were beginning to think about the long-term future of the company.

RAC continued to grow rapidly under THORN EMI ownership by a combination of new store openings and acquisitions. By 1989, it had 745 stores and, by 1991, these had expanded to over 1,000. In 1991, jewellery was added to the items rented through RAC outlets. In the following year, a second rent-to-own operation, Remco – which aimed at a slightly better-off customer – was acquired in the US, for $53 million. After this acquisition, Rental had nearly 1,200 outlets in North America.

In 1992, Jim Maxmin left the company to become chief executive of the retailing and fashion group Laura Ashley. He was succeeded by Michael Metcalf, who had been finance director of Rental from 1985 to 1988, and understood the business well. He had been moved from that position by Southgate to become deputy finance director of THORN EMI, taking over as finance director in 1989 when Bob Nellist left the company. Metcalf had brought with him a detailed understanding of the rental business, and his views on its future were similar to those of Southgate. Southgate saw him as a future chief executive of Rental, and he was the obvious successor to Maxmin.

While the business Metcalf inherited continued to grow outside the UK, the original UK business went through a recurring process of rationalisation and cost reduction, as its traditional market continued to shrink. By 1992, the number of outlets in the UK had been substantially reduced and effort was concentrated on

the Radio Rentals brand. In that year, it was decided to withdraw
from general electrical retailing in the UK, at a cost of £56 million,
a consequence of not having sold the Rumbelows business three
years earlier. The Rumbelows stores were converted into a second
low-cost rental chain, but Rumbelows was to prove no more
successful in this guise and was finally closed in 1995, at a cost
of a further £98 million.

Rental's financial record in the late 1980s and early 1990s had
been patchy as a result of the complex restructuring it had to
undergo. Operating profits fell from £146 million in 1989/90 to
£106 million in 1991/92. By 1993, however, under the leadership
of Michael Metcalf, Rental had formed a clear idea of its mission.
The 1993 annual report explains that:

> Rental is too narrow a word to define our broad business potential.
> The business spans that sector of the household durables market
> where consumers, unable or unwilling to make an outright
> retail purchase, want financial flexibility and product service
> back-up. The size of this consumer sector varies considerably
> from country to country, but THORN EMI Rental estimates
> that it typically represents up to 50% of the overall market for
> consumer durables.

By combining elements of the traditional UK rental business with
what it had learnt from the acquisition of RAC, a new, flexible
and internationally applicable formula – or series of formulae –
had been developed. It was no longer simply in the business of
long-term rental of television sets and video recorders but was
a provider of a range of financing options – credit, rent-to-own,
rent-with-purchase-option and the traditional rent-to-rent – to
give consumers access to a variety of products. These include,
alongside the traditional television sets and video recorders, a
range of household appliances, stereo systems, telephones and
faxes, personal computers and furniture. Jewellery, so far, has
been restricted to the US.

By breaking out of the mould of its historical business, Thorn
Group has moved from a declining market to a growing one. While
many of the typical middle-income customers of the traditional UK
rental business are now wealthy enough to purchase television sets

and video recorders on their credit cards, the last decade has seen a huge increase in another type of potential customer. These are people who aspire to owning products that have become a part of modern life, and who are surrounded by images of them in the media and in shop windows, but who do not have access to credit cards, bank overdrafts or other lines of credit that the better-off take for granted. In the West, their situation is a result of the polarisation, over the last decade, between those in well-paid, full-time employment, at whom much advertising is aimed and who are the customers for the smart high-street shops, and the increasing proportion who are in risky, poorly paid, mostly part-time employment, but still aspire to the modern lifestyle that they see around them. In Britain, the proportion of households that fall into this category is somewhere between 40 and 50 per cent and rising. Thorn Group's Crazy George chain, started in 1994 in Britain, now has more than twenty outlets and is expanding fast. It is a concept that is equally applicable to the developing world. In eastern Europe, Asia and South America, there is a rising class of industrial and office workers, only recently exposed to Western-style consumption and to the availability of many consumer durables, but with income levels, and access to credit well below their Western counterparts. In fact, the potential for Thorn Group in these varied customer groups across the world extends beyond giving them access to consumer durable products: it could become a means of providing 'liquidity to the liquidity constrained.'

The benefits of the new strategy are reflected in the financial results since 1991/92:

£ million	1991/92	1992/93	1993/94	1994/95	1995/96
Turnover	1,372	1,388	1,484	1,589	1,537
Profit (a)	106	115	129	152	187
RoS	7.7%	8.3%	8.7%	9.6%	12.2%

(a) Before interest and tax

Faced with the decline of the traditional British rental habit, the typical conglomerate would have placed Rental in the 'cash cow' category of its portfolio. Finding a new role for it would have seemed too much like hard work, compared to a readjustment of the portfolio. It was because THORN EMI chose to focus on Rental that it received the attention, effort and investment that enabled it to rediscover a growth path. Now operating in twenty countries around the world, the business has come a long way from the shop renting radios in Twickenham which Jules Thorn reluctantly acquired in the 1930s.

17

Relentless Focus

The idea of concentrating its resources and focusing its attention on a very small number of industries has been the dominant strand in THORN EMI's strategic thinking over the last decade. It is unlikely that the revival of the music business or the transformation of the rental business would have been achieved if the group's resources had been spread more thinly, or the attention of its management spread more widely.

A corollary to this idea is that those businesses of THORN EMI which were in industries it no longer wished to remain in would fare better under owners who had chosen to concentrate on those particular industries. Since those businesses should, on this reasoning, be worth more to focused owners, THORN EMI would also stand a better chance of selling them for more than they were worth to it. In reality, of course, the market for specific businesses at any particular time is limited and, as the economists would put it, information about them is imperfect. As a result, businesses are regularly sold for greater or lesser sums than subsequent events show them to be worth. However, if the superiority of concentration and focus over diversity and balance is real, one would expect to find a general tendency for businesses to perform better, under focused owners, than they had done as part of a diversified conglomerate.

Of the businesses that THORN EMI sold, a number went to focused buyers who were dominant in the particular industry. The sale of Ferguson to Thomson and the major domestic appliance business to Electrolux fall into this category. For those businesses, it is impossible to compare their performance, past and present, in any meaningful way, since they no longer exist as distinct entities, having been integrated into the buyer's business. Of course, factors other than change of ownership may also have had a significant impact on subsequent performance. In the case of Ferguson, where it appears that little of the original business now remains, the competitive forces in the global consumer electronics industry must have swamped any benefit it might have derived from being part of a focused group.

There is one category of disposals, however, where a more meaningful comparison is possible. A number of THORN EMI's businesses were sold to their management, with financial backing from venture capitalists and banks. The relatively easy availability of venture capital to finance management buyouts, starting in the early 1980s, coincided with the period when THORN EMI's disposal programme was at its most active. A number of these management buyouts have since been sold on to other corporate owners, in some instances to conglomerates, indicating that belief in diversification is by no means dead. But some have been floated on the stock market and it is these which provide an opportunity to consider whether focused management has improved performance. They also provide a test of another feature of current thinking, which is that business performance is improved where managers have a considerable personal stake in their businesses.

Two notable buyouts from THORN EMI which have subsequently been successfully floated on the London Stock Exchange are Kenwood Appliances plc and TLG plc, the holding company of the Thorn Lighting fixtures and fittings business. The latter has a relatively short history as an independent business: it was sold by THORN EMI in August 1993 and floated in November 1994. Kenwood Appliances has a longer track record as an independent company: it was bought out in September 1989 and floated in June 1992. It is also a particularly interesting example of trends in the management of manufacturing industry in Britain since the Second World War and their influence on its international competitiveness.

Kenwood, it will be recalled, became part of Thorn in 1968 when it was acquired by Sir Jules Thorn. Compared with most British manufacturers of the 1950s and 1960s, its founder, Kenneth Wood, was an exceptional individual. He had an understanding of the importance of design and of international marketing decades ahead of his contemporaries. Having founded the business in 1947, his first product was an electric toaster. This was closely followed by the electric mixer which, further refined as the Kenwood Chef, has sold in many millions around the world as a multi-purpose kitchen appliance and has almost become a generic name for food preparation equipment. The design and engineering of the Kenwood Chef, which reflected Kenneth Wood's interest in product design, was a major reason for its success.

He also saw the importance of establishing the Kenwood Chef as an international product at a time when it had no competitors. With a far-sightedness that puts many larger British manufacturers, including Thorn, to shame, by the late 1960s he had established companies in every major European country and had associates as far afield as Mexico and Argentina. He is an exception to the rule among the majority of British manufacturers of consumer durable goods, who tended to stick to the domestic market and not to exploit the advantage of an early lead in establishing an international business.

Thorn's offer for the business valued it at £11.5 million. It was a generous price, representing a premium of nearly 80 per cent over the market price and a price-to-earnings multiple of twenty-nine. It was made affordable by the fact that it was paid for in Thorn shares, which themselves commanded a price-to-earnings multiple of thirty. Kenwood was absorbed into Thorn's major domestic appliance business, which made cookers, refrigerators and domestic heating appliances. The sales forces and administrative systems of the two businesses in the UK were merged. Kenwood's international network of companies was given the role of marketing Thorn's other domestic appliances. Kenneth Wood himself stayed on as a consultant for a few years, but no longer had an executive role. Little of his internationalism or interest in design seems to have been transferred over to Thorn.

Thorn's major domestic appliance business was founded on selling generally unimaginative products to the UK consumer through the showrooms of the gas and electric utilities. Kenwood, with its tradition of innovative design and international marketing, sat uneasily alongside its culture and, over the years, seems to have lost much of its original flair. Product innovation was not highly regarded by the conservative gas and electricity utilities.

Few of the larger domestic appliance products had been designed in a way that made them suitable for selling in international markets. The idea of establishing and maintaining an international brand through a worldwide network of businesses was alien to the thinking of the major domestic appliance business, where international business was synonymous with exporting. In the absence of any strategic imperative, the approach to Kenwood's international businesses became narrowly financial: international companies were treated as export outlets for the UK factory and judged on the contribution they could earn. As a result, some were eliminated – most importantly, one in Germany – and the international network was contracted. During the same period, Kenwood's major competitor, Moulinex, was expanding its international operations and would, in time, come to dominate the market.

In 1985, Kenwood was separated from the major domestic appliance business and re-established as a separate company under a new and remarkably young chief executive, Tim Parker. He brought in a new management team and set about changing the culture of the business. Costs were reduced, over 200 jobs were eliminated, and investment in new manufacturing equipment was increased. In two significant ways, he went back to the original Kenwood culture. Product design and innovation were once again given a high priority and a host of new product lines were added. And the attitude of being a UK-based exporter, inherited from the major domestic appliance business, was replaced with that of being an integrated, international marketing organisation.

Although the major domestic appliance business was sold to Electrolux in 1987, Kenwood was retained by THORN EMI as a niche business of some interest. Following Colin Southgate's strategic review in 1988, however, it was decided to sell Kenwood. It did not fit the criterion of being a business with a profit potential in excess of £50 million and, though significant capital expenditure had been made on it, THORN EMI was in no mood to support the sort of expansion plans that Tim Parker had in mind.

Although by 1989 Kenwood was a sounder business than it had been five years earlier, it still had a patchy financial record, affected by the restructuring after its separation from the major domestic appliance business.

£ million	1985/86	1986/87	1987/88	1988/89
Sales	52.3	58.7	63.1	62.6
Profit (a)	1.6	4.1	0.7	4.1
RoS	3.1%	7.0%	1.1%	6.5%

(a) Before interest and tax

Commenting on the decision to sell the business in 1989, Tim Parker says: 'The actions we had taken needed three years to show results. It was fortuitous [from the buyout's viewpoint] that THORN EMI decided to sell early.' Parker's management buy-out team, which was backed by the venture capital group Candover, offered a significantly higher price than the other bidders for the business. The deal involved a payment of around £56 million, together with an 8 per cent holding for THORN EMI in the buyout company. It appeared to value the business fully on the basis of its past record, since it represented a price of around twenty-five times the previous year's profits, adjusted for tax. With heavy borrowings taken on to finance the buyout, it was clear that the business would have to improve its performance rapidly if it was to survive.

Within hours of completing the buyout, Parker removed a whole tranche of middle management from the company – eighty people out of around 200 in administrative jobs, saving perhaps £1.5 million in salaries and wages. News of this caused jaws to drop in THORN EMI's head office – if this was a sensible move, why hadn't he done it under THORN EMI ownership? Parker's explanation is instructive:

> It was a very risky move as no one was certain what the effect would be. But we were prepared to take risks we wouldn't have taken without the MBO. There is definitely a 'buyout effect' on management. It was a once in a lifetime chance and we were a youthful team who could afford to take risks.

Parker's explanation points to one of the major problems of managing rapidly changing businesses within a conglomerate. It is a similar problem to the one that Jim Fifield tackled in EMI Music when he gave his people the 'freedom to fail'. The natural style and pace of management in a conglomerate is to maintain stability. Radical decisions need to be convincingly justified to people far removed from the details of the business before they are taken. The risk of being wrong vastly exceeds the reward for being right. Where industries are changing rapidly, this puts businesses run by conglomerates at a significant disadvantage. The asymmetry between risk and reward causes their managers to be less adventurous in their decision-taking. The result, as Jim Fifield pointed out in his letter to the staff, is to guarantee mediocrity.

Despite the cost-cutting undertaken at the outset, Kenwood's first year as an independent company was extremely tough. In 1990, interest rates rose to 15 per cent and, with the high level of borrowings taken on for the buyout, the company just managed to keep its head above water. In the sixteen-month period to the end of September 1990, operating profits of £8.1 million barely covered interest charges of £7.4 million. Candover had to subscribe for additional capital in the company to avoid the risk of it breaching its covenants with its banks.

However, Kenwood survived this early crisis and, by 1992, its financial situation was much sounder. By 1993, Kenwood had made enough progress to justify floating it on the London Stock Exchange, valuing the business at £105 million. In 1994, other elements of Parker's strategy were put into place with acquisitions in the UK, Italy and China, which widened the product range and increased the international presence. The following table shows the development of the business since the buyout:

£ million	1989/90	1990/91	1991/92	1992/93	1993/94	1994/95
Sales	66.7	76.0	92.1	101.6	120.4	142.4
Profit (a)	4.2	6.6	9.5	10.4	12.3	14.8
RoS	6.3%	8.7%	10.3%	10.2%	10.2%	10.4%

(a) Before interest and tax

There is no doubt that the performance of Kenwood has been much better as an independent company than as part of THORN EMI. It has been able to make the strategic moves and implement the radical changes necessary to survive and prosper in its competitive and rapidly changing industry. Since this was achieved by essentially the same people who were running the business for THORN EMI, it suggests that much of the reason for the transformation lies in the change from being a small part of a diversified conglomerate to being an independent, focused company in which the management had a considerable personal stake.

Thorn Lighting, which was bought out from THORN EMI in August 1993, has had a less radical change in performance as an independent company, but has made steady progress. Its management is essentially unchanged and the strategy it is following was formulated by Hamish Bryce, its chief executive, during its ownership by THORN EMI. The most significant recent decision in the history of the business, to sell the lamp manufacturing activities, was taken and implemented while it was part of THORN EMI. Hamish Bryce believes that the main change has been a psychological one: the expression of confidence in the future of the business by new investors putting money into it. In November 1994, the holding company of Thorn Lighting was floated on the stock market, valuing the business at £205 million.

Not all buyouts from THORN EMI have been unqualified successes. Owner management and focus cannot necessarily overcome adverse changes in the industrial environment or fundamental strategic disadvantage. For example, THORN EMI's computer software and services business was sold in 1991 to a management buy-out team, backed by the venture capital group CINVen, for around £70 million, together with a 20 per cent shareholding in the buy-out company, Data Sciences. In the year prior to their sale, these businesses had made pre-tax profits of £6.2 million on sales of £117 million, but their subsequent performance was considerably worse, affected by a sharp downturn in the markets they served. At one point, Data Sciences' shares were almost worthless, but the company has since staged a recovery and its profits in the year to 30 September 1995 were reported as £6.1 million, on sales of £106 million. It has recently been sold to IBM for £95 million, a modest increase on the price paid to THORN EMI five years earlier.

It would be misleading to give the impression that sales to focused owners or buyouts were universal panaceas for THORN EMI's former businesses. Some, such as Ferguson, were swallowed up in the restructuring of their industries and simply disappeared. Others, particularly smaller ones sold in buyouts, improved their performance in the short term, but were faced

with the same strategic issues that had confronted them during
their ownership by THORN EMI in the long term. The general
trend, however, among the smaller businesses sold by THORN
EMI to more focused owners has been towards a significant
improvement in performance, paralleling the improvement in
performance of the businesses retained by it. This does provide
circumstantial evidence to suggest that focus and concentration
have indeed improved performance. We have seen some of
the reasons why this may be so. The problems of managing
businesses in complex, rapidly changing industries is one that
the diversified conglomerate is particularly bad at. Conglomerates
were suited to the environment of steady growth which prevailed
for the first three decades after the Second World War. Their
main skill – rigorous financial control – was well employed in
getting incremental improvements in medium-sized businesses
in stable industries, little troubled by technological change or
new competitors. Superior financial management combined with
adroit deal-making, enabling businesses to be bought cheaply,
proved to be a winning formula for many conglomerates for a
considerable period.

It is no coincidence that the decline in popularity of the
conglomerate with investors was preceded by the emergence,
in most industries, of new, international competitors and rapid
technological change. The virtues sought by the conglomerate
– steady, incremental improvement; balance between a number
of industries; avoidance of risk – became handicaps in this new
environment. To stay competitive, it was not enough to do just
a little better what had been done before. Entirely new ways of
designing, making and selling things had to be devised. Change
was not incremental but revolutionary. The idea of balance did
not sit well with the requirement to back a particular business
to the point where it dominated its market, or else to get out of
it. Avoidance of risk often meant steady and certain decline. The
uniform criteria applied by conglomerates across their business
portfolio handicapped businesses with unusual characteristics,
particularly in areas such as entertainment and high technology.

By the late 1970s, these conditions applied to most of the
industries in which THORN EMI was present. It is significant,
however, that the majority of the strategic moves made by the

company in the late 1970s and early 1980s were not in support of any of its existing businesses, but rather in new areas. It was only when THORN EMI had decided that its future lay in a very small number of businesses that it had the confidence to make the radical moves required to make a success of them. By the same token, it was only after many of its businesses were sold that they were able to make the radical changes required to succeed in their own industries.

Thorn's earlier history, in Sir Jules's heyday, suggests a more focused approach and a clearer understanding of the value of dominating markets, albeit within a national rather than global arena. Until the late 1960s, Thorn was essentially in two industries – lighting and consumer electronics, with domestic appliances providing a smaller, third leg. All of Sir Jules's major deals – up to and including the acquisition of Radio Rentals – were done in order to increase the company's domination in the lighting and consumer electronics market. It was in the late 1960s that the idea of balancing the company's exposure to the UK consumer prompted diversification into other areas. At the same time, of course, its two major businesses found they were no longer big fish in a national pool but, increasingly, small fish in a global pool. The policies that had led to success in the home market – control of distribution channels, proliferation of brands, sparse investment in technology and manufacturing facilities – were little help in the larger arena.

EMI had been, predominantly, a music company until the Second World War. Its role in the development of television, and in military electronics during the war, took it into new areas after the war. The idea of 'balance' appears to have played an important role in the thinking of successive post-war chairmen of the company; indeed, it appears to have been the dominant theme in its strategy. Arguably, this 'balance' was achieved at the expense of sacrificing opportunities in its original music business and also failing to develop opportunities available to its military electronics and television equipment businesses immediately after the war.

Diversity and 'balance' continued to dominate the strategy of THORN EMI in the early 1980s, again at the expense of building a strong competitive position in one or two of its existing businesses. By then, however, the global business environment had altered to the point where notions of diversity and balance were positively damaging for the company. In a world of global industries, only the very largest companies in the world can afford both to prosper in the industries they operate in and aspire to diversity and balance. It is no coincidence that the only conglomerate to emerge from the 1980s with its reputation enhanced is the US giant General Electric, one of very few that fits into this category since each of its businesses is number one or number two in its industry, on a worldwide basis.

18

Demerger

The probability that demerger into two or more businesses was a likely conclusion to the process of focusing was recognised by Colin Southgate by 1989. Internally, the core of the company was seen as consisting of Music, Rental and the smaller HMV music retailing business. Although the 1990 annual report gave considerable prominence to Lighting, as well as to Music and Rental, the growing problems in the lamp manufacturing industry, referred to in Chapter 14, had led to a change in perception about its long-term future. THORN EMI still had many of its technology-related businesses – in defence electronics, computer software and security – but it was recognised that these would, in time, be sold. The decision to put the defence electronics business up for sale had actually been announced in June 1989.

While demerger was recognised as a long-term probability, much work still remained to be done before it could be seriously considered. Music was well on the road to recovery, but it needed time and more investment to be strong enough to establish itself as an independent company. Rental was still in the process of finding a future role for the UK rental business, whose traditional market was in decline. The HMV chain was in the early stages of transforming itself from a largely UK-based business to an international one. The centre of THORN EMI still had a role, for some time, in assisting these businesses to realise their ambitions, although it was recognised that once these ambitions were achieved there might be no further role for the centre. The other crucial role for the centre, in the short-term, was to sell the remaining businesses, and this task was to be more difficult, and take longer, than was anticipated in 1989.

In the summer of 1989, Colin Southgate was considering two possible routes for moving forward in what he regarded as the third phase in the recovery of THORN EMI. The first, which he labelled, with his customary directness, 'Mr Plod', was essentially a continuation of the strategy that had been followed to date: more investment in Music to strengthen its competitive position; redefining the strategy for Rental and supporting it with investment; sale of the defence electronics business; and continuing development of the smaller computer software, security and HMV businesses, almost as an investment trust. At some point in the future, this route would have led to a demerger into two or three businesses: a music company, which might by then have expanded into related areas of entertainment; a rental and financial services company; and, possibly, a high-growth investment trust.

The alternative route was similar as far as Music and Rental were concerned, but sought to take advantage of an anomaly that had developed in the share price of another diversified electronics company, Racal, which also, incidentally, highlighted the stock market's growing disenchantment with diversified companies. During the 1980s, Racal had diversified beyond its original business in military communications equipment by acquiring the radar business of Decca and the Chubb fire and security business. Its most important diversification, however, was in the cellular telephony business, where it set up, in association with a small American partner, the Vodafone network, one of the two cellular phone networks in the UK at the time. The cellular phone market had enjoyed explosive growth in the 1980s, not all of which was reflected in the share price of Racal. In an effort to correct the stock market's perception of its value, Racal had, in October 1988, floated shares in the cellular phone subsidiary Racal Telecommunications, on the stock market, while retaining an 80 per cent shareholding in the business. Racal's intention, presumably, was that once the stock market was able properly to value the shares in Racal Telecommunications that had been floated, it would apply a similar valuation to the 80 per cent of the shares that Racal still owned, thereby increasing the value of Racal itself.

The stock market's response was, on the face of it, anomalous. The shares in Racal Telecommunications rose nearly threefold by the summer of 1989, and its parent's wish to see it properly valued by the stock market was fulfilled. But little of the revaluation appeared in the shares of Racal. By the summer of 1989, Racal's holding in Racal Telecommunications was worth £2.9 billion, but Racal itself was valued at only £2.8 billion. The implication was that the rest of Racal, a collection of businesses with profits of over £100 million and net assets of over £600 million, excluding its holding in Racal Telecommunications, operating in defence electronics, security and communications, had no value at all, in fact was valued at minus £100 million. This was as clear a case of the discount applied to a conglomerate by the stock market as any.

The opportunity that THORN EMI sought to exploit was to acquire the rump of Racal, in the process floating its 80 per cent shareholding in Racal Telecommunications on the stock market, and then to combine its own defence electronics, security and computer software businesses with those of Racal. This combined business would then be demerged. It seemed to be an elegant solution to the problems faced by both Racal and THORN EMI. The proposal was put to Racal by THORN EMI, but failed to generate any enthusiasm. The idea of trying to push ahead without the co-operation of Racal's management was examined by THORN EMI's advisers, but there were technical problems that would have made it extremely difficult to complete the transaction if it had been opposed by even a small minority of Racal shareholders. In any event, the THORN EMI board was reluctant to get involved in a complex and high-profile hostile bid. The idea was therefore dropped by THORN EMI but, interestingly, Racal itself demerged Racal Telecommunications (now Vodafone Group plc) in 1991 and also demerged its Chubb security business in 1994.

Demergers, now very much *à la mode*, had begun to achieve prominence by the late 1980s in the UK. The British Government had passed legislation in 1980 in order to simplify the tax and legal mechanics of demergers, but much of British industry, at the time, was still bent on diversification rather than on focus. An episode that helped to raise the profile of demergers, and which also introduced a new word into business vocabulary, was the attempt by Sir James Goldsmith and his band of wealthy adventurers to 'unbundle' BAT, the tobacco, retailing and financial services conglomerate. Sir James's little group, which operated as a consortium by the name of Hoylake, received a generally unfavourable reception in the press and was, of course, fiercely resisted by the management of BAT. The participants in Hoylake were dubbed 'an ad hoc troupe of financiers', suggesting a footloose band of slightly disreputable characters willing to turn their hand to anything that might generate a quick profit. Sir James himself sought to draw a tenuous distinction between the asset-stripping philosophy of the 1970s and his concept of unbundling. He explained that asset-stripping involved companies that were 'worth more dead than alive'. Unbundling, he claimed, was the opposite. It was 'taking companies which are being stifled by bureaucracy and liberating them'.

The argument underlying unbundling, the view that diversified conglomerates tended to reduce rather than increase the value of their businesses, was accepted by many UK institutional investors by the late 1980s. As this book has attempted to show, however, the reasons for this characteristic of conglomerates are considerably more complex than the effects of stifling corporate bureaucracies. What the investors in BAT were not prepared to accept was that any increase in value from unbundling should be shared with a band of outsiders, newly arrived on the scene, and it was this which led to the failure of Hoylake's bid. However, Sir James's enterprise did bring home to managements of large, diversified British companies both the intellectual arguments for focus and their companies' vulnerability to other 'ad hoc troupes of financiers' able and willing to take on the job of unbundling, if they did not do the job themselves. BAT itself went on to demerge its retailing interests in 1990.

The decision, in 1988, by the chemicals and textiles group Courtaulds to demerge into two separate companies was an influential example for many British company directors, particularly as it was made without the threat of a predator. Here was a successful and respected company whose board had decided that they, as a group, were uncomfortable with directing two very different businesses. In 1992, ICI, one of Britain's largest companies, also decided to demerge, although its decision was partly motivated by the unwelcome attentions of that arch conglomerator Lord Hanson.

THORN EMI made considerable progress in building up its core music and rental businesses in the early 1990s, and continued the steady disposal of many of its peripheral interests. The one business it was not able to sell in accordance with its timetable was its defence electronics business, THORN EMI Electronics. As we have seen, the tearing down of the Berlin Wall and the collapse of the Soviet Union made the task of selling a company in the defence industry considerably more difficult. Arguably, THORN EMI clung to an unrealistic valuation of the business in the changed environment. The price recommended to the board as realistic, around £250 million, would have represented a price-to-earnings multiple of fourteen. Such a figure would have been reasonable had the defence industries' growth merely slowed down. In fact, defence expenditure was cut back very severely, and the market was contracting. THORN EMI Electronics' problems were made worse by the fact that it had started to lose money on many of its contracts. In the mid-1980s, in an attempt to bring greater efficiency and reduce waste in the production of defence equipment, the Ministry of Defence had moved away from its previous cosy system of awarding 'cost plus' contracts, where the risks were largely borne by the taxpayer, to fixed price contracts awarded by competitive bidding. The culture of most defence contractors, however, retained elements of the 'cost plus' era. By the early 1990s, fixed price contracts taken on in the 1980s were coming to completion, and THORN EMI Electronics, along with other defence contractors, was having to recognise that it would make considerable losses on many of these contracts.

In 1991, the idea of an early sale of THORN EMI Electronics was shelved and the business was grouped with THORN EMI's security interests and the Central Research Laboratories to form an industrial and technology-based conglomerate called Thorn Security and Electronics (TSE). The other remaining technology-related interest, in computer software, was sold in a management buyout in the summer of 1991. Soon after, THORN EMI acquired Virgin Music, thus fulfilling one of Colin Southgate's major objectives. This once again raised the urgency of disentangling THORN EMI from everything but its central core of music, music retailing and rental. The arrival of a new finance director, Simon Duffy, previously with Guinness, gave added impetus to getting on with the process. In 1992, TSE and the remains of Thorn Lighting were once again up for sale. This time, it seemed as if THORN EMI's efforts would be blessed with greater success. It received an offer from the industrial conglomerate Williams Holdings, which valued the combined businesses at around £400 million. While this was less than the value THORN EMI might have set on them a few years earlier, it was still a good deal, from its point of view, in the changed circumstances. The deal came very close to being completed in the summer of 1992 – the two sides actually initialled a contract – but it was not to be. It was conditional on Williams raising funding for the purchase on the stock market and it seems clear that Williams was not able to convince the City that it should swim against the prevailing corporate tide by further diversification. In fact, Williams' interest in the defence electronics business had always seemed odd. Although it had flirted with activities on the periphery of the defence business, it had not had any involvement in mainstream, high-technology military equipment. For it to enter the arena at a time when the market was shrinking, and long-established players were seeking to get out, appeared to be a curious move. It is interesting to note that, following its encounter with THORN EMI, Williams itself changed to a more focused strategy, selling off a number of its businesses and concentrating on a few. It bought THORN EMI's fire appliance business and has since gone on to build up a substantial global presence in the fire protection market.

The failure of the deal with Williams set back THORN EMI's plan to be rid of all its non-core interests by 1994. The lighting business was eventually sold to an investment group, Investcorp, in 1993, and the security business was sold in a management buyout in 1994, with THORN EMI retaining a 40 per cent holding. The defence electronics business was eventually sold in 1995, the majority of it going in two separate transactions: one with the French group Thomson-CSF and the other with Racal Electronics. What it received for the defence businesses in total was, however, considerably less than the figure of £250 million it had hoped for in 1989. THORN EMI still retains the Central Research Laboratories, the birthplace of a significant portion of Britain's technological achievements in the twentieth century.

However, CRL works almost entirely for customers outside THORN EMI.

As the frustratingly slow final stages of the disposal process ground on through 1993 and 1994, Sir Colin, as he now was, and Simon Duffy increasingly turned their thoughts to the long-term rationale for THORN EMI continuing to exist as one business. The core businesses – Music, Rental and HMV – had little in common beyond a consumer orientation. They shared no core skills and resources and had very different cultures and styles. Indeed, it was a matter of some satisfaction that each of the businesses had developed skills and a culture appropriate to its own industry, without regard to some over-arching corporate culture or set of values. That characteristic lay at the heart of the principle of focusing on, and excelling in, a particular industry. Once each business had attained a sufficient size, maturity and power in relation to its competitors, was there any reason for it to remain under a THORN EMI corporate umbrella?

One possible justification for a continuing role for THORN EMI could be found if, for some reason, there was a case for building yet another business alongside the three core businesses. Given the company's recent history of getting out of a range of businesses, this possibility was viewed with some scepticism. Nevertheless, it was a question that had to be explored. It was unlikely that diversification into an area unrelated to its existing businesses would make any sense, but was there, for example, a case for entering another area of the entertainment industry which might be related, in some fashion, to music? Most of EMI Music's competitors had interests in other entertainment or media industries: Time Warner in book and magazine publishing, films and television, satellite and cable channels and cable networks; Sony in films and television and entertainment hardware; MCA in films, venue management and book publishing; and PolyGram in films and television.

THORN EMI still had an interest in television through its ownership of Thames Television. The stake in Thames went back to the acquisition of ABPC by EMI in the 1960s, at a time when EMI's management was attempting to build a diversified entertainment conglomerate. For many years, Thames, which owned the commercial television franchise to broadcast to the London area during weekdays, had been jointly owned by THORN EMI and the industrial services conglomerate, BET. In 1986, in the early days of Sir Colin's restructuring of THORN EMI, an agreement had been reached to sell Thames to Carlton Communications, then a mini-conglomerate. This deal had been blocked by the IBA, which regulated commercial television broadcasting at the time. THORN EMI and BET had then floated Thames Television on the London Stock Exchange, reducing their shareholding in the process to 28 per cent each.

In 1991, existing commercial television franchises came to an end and new franchises were offered in an auction, under new rules devised by the Thatcher government, which ensured that commercial television was no longer the licence to print money which it had once been described as being. It was known that Carlton, still smarting from its rejection by the IBA, was bent on getting the London franchise itself and would put in a very competitive bid. Reluctant to back Thames in a tough bidding process, and taking advantage of a more liberal regime on the ownership of commercial broadcasting companies, BET decided to put its stake in Thames up for sale in 1990. BET persuaded THORN EMI that higher offers would be received if their shareholdings were marketed together as offering majority ownership of Thames. The offers they received for their shareholdings were lower than THORN EMI's expectations and it decided that it would be a better bet to back Thames through the auction. THORN EMI bought BET's stake, thus becoming the majority shareholder. As stock market rules required it to make an offer to the other shareholders in Thames, THORN EMI's shareholding actually increased to approximately 59 per cent, the additional 31 per cent having cost it around £18 million.

In the event, the bidding process for the London franchise was every bit as competitive as had been expected and was won by Carlton for a price well in excess of what Thames itself could offer, taking account of its other commitments. Sir Colin regrets not having encouraged Thames' management to be more aggressive in their bid and, in particular, for not having pushed harder for Thames to bid for the London weekend franchise as well. This was won by the incumbent, LWT, on favourable terms.

The loss of the franchise was a major blow to Thames, which had to be extensively downsized to fit its new role as an independent television production company. At a stroke, Thames' profits fell well below the threshold that THORN EMI had established as a criterion for retaining businesses in the group, raising the question of whether, in this new role, it could become a vehicle for broadening THORN EMI's interests in entertainment beyond music. Independent television production, however, was felt to be a business with a number of unfavourable characteristics in the US and the UK, and there was little interest in expanding into that area. The alternative television-related opportunities, such as cable and satellite television and a re-entry into terrestrial television by acquisition, were also ruled out, because of the scale of investment required to achieve a leading position; because of media ownership rules; and because there was no discernible synergy between music and television production and broadcasting. As a result of these considerations, the company decided to sell its stake in Thames to Pearson plc in 1993, for £58 million. In spite of the loss of the London weekday franchise, THORN EMI was able to realise a profit of £34 million from the sale.

A related entertainment area which had tempted many of EMI Music's competitors was feature film production. PolyGram, for example, had entered the film production business partly because it felt there were some genuine advantages in being in both filmed and audio entertainment, including overlaps in distribution and, in the future , in technology; the growing interest of music superstars in appearing in films; and the increasingly visual nature of the music business. Given THORN EMI's own unsatisfactory past involvement in film production and distribution, and the fact that Sir Colin himself had been instrumental in extracting the company from the film business, it would take an extremely persuasive case for him to consider re-entering it.

In fact, an examination of the feature film industry, a decade after THORN EMI pulled out of it, suggests that the characteristics that made it unattractive then are, if anything, even more pronounced now. The cost of making and marketing feature films has increased considerably faster than inflation: figures from the Motion Picture Association of America show that, for Hollywood films, production and marketing costs have risen at over 10 per cent per annum in the decade to 1995. While production and marketing costs have also risen in the music industry, there the increase has been accompanied by an even faster rate of increase in revenue, together with efficiencies in distribution. As a result, music industry margins have been on a rising trend. In contrast, film industry revenues have not increased as fast and film industry margins have shrunk over the last decade. Moreover, there is an inherent difference in the nature of the investment in artistic talent in the film and music industries. While both music and film companies are concerned with exploiting artistic talent, the relationship between artist and company is significantly different. In the music industry, the company has a developing, and usually long-term, relationship with the artist, so that the artist is an asset with a value beyond his or her back catalogue. That is a situation that does not exist in the film industry, where stars generally have no affiliation to a particular studio. Finally, the most financially unattractive feature of the film industry, the fact that film production companies must place a small number of very large bets each year, remains as prominent as ever. Again, it compares unfavourably in this respect with music: whereas a large music company typically releases hundreds of new records each year, with costs of production and marketing averaging a few hundred thousand dollars or less per release, even a large Hollywood film production company (or 'major') cannot release more than, say, two dozen films a year, at an average cost of tens of millions of dollars per film. Combine that with a lower average return on film production, and the contrast between music and film industry economics is apparent.

Given this catalogue of unfavourable characteristics, and the fact that EMI Music did not feel itself to be disadvantaged by not being associated with a major film studio, Sir Colin was never really tempted to consider re-entering the film business. One industry that did, however, catch THORN EMI's eye was US book publishing. Book publishing was regarded, within THORN EMI, as the most financially attractive of related industries. It shared some of the business characteristics of the music industry: a large number of relatively small creative transactions, allowing the risk to be spread; the leading role of Anglo–American material; the importance of back catalogue and its skilful management; and the prominence of heavily marketed popular blockbusters. It was, of course, recognised that the creative cultures of music and book publishing were worlds apart. Nevertheless, the interest in book publishing was serious enough to encourage the company at least to fly a kite at a meeting with investors. However, the company's target acquisition did not become available and so the idea moved somewhat into the background.

THORN EMI's refusal to be enticed into related diversifications is an indication both of the history of focusing down and of the rigour applied to thinking about the future by Sir Colin and his colleagues. Much diversification within the entertainment industry has been based on apparent similarities or relationships: the apparent similarities between filmed and musical entertainment or the relationship between entertainment production and distribution or between entertainment hardware and software. It was, of course, reasoning based on such relationships which was used to justify the acquisition of EMI by Thorn. Lessons learned over the decade and a half since then had forced THORN EMI to look much more rigorously, and more sceptically, at the real advantage that such similarities and relationships bring. The conclusion that it arrived at each time was that they do not form a basis for the company to diversify; that there is no such thing as the entertainment industry, only a range of products and services on which consumers spend money to entertain themselves; and that if its shareholders wished to broaden their exposure to the entertainment sector, they were better off doing it directly rather than through THORN EMI.

This conclusion led naturally to a questioning of the continued existence of THORN EMI as one company, once its peripheral businesses had been sold and its core businesses were sufficiently mature to manage their own futures. The question of demerging the group was first seriously discussed by the board in 1994, but it was decided that work still remained to be done by the THORN EMI corporate centre. By 1995, the last major disposal, of the defence electronics activities, had been completed and the music and rental businesses, now given their own identities as EMI and Thorn respectively, had been further strengthened. The managements of both major businesses were keen to demerge: EMI's to enhance the company's profile in the global music industry and to highlight its superior financial performance, and Thorn Group's to emerge from the shadow of its more glamorous cousins in the music business and to carve out its own future. There were few financial synergies to be gained from keeping THORN EMI together. The loss of some tax advantages was more than offset by the business advantages. Simon Duffy, the finance director of THORN EMI, was a firm believer in the logic of demerger. He believed that the group had reached a point where the corporate centre had ceased to add any value.

Although cold logic pointed in the direction of demerger, it was not an easy decision for Sir Colin personally. He had been running THORN EMI for a decade, had led it through one of the most far-reaching corporate restructurings of the 1980s, and had taken it from near-disaster to considerable success. He felt a personal identification with the company, stronger than any of its leaders since Sir Jules Thorn. Demerger would certainly leave EMI much more exposed to the threat of a takeover, which might once again remove the name of EMI from the list of independent companies. That was certainly the expectation of the stock market after the decision to demerge was announced. It is to Sir Colin's credit that the logic of what was best for the businesses and the shareholders ruled over such considerations.

EMI's forebears, The Gramophone Company and The Columbia Gramophone Company, started in business nearly one hundred years ago, in 1897. The Electric Lamp Service Company, which became Thorn Electrical Industries, was founded almost seventy years ago. Like most new companies, they were founded on specialist skills and knowledge: in the case of EMI, skills in sound recording and reproduction and, in the case of Thorn, knowledge of the electric lamp market. As they grew, both companies became more diverse. In the case of EMI, this was initially a result of applying its technical skills to produce products for other markets. For Thorn, it was a result of applying its skills in manufacturing management into other markets. With both companies, diversity mushroomed after the Second World War and particularly in the 1960s. Interestingly, this period also saw the rise of the professionally trained manager and, with him, the idea that the application of professional management techniques, particularly in finance and accounting, would give companies a competitive advantage across a broad range of industries. That, indeed, was true for a period, while these skills were in short supply and, therefore, valuable. Applying their management skills across a range of industries proved to be a profitable route to growth for a number of companies.

Diversification gained further intellectual respectability in the 1970s with the concept of related diversification – the idea that there was some advantage in being in a range of industries whose products or markets were related in some way. It was this idea which dominated THORN EMI's strategy in the early 1980s and continues to appeal to many companies, particularly in the media and entertainment industries. One manifestation of this is the hardware/software relationship, in which THORN EMI was an early believer. However, given the very different characteristics of the hardware and software businesses, and the difficulty of managing the interface between them, there seem to be few situations in which being in both is an advantage.

One such situation, as demonstrated by the early history of EMI, is when a completely new market is being created. In the early days of recorded music, it was not just advantageous but essential to sell both records and record players. As the market matured, however, EMI found that it was not particularly good at making gramophones and it did not need to make them in order to sell music. Later moves to marry hardware and software to advantage, by THORN EMI and by some of the major Japanese electronics companies, for example, have been failures. The early years of the computer industry were also marked by a successful combination of hardware and software. Once the barriers of proprietary hardware and operating systems were removed, however, the benefits of being in both hardware and software vanished.

By the 1980s, increasing volatility, rapid social and technological change, transfer of power from producers to consumers, all made the task of management much more demanding. Managing across a diverse range of businesses, whether related or unrelated, added another layer of complexity to all the others that had to be coped with, while offering little benefit. At the same time, the generalist skills, which diversified companies had deployed so successfully in earlier decades, were now widely available and hence conveyed little competitive advantage. They were taken for granted by most businesses. It was the specialist skills – specialised knowledge of particular markets, customers or technologies – which now gave companies a competitive edge. The balance of advantage had tilted back, from the generalist to the specialist, from diversity to focus. The histories of both Thorn and EMI have followed the complete cycle, from focus to diversity and back to focus.

APPENDIX I

List of Interviewees

The following individuals were interviewed in the course of research for this book. Their assistance is gratefully acknowledged. The designations given against each name are intended to give an indication of the main areas on which they were interviewed, bearing in mind that many held a number of positions in the organisation.

Charles Ashcroft	Partner, Rowe & Maw
Sir William Barlow	Director, THORN EMI, 1980–89; Chairman, Engineering Group, 1980–84
Steve Bates	EMI CAT Scanner development team
Hamish Bryce	Chief Executive, Thorn Lighting (later TLG plc), since 1986
William Cavendish	Personal Assistant to Sir Joseph Lockwood, 1964–74
Robin Charlton	Company Secretary, THORN EMI, since 1982
Ian Christians	Director of Strategic Development, THORN EMI, 1986–88
Simon Duffy	Group Finance Director, THORN EMI, since 1992
Claire Enders	Manager, Corporate Development, THORN EMI, since 1992
James Fifield	President & Chief Executive, EMI Music, since 1989; President & COO, EMI Music, 1988–89

Len Govier	Various management roles in Thorn, 1949–65; later with THORN EMI Home Electronics
Dr Ken Gray	Director of Technology, THORN EMI
Alan Harford	Director of Human Resources, EMI Music, 1979–89
Peter Hayman	Treasurer, EMI, 1976–80; Director of Special Projects, THORN EMI, 1987–89
Leslie Hill	Chief Executive, Thorn Lighting, 1973–85
Sir Godfrey Hounsfield	Inventor of EMI CAT scanner
Dr Richard Hurst	Head of Patents, THORN EMI, 1981–95
Alan Hurst-Brown	Partner, Rowe & Pitman
John Kuipers	Director, EMI, 1967–79
Peter Laister	Chairman, THORN EMI, 1984–85; Managing Director, 1979–83
Guy Marriott	Senior Vice President and General Counsel, EMI Music, since 1990
Nigel Graham Maw	Senior Partner, Rowe & Maw, 1976–93
Tom Mayer	Chairman, THORN EMI Electronics, 1981–90
Stuart McAllister	Chief Executive, HMV Group, since 1986; Human Resources Director, THORN EMI Home Electronics, 1984–86
Bhaskar Menon	Chairman, EMI Music, 1978–90
Harold Mourgue	Finance Director, THORN EMI, 1970–85; Vice Chairman 1984–88
Robert Nellist	Finance Director, THORN EMI, 1985–89
Richard 'Dickie' Norman	Chief Executive, Thorn Consumer Electronics, 1972–85
Jean Orr	Personal Assistant to Sir Jules Thorn

Tim Parker	Chief Executive, Kenwood (later Kenwood Appliances plc), 1985–95
Sir John Read	Chief Executive (later Chairman), EMI, 1969–79
John Richards	Director of Personnel, THORN EMI, 1979–87
John Sibley	Director, THORN EMI, 1974–85
John Skolas	President, THORN EMI, Inc., since 1992
Sir Colin Southgate	Chairman, THORN EMI, since 1989; Chief Executive since 1987; Managing Director, 1985–87
David Steadman	Managing Director, EMI Medical, 1978–80
Douglas Stevenson	Managing Director, Inmos International, 1985–88
G Jack Strowger	Managing Director, Thorn Electrical Industries, 1970–79
Sir Graham Wilkins	Chairman, THORN EMI, 1985–89; Non-Executive Director, 1978–85
Peter Wilmot-Sitwell	Senior Partner, Rowe & Pitman
Leonard Wood	Director, EMI Music, 1966–79; Managing Director, EMI Records (UK), 1959–1966
Colin Woodley	Manager, Corporate Communications, THORN EMI
Don Young	Director of Human Resources, THORN EMI, 1987–90

APPENDIX II

Share Price Performance

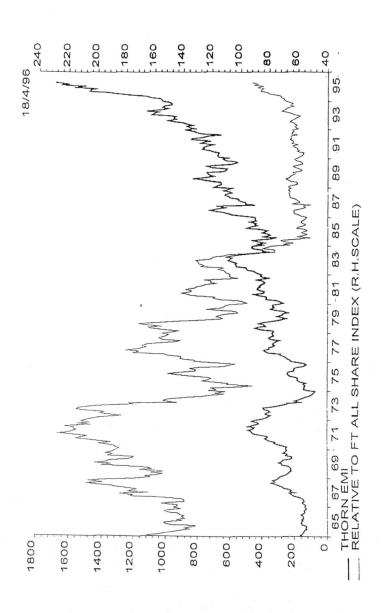

THORN EMI
RELATIVE TO FT ALL SHARE INDEX (R.H.SCALE)

18/4/96

APPENDIX III

Thorn Electrical Industries

£ million — Group Financial Statistics

Year to 31 March	1970	1971	1972	1973	1974	1975	1976	1977	1978 (a)	1979 (a)
Sales	294	343	413	507	619	707	807	993	1092	1208
Profit before Interest and Tax	35	41	53	74	81	77	79	108	116	122
Profit after Tax (b)	19	23	30	34	37	31	37	51	73	79
Earnings per Share (b)	13.6	16.7	21.7	30.0	26.2	23.0	27.5	36.1	52.1	55.1
Fixed Assets	54	59	66	70	82	98	99	114	132	140
Rental Assets	57	75	102	109	126	131	150	171	183	200
Trade and other Investments	9	15	12	13	33	24	18	13	12	11
Net Current Assets	29	25	22	33	37	66	91	112	128	178
Total Assets less Current Liabilities	150	174	202	225	278	319	358	409	455	529
Shareholders' Funds	99	116	139	161	181	196	218	251	352	420
Minority Interests	6	6	6	7	8	8	8	8	9	10
Deferred Taxation	7	12	19	23	55	82	104	126	69	79
Loans	38	41	37	35	33	34	27	25	25	19
Capital Employed	150	174	202	225	278	319	358	409	455	529
Return on Sales	12%	12%	13%	15%	13%	11%	10%	11%	11%	10%
Return on Operating Assets	23%	24%	26%	33%	29%	24%	22%	26%	25%	23%
Return on Equity	18%	19%	21%	20%	20%	15%	16%	20%	20%	18%

Notes:
(a) The company changed its policy on accounting for deferred tax in 1979.
1978 has been restated to reflect the new policy.
(b) Before extraordinary items

Source: TEI 1979 Report and Accounts

Thorn Electrical Industries

£ million   Segment Data

Year to 31 March	1972	1973	1974	1975	1976	1977	1978	1979
Sales								
Consumer Electronics	93	138	176	332	371	430	397	446
Rental (a)	90	113	137					
Domestic Appliances	92	119	144	173	222	298	329	373
Lighting	125	163	204	168	196	227	251	260
Engineering	73	66	77	126	144	193	215	245
Intra-Group / Other	-60	-92	-119	-92	-126	-155	-100	-116
Total	**413**	**507**	**619**	**707**	**807**	**993**	**1092**	**1208**
Profit before interest								
	(b)	(b)	(b)					
Consumer Electronics	12	17	13	46	53	63	65	73
Rental (a)	19	25	28					
Domestic Appliances	7	12	13	15	15	20	21	21
Lighting	7	12	11	8	8	13	14	14
Engineering	5	4	8	13	12	15	16	14
Discontinued Activities				-5	-8	-3		
Total	**49**	**70**	**74**	**77**	**79**	**108**	**116**	**122**

Notes:
(a) Rental included in Consumer Electronics after 1974
(b) Profit after interest
(c) Figures prior to 1972 have not been included because of frequent changes
in classification   Source: TEI Reports and Accounts

APPENDIX IV

EMI

£ million   Group Financial Statistics

Year to 30 June	1970	1971	1972	1973	1974	1975	1976	1977	1978	1979
Sales	215	231	251	321	400	503	671	851	873	869
Profit before Interest and Tax	25	14	23	34	41	43	65	75	38	29
Profit after Tax (a)	11	5	10	14	16	15	28	32	10	3
Earnings per Share – pence (a)	12.1	6.1	9.8	14.2	17.0	15.8	25.8	28.8	7.6	1.8
Fixed Assets	69	81	85	104	113	130	150	179	234	235
Goodwill and Intangible Assets	61	64	64	81	82	80	83	108	85	94
Trade Investments	15	16	15	14	12	12	14	18	18	13
Net Current Assets	7	18	17	23	27	23	39	62	48	67
Total Assets less Current Liabilities	152	179	181	223	233	246	285	367	384	409
Shareholders' Funds	108	110	115	131	145	154	177	218	237	247
Minority Interests	13	12	13	15	10	11	13	13	11	10
Deferred Taxation	0	0	0	1	2	6	15	26	16	9
Loans	31	57	54	76	77	75	80	109	120	143
Capital Employed	152	179	181	223	233	246	285	367	384	409
Return on Sales	12%	6%	9%	11%	10%	9%	10%	9%	4%	3%
Return on Operating Assets	16%	8%	13%	15%	18%	17%	23%	20%	10%	7%
Return on Equity	9%	4%	8%	10%	10%	9%	15%	14%	4%	1%

Notes:
(a) Before extraordinary items   Source: EMI 1979 Report and Accounts

EMI

£ million	Segment Data

Year to 30 June	1970	1971	1972	1973	1974	1975	1976	1977	1978	1979
Sales										
Music	129	128	138	170	214	258	345	430	439	430
Leisure	33	36	38	45	54	67	81	95	132	146
Television Services	11	14	17	22	23	29	38	51	61	72
Electronics (non Medical)	43	53	58	84	105	129	165	182	174	177
Medical Electronics				0	5	20	42	93	67	44
Total	215	231	251	321	400	503	671	851	873	869
Profit before Interest										
Music	16	2	9	17	26	20	27	33	17	2
Leisure	4	4	5	4	3	6	6	7	12	19
Television Services	1	4	5	6	5	3	6	8	9	8
Electronics (non Medical)	3	3	1	5	6	5	14	12	14	13
Medical Electronics				0	1	9	13	15	-13	-13
Property		1	2	2	0	0				
Group Profit **before Interest**	25	14	23	34	41	43	65	75	38	29

Source: EMI 1979 Report and Accounts

APPENDIX V

THORN EMI

£ million — Group Financial Statistics 1980–1989

Year to 31 March	1980 (b)	1981	1982	1983	1984	1985	1986	1987	1988	1989
Sales	1621	2229	2436	2716	2821	3204	3317	3203	3054	3291
Profit before interest and tax	139	129	141	164	190	172	154	192	244	320
Profit after Tax (a)	89	67	72	69	91	71	66	103	146	193
Earnings per Share – pence (a)	57.6	34.5	37.9	35.4	47.8	29.9	26.5	43.9	53.1	64.2
Fixed Assets	377	334	361	372	382	445	368	375	387	448
Rental Assets	252	302	399	461	483	455	428	441	546	638
Investments	30	30	31	35	37	73	65	58	52	97
Finance Subsidiary Net Assets								7	11	18	27
Net Current Assets	121	112	18	9	66	107	150	112	82	-87
Total Assets less Current Liabilities	781	779	809	876	967	1079	1018	996	1085	1123
Shareholders' Funds	548	577	608	605	639	623	581	630	645	590
Minority Interests	16	17	12	14	12	23	23	28	126	229
Deferred Taxation	83	81	71	65	93	64	26	25	26	35
Other Provisions					64	172	161	164	167	167
Loans	133	104	118	192	159	197	228	149	121	102
Capital Employed	781	779	809	876	967	1079	1018	996	1085	1123
Return on Sales	9%	6%	6%	6%	7%	5%	5%	6%	8%	11%
Return on Operating Assets	18%	17%	17%	19%	20%	16%	15%	19%	22%	30%
Return on Equity	16%	11%	12%	11%	14%	11%	11%	16%	19%	24%

Notes:
(a) Before extraordinary items. 1980 and 1981 not adjusted for subsequent Rights Issues
(b) Includes EMI for 4 months only

Source: TEMI Financial Data Book

THORN EMI

£ million   Segment Data 1980–1989

Year to 31 March	1980	1981	1982	1983	1984	1985 (a)	1986	1987	1988	1989
Sales										
Rental, Retail and Consumer Electronics (b)	507	581	685	778	850	832	884	991	1151	1326
Technology / Engineering	285	594	607	662	703	649	679	669	769	592
Music and Thames TV (c)		412	487	501	488	582	579	648	663	766
Domestic Appliances and Lighting (b)	708	690	737	839	872	325	348	378	417	523
Films, Video, Cable TV		92	97	110	111					
EMI (4 months 1980 only)	279									
Discontinued Operations		25				993	1018	661	98	84
Intra Group	-158	-165	-177	-174	-203	-177	-191	-144	-44	
Total	1621	2229	2436	2716	2821	3204	3317	3203	3054	3291
Profit before Interest										
Rental, Retail and Consumer Electronics (b)	73	70	73	83	85	87	96	128	148	159
Technology / Engineering	19	30	20	28	33	36	9	29	39	55
Music and Thames TV (c)		20	37	21	16	16	9	27	38	54
Domestic Appliances and Lighting (b)	35	7	22	36	46	21	15	5	20	44
Films, Video, Cable TV		3	-10	-5	9					
EMI (4 months 1980 only)	11									
Discontinued Operations						13	25	-26	-2	10
Property and Investment Profits								27		
Total	139	129	141	164	190	172	154	192	244	320

Notes:
(a) Segment classification changed in 1985
(b) Retail included in Domestic Appliances and Lighting until 1985
(c) Thames TV included for 1985–1989 only   Source: TEMI Financial Data

THORN EMI

£ million Group Financial Statistics 1990–1996

Year to 31 March	1990	1991	1992	1993	1994	1995	1996
Sales	3571	3660	3954	4452	4292	4507	5056
Operating Profit (a)	343	296	281	379	383	455	575
Profit before Tax (b)	330	160	131	274	327	271	478
Profit after Tax (b)	230	85	61	166	205	114	240
Earnings per Share – pence (b)	76.7	27.2	20.5	43.6	48.2	25.0	52.3
Adj. Earnings per Share–pence (c)	58.6	48.4	40.8	52.1	53.2	62.5	76.3
Music Publishing Copyrights	217	270	273	392	401	380	409
Property, Plant, Equipment	446	502	503	559	503	710	750
Rental Assets	650	660	655	664	656	692	728
Investments	129	120	123	142	132	52	34
Net Current Assets	-93	-86	153	-409	-360	-448	-548
Total Assets less Current Liabilities	1349	1465	1707	1348	1332	1385	1373
Shareholder's Funds	592	600	716	453	735	584	558
Minority Interests	8	22	15	7	2	74	66
Deferred Taxation	36	37	23	22	19	17	26
Other Provisions	169	235	321	305	209	303	382
Loans	544	572	632	562	366	407	341
Capital Employed	1349	1465	1707	1348	1332	1385	1373
Return on Sales	10%	8%	7%	9%	9%	10%	11%
Return on Operating Assets	25%	20%	16%	28%	29%	33%	42%
Return on Equity	38%	14%	8%	36%	28%	17%	38%

Notes:
(a) Before financing charges and exceptional items
(b) After exceptionals
(c) Before exceptionals

Source: TEMI Financial Data

THORN EMI

£ million   **Segment Data 1990–1996**

Year to 31 March	1990	1991	1992	1993	1994	1995	1996
Sales							
EMI Music	884	1016	1129	1507	1761	2189	
THORN	1253	1259	1372	1388	1484	1589	
HMV	165	207	262	323	404	503	
Other and Discontinued	1270	1178	1192	1234	643	225	
Total	**3571**	**3660**	**3955**	**4452**	**4292**	**4506**	
Operating Profit (before exceptional items)							
EMI Music	92	103	125	197	246	295	
THORN	146	117	106	115	129	152	
HMV	6	4	1	3	6	14	
Other and Discontinued	99	72	49	65	1	-6	
Total	**343**	**296**	**281**	**379**	**383**	**455**	

Source: TEMI Financial Data

APPENDIX VI

THORN EMI Disposals

1980–1995

Year	Company	Business Sector	Acquirer
1980	Tricity Finance Ltd	Rental (Leasing)	Lombard North Central Ltd
	EMI Hotels & Restaurants Angus Restaurants EMI Royal London Hotels King & Queen Golden Egg Properties Golden Egg Properties Investments	Leisure	Scottish & Newcastle Breweries
	THORN EMI Leisure Associated British Leisure Bernard Delfont Organisation Chichester Yacht Basin County Squash Rackets Delfont Music Ember Entertainments Blackpool Tower Company EMI Dancing Grade-River Ivy Productions London Presentations Prime Productions	Leisure	Trusthouse Forte Hotels Ltd
	EMI Medical	Medical Electronics	GE Medical Systems
1983	**Evershed & Vignoles**	Engineering	Bestobell
	Martin Thomas Ltd	Engineering	Andover Group
	Monks & Crane Ltd	Engineering	Trackplace Ltd
	THORN EMI Social Centres	Leisure	Bass Leisure Ltd
1984	**Goodmans' Loudspeakers and Goodmans' Industries Ltd**	Consumer Electronics	Actclose Ltd
	Bradford Cylinders Ltd	Engineering	MBO
	Coventry Dies	Engineering	Deeming Taylor Ltd
	Pantak Ltd	Engineering	Scanray Corporation

	SMC Varme Tehnik A/S	Engineering	J V Anderson
	THORN EMI Industrial Boilers Ltd and THORN EMI Energy Development Ltd	Engineering	Pound Ltd
	Towler Hydraulics GmbH	Engineering	Parker Hannifin NMF-GmbH
1985	Carbon Taps Dies & Handtools	Engineering	Karolyi Associates Ltd
	Foster Electrical Supplies Ltd	Engineering	Parkfield Group plc
	High-Speed Taps & Dies	Engineering	Osborn Mushet Tools Ltd
	THORN EMI Building Services	Engineering	Axisminster Services Ltd
	THORN EMI Diescastings Ltd	Engineering	Lupton & Place Ltd
	Towler Hydraulics (UK) Ltd	Engineering	Oilgear USA
	Brighton Marina Co. Ltd	Leisure	Brent Walker Holdings Ltd
	THORN EMI Autopayment Ltd	Technology	Godwin Warren Control Systems plc
1986	THORN EMI Heating Ltd	Appliances	Myson Group plc
	REW Video Duplication	Consumer Electronics	MBO
	THORN EMI Video Facilities	Consumer Electronics	Soho Vision Ltd
	CGS Resistance Company Ltd	Engineering	Holsworthy Electronics plc
	International Twist Drill Co. Ltd	Engineering	Grampian Tools Ltd
	Metal Industries Ltd	Engineering	Expamet International plc
	Pressed Parts Division (Keyswitch Varley)	Engineering	A D Precision Presswork Ltd
	THORN EMI Engineering Components Division	Engineering	FKI Electronics plc
	THORN EMI Screen Entertainment Ltd	Entertainment	Bond Corporation
	Record Merchandisers Ltd	Music Retailing	Woolworth Ltd
	THORN EMI Cable Television (49%) and Swindon Cable	Television	British Telecom
	Premiere Partnership (41.2%)	Television	Mirror Group Newspapers

	Television Entertainment by Cable	Television	Cable and Television Holdings Ltd
	Starstream Limited (1/3rd share)	Television	Thames Television
	The Music Channel Ltd (50%)	Television	Virgin Group
	Data Products Division (Datatech)	Technology	Emidor
	Gothic Crellon Ltd and Gothic Electronic Components Ltd	Technology	MBO
	Recordacall Ltd	Technology	Vanderhoff
	THORN EMI Brimar Ltd	Technology	The Rank Organisation
	THORN EMI Dynatel Ltd	Technology	MBO
1987	J2T Video (Newhaven Ltd)	Consumer Electronics	Thomson Grand Public
	THORN EMI Ferguson Ltd	Consumer Electronics	Thomson Grand Public
	Visionprint	Consumer Electronics	Continu-forms Holdings plc
	THORN EMI Major Domestic Appliances Ltd	Domestic Appliances	Electrolux
	Modutec Inc. & EMICO Inc.	Engineering	Hawker Siddeley (USA)
	THORN EMI Measurement Ltd	Engineering	MBO
	Nuclear Enterprises Ltd and EMI Technology SA	Technology	MBO
	On-Line Information (Datasolve 33%)	Technology	Financial Times Group
	THORN EMI Robotics	Technology	MBO (part), closed down rest
	THORN Simtec	Technology	Jasmin Electronics PLC
1988	JVC Distribution Businesses	Consumer Electronics	Victor Company of Japan Ltd
	THORN EMI Electronics Australia Pty Ltd	Consumer Electronics	AWA Limited
	Monk Metal Windows (1961) Ltd	Engineering	Rea Metal Windows Ltd
	THORN Ericsson Telecommunications Ltd (51%)	Technology	L M Ericsson of Sweden
1989	THORN EMI Colour Tubes Ltd	Consumer Electronics	Closed down/

			ceased trading
	THORN Ferguson Finance Limited	Consumer Electronics	MBO
	THORNPHONE	Consumer Electronics	Racal-Vodac Ltd
	Kenwood Ltd	Domestic Appliances	MBO
	Computer Aided Engineering Software (Software Sciences)	Technology	MBO
	Inmos Limited	Technology	SGS-Thomson Microelectronics
	IPSYS	Technology	MBO
	THORN EMI Datatech Ltd	Technology	NE Technology (part) Penny & Giles (part)
	THORN EMI Meters Division	Technology	Schlumberger Industries Ltd
1990	THORN EMI Financial Services plc	Electrical Retailing (Leasing)	Lombard Tricity Finance Limited
	Trinity House Finance plc	Electrical Retailing (Leasing)	Lombard Tricity Finance Limited
	Holophane S A	Lighting	Fidenza Vetraria SpA
	Micrologic	Technology	Closed down/ ceased trading
	Parsys Ltd	Technology	MBO
	Systron Donner Corporation Inertial Division Duncan Electronics Division Edcliff Division Seaton-Wilson Division	Technology	BEI Electronics
	THORN EMI Computer Software (part)	Technology	Pilot Software
1991	Thorn Lighting (Light Sources)	Lighting	GE (USA)
	HMV New Zealand	Music Retailing	Brash Pty Ltd.
	MEL's Communications Business	Technology	Thomson-CSF (France)
	THORN EMI Software Ltd	Technology	MBO
1992	Atlantis Stores (part)	Electrical Retailing	Scottish Power
	Atlantis Stores (part)	Electrical Retailing	Norweb plc
	Atlantis Stores (part)	Electrical Retailing	Seeboard plc
1993	THORN Lighting	Lighting	MBO
	Thorn Security (Fire Appliances)	Security	Williams Holdings

	Systron Donner Corporation Microwave Division Instrument Division	Technology	Signal Technology Corp.
	Thames Television plc (59%)	Television	Pearson PLC
1994	**GB Glass (50%)**	Lighting	MBO
	Lamp Metals – Gateshead	Lighting	Closed down/ ceased trading
	THORN Security Ltd	Technology	MBO
	Babcock Thorn (35%)	Technology	Babcock
	Systron Donner Corporation Safety Systems Division	Technology	Whittaker Corporation
	THORN Automation Ltd	Technology	MBO
	THORN EMI Computeraid	Technology	MBO
	THORN EMI Electron Tubes Ltd	Technology	MBO
	THORN EMI Malco, Inc.	Technology	Schlumberger Technologies, Inc.
1995	**THORN EMI Electronics (Defence)**	Technology	Thomson CSF
	THORN EMI Electronics (Sensors)	Technology	Racal
	THORN EMI Microwave Devices	Technology	MBO

APPENDIX VII

THORN EMI Acquisitions

1980–1995

Year	Company	Business Sector
1980	Andrew Fraser & Co	Engineering
	Emico Division of Sheller-Globe Corporation	Engineering
1981	J2T (VCR Manufacturing Joint Venture)	Consumer Electronics
1982	Computer Systems Division of BOC Group plc	Technology
1983	Sealed Motor Construction Co Ltd	Domestic Appliances
1984	Brady's (Music) Ltd	Music Retailing
	Inmos International plc	Technology
	Ediciones Musicales SA	Music
1985	Hispavox SA	Music
	EPS Consultants Ltd	Technology
	SMB Computers Ltd	Technology
1986	Revolver Records	Music Retailing
	Granada Telerent AB	Rental
	Babcock Thorn Ltd	Technology
	(Rosyth Dockyard Joint Venture)	
	Production Control (Ericsson) Ltd	Technology
1987	Vallances Ltd	Electrical Retailing
	Jarnkonst Group (ASEA AB)	Lighting
	Granada's European Rental Companies	Rental
	Murphy Tele-Rents	Rental
	Norman Thorp Ltd	Rental
	Rent-A-Center, Inc.	Rental
	Computer Maintenance Division of ISG Ltd	Technology
	Computer Maintenance Division of Zygal Services Ltd	Technology
	JEL Energy Conservation Services Ltd	Technology
	LA Computer Services Ltd	Technology
1988	Ketts Ltd	Electrical Retailing
	Uprate Ltd	Electrical Retailing
	Holophane SA	Lighting
	Howard Smith Lighting Group	Lighting

	Colour TV Rentals Ltd	Rental
	Visionhire Holdings Pty Ltd	Rental
	Calder Valley Fire Protection Engineers	Technology
	Financial Trading Systems, Inc.	Technology
	Informatik Forum GmbH	Technology
	Kidde Automated Systems Inc.	Technology
1989	Chrysalis Records Ltd (50%) and Tenwright Records, Inc. (50%)	Music
	SBK Entertainment World, Inc. and Combine Music Corporation	Music
	Cumberland Television Pty Ltd	Rental
	Fletcher Rentals (Television) Ltd	Rental
	Rediffusion Business Electronics Ltd	Rental
	SS Clorius	Technology
1990	Filmtrax plc	Music
	IRS Records Ltd	Music
	Hospital Television Services Ltd	Rental
	Rental business of Bennett & Fountain Group	Rental
	R F Sweeney Radio Ltd	Rental
	Fire Safety Equipment Ltd	Technology
	Rex Fireprevention Ltd	Technology
	Autocall, Inc.	Technology
	MEL Division of Philips Group	Technology
1991	Chrysalis Records Ltd (purchase of outstanding 50%)	Music
	Lothian Fire Protection	Security
	Thames Television plc (purchase of BET shareholding)	Television
1992	Medley Records AS	Music
	Sparrow	Music
	Virgin Music Group Ltd	Music
	Remco America, Inc.	Rental
1994	Food Ltd	Music
	Intercord GmbH	Music
	Star Song Communications	Music
1995	Dillons The Bookstore Ltd	Retailing
1996	Advantage Companies, Inc.	Rental
	Tidewater Rental Corp.	Rental

INDEX